REPUTATION, STOCK PRICE, AND YOU

WHY THE MARKET REWARDS SOME COMPANIES AND PUNISHES OTHERS

Dr. Nir Kossovsky

apress®

Reputation, Stock Price, and You: Why the Market Rewards Some Companies and Punishes Others

Copyright © 2012 by Nir Kossovsky

All rights reserved. No part of this work may be reproduced or transmitted in any form or by any means, electronic or mechanical, including photocopying, recording, or by any information storage or retrieval system, without the prior written permission of the copyright owner and the publisher.

ISBN-13 (pbk): 978-1-4302-4890-3
ISBN-13 (electronic): 978-1-4302-4891-0

Trademarked names may appear in this book. Rather than use a trademark symbol with every occurrence of a trademarked name, we use the names only in an editorial fashion and to the benefit of the trademark owner, with no intention of infringement of the trademark.

President and Publisher: Paul Manning

Acquisitions Editor: Jeff Olson

Developmental Editor: Robert Hutchinson

Editorial Board: Steve Anglin, Mark Beckner, Ewan Buckingham, Gary Cornell, Louise Corrigan, Morgan Ertel, Jonathan Gennick, Jonathan Hassell, Robert Hutchinson, Michelle Lowman, James Markham, Matthew Moodie, Jeff Olson, Jeffrey Pepper, Douglas Pundick, Ben Renow-Clarke, Dominic Shakeshaft, Gwenan Spearing, Matt Wade, Tom Welsh

Coordinating Editor: Rita Fernando

Copy Editor: Terry Kornak

Compositor: Bytheway Publishing Services

Indexer: SPi Global

Cover Designer: Anna Ishchenko

Distributed to the book trade worldwide by Springer-Verlag New York, Inc., 233 Spring Street, 6th Floor, New York, NY 10013. Phone 1-800-SPRINGER, fax 201-348-4505, e-mail orders-ny@springer-sbm.com, or visit www.springeronline.com.

For information on translations, please contact us by e-mail at info@apress.com, or visit www.apress.com.

Apress and friends of ED books may be purchased in bulk for academic, corporate, or promotional use. eBook versions and licenses are also available for most titles. For more information, reference our Special Bulk Sales–eBook Licensing web page at www.apress.com/bulk-sales. To place an order, e-mail your request to support@apress.com

The information in this book is distributed on an "as is" basis, without warranty. Although every precaution has been taken in the preparation of this work, neither the author(s) nor Apress shall have any liability to any person or entity with respect to any loss or damage caused or alleged to be caused directly or indirectly by the information contained in this work.

For Bear

Contents

About the Author vii

About the Contributors ix

Acknowledgments.. xi

Part I Précis 1

Chapter 1: Avoiding Hara-Kiri.. 3

Chapter 2: A $54 Billion Reputation.. 11

Part II Profit and Loss.. 29

Chapter 3: Customers... 31

Chapter 4: Employees 53

Chapter 5: Suppliers 93

Chapter 6: Creditors 127

Part III Controls 141

Chapter 7: Equity Investors... 143

Chapter 8: Boards of Directors 165

Chapter 9: Analysts... 201

Chapter 10: Regulators.. 225

Part IV Perspectives... 239

Chapter 11: Cultural Context 241

Chapter 12: Metrics 249

Chapter 13: Consider These.. 273

Index 287

About the Author

Dr. Nir Kossovsky is an authority on business process risk and reputational value. With a career spanning the worlds of risk, probability, and intangibles, Kossovsky is cofounder, chief executive, and director of Steel City Re, reputational value specialists. Kossovsky holds more than a dozen patents, including an algorithmic reputational value measurement system currently enabling insurance solutions (patent pending), third-party investment strategies, and governance products. He is the executive secretary of the Intangible Asset Finance Society, a professional organization, for which he edits the *Mission:Intangible* blog under the *nom de plume* Huygens.

He served on the boards of Patent & License Exchange and Littlearth, Inc.; was a consultant to the U.S. Food and Drug Administration's medical device advisory panels; and is featured in case studies from Harvard and Darden Schools of Business. Formerly a practicing physician with an M.D. degree from the University of Chicago, Kossovsky earned an MBA from the University of Southern California and a BA in Philosophy from the University of Pittsburgh. Kossovsky was a tenured member of the faculty of the UCLA School of Medicine, Chief of the UCLA Medical Center's Autopsy Service, and a Deputy Coroner in Los Angeles County. He is a Trustee of Excela Health Systems, a community-based healthcare provider. He graduated from the U.S. Navy War College and was honorably discharged with the rank of Captain from the U.S. Navy Reserves. He is the author of more than 200 scholarly articles, lay articles, and books.

About the Contributors

Michael D. Greenberg is a senior behavioral scientist with the RAND Corporation and director of the RAND Center for Corporate Ethics and Governance. He is a clinical psychologist and an attorney by training. Greenberg's work at RAND has involved designing and leading empirical research projects on topics spanning healthcare, civil justice, national security, and law and business issues. He has led or co-led projects in all of these areas, and some recent examples of his work include studies on fair value accounting and systemic risk; medical malpractice litigation and hospital-based patient safety; and the impact of the 2008 financial crisis on the U.S. civil justice system. In his role as the Director of RAND's Center for Corporate Ethics and Governance, Greenberg leads RAND Corporation efforts in developing new research and path-breaking round-table events designed to contribute to better policy on matters ranging from organizational compliance and behavior, to government regulation of business organizations, to the role of organizational boards in institutional oversight. RAND reports authored by Greenberg include *Directors as Guardians of Compliance and Ethics Within the Corporate Citadel* (2010); *For Whom the Whistle Blows: Advancing Corporate Compliance and Integrity Efforts in the Era of Dodd-Frank* (2011); and *Corporate Culture and Ethical Leadership Under the Federal Sentencing Guidelines* (2012).

In addition to his work at RAND, Greenberg has held adjunct and teaching appointments at the University of Pittsburgh School of Law, the University of Pittsburgh School of Medicine, and the Heinz College of Public Policy at Carnegie Mellon University. He received his Ph.D. degree in clinical psychology from Duke University, and following an internship at Dartmouth Medical Center in New Hampshire, he entered law school, received his J.D. degree from Harvard, and worked as an attorney at Ropes & Gray, a Boston law firm.

About the Contributors

Robert C. Brandegee was cofounder and principal of Brandegee, Inc., Pittsburgh-based management consulting/communications firm. He served as VP of Creativity and played a lead role on many assignments related to the management of change in business organizations, as well as in nongovernmental organizations (NGOs) and government agencies. Clients included Westinghouse, Alcoa, U.S. Steel, PPG, Heinz USA, Cyclops/Armco Steel, University of Pittsburgh, Carnegie Mellon University, Chatham University, the City of Pittsburgh, and Allegheny County, as well as U.S. government agencies Departments of Energy, Defense, and Transportation (DOE, DOD, and DOT).

For many of these assignments, Brandegee pioneered a change management technique called strategic concept mapping that uses visual/verbal displays of evolving strategic frameworks. These were a key tool in iterative planning with client groups for corporate culture change, and yielded a common model of problems and needs shared among management and employees. The output was a strategic action plan distilled to a single page. This provided ongoing guidance and encouraged regular reference and ease of revision as change processes progressed.

Brandegee is a graduate of Williams College. Now retired from Brandegee, Inc., he continues to advise and write for selected clients in fields he has identified as having significant potential for broad societal improvement.

He also designs and markets contemporary furniture, combining antique hand hewn beams, logs, and barn siding with glass and other materials.

Acknowledgments

This is a "how-to" book providing a governance framework and a diversity of execution strategies to help the market recognize and reward companies for creating authentic reputational value. I expect readers will enjoy this book's content and style only because my own effort in channeling the wisdom and experience of many has been heroically augmented by the superior communications skills of a few.

For sharing their thoughts, time, and/or enabling me to experiment, I thank (in alphabetical order) Mary Adams, Alex Arrow, Urmi Ashar, Jonathan Salem Baskin, Andreus Beck, Jeffrey Brandt (ZL), Tim Campbell, Scott Childers, Mary Choi, Robert Congel, Dennis Dalton, Manuel Dujovny, Alfred Fasola, Judith Giordan, Bryan Gransden, John Griggs, Kenan Jarboe, Robert Johnson, Takashi Kiuchi, Yuval Kossovsky, Bruce Lehman, Robert P. Liscouski, William McGinty, Barbi Mittleman, Pamela Newman, Takaaki Nimura, Hidieki Otsuyama, David Petrie, Richard Pietrafesa, David Porter, Dale Predmore, Christina Ray, Robert Rittereiser, Greg van Dyke, Joff Wild, and Glenn Yago.

For helping me express my thoughts judiciously, I owe much to Robert Hutchinson and Jeff Olson from Apress and Ada and Robert Brandegee, formerly with Brandegee, Inc. For producing this book efficiently with panache, I thank Rita Fernando and Terry Kornak.

For just about everything related to the business of reputational value risk insurance, I thank my Steel City Re cofounder and long-suffering business partner, Peter Gerken.

PART I

Précis

CHAPTER

1

Avoiding Hara-Kiri

A reputation for a thousand years may depend upon the conduct of a single moment.

—Ernest Bramah

In one of the final scenes in the 1993 murder mystery film, *Rising Sun*, a police inspector stands in a Japanese corporate boardroom at the top floor of a towering office building. In front of the entire board, he prepares to accuse one member of criminal culpability. With tension rising, fellow board members begin to distance themselves physically from the soon-to-be-accused. Taking the cultural cue, the executive takes the honorable route and leaps out of a window, mercifully ending the crisis for all.

In an example of real life imitating art, the scene was replayed on Tuesday, 15 June 2010, when five major oil company executives lined up at a witness table for a House Energy and Commerce Committee hearing to investigate the Deepwater Horizon oil rig disaster, which at the time was still pouring 50,000 barrels of oil a day into the Gulf of Mexico. Exxon Mobil CEO Rex Tillerson said, "We would not have drilled the well the way [BP] did." Chevron CEO John Watson and Shell Oil Co. president Marvin Odum concurred. Rep. Joseph Cao, who had emigrated from Vietnam, closed the scene: "In samurai days, we would just give…[the Chairman of BP]…a knife and ask [him]…to commit hara-kiri."[1]

But the simple solution of seppuku that might have sufficed in an earlier Japanese culture is not available in our complex multifaceted world. BP did not have the luxury of quickly and mercifully ending the fallout from the

Chapter 1 | Avoiding Hara-Kiri

corporative event that best exemplifies a modern reputational crisis: the explosion of the Transocean Deepwater Horizon oil-drilling rig in the Gulf of Mexico.

The explosion on 15 April 2010 of the Deepwater Horizon platform, situated 40 miles southeast of New Orleans on the Macondo Prospect oil field, killed 11 and critically injured 17 of the 126-member crew. Within hours, Deepwater Horizon was completely destroyed. As it burned and sank, severance of the connection between the well-head and the rig opened the spill of oil into the Gulf of Mexico. On the day of the Energy and Commerce Committee hearing, a government panel confirmed that this oil spill was the largest in U.S. history.

Anatomy of a Reputational Crisis

The Deepwater Horizon disaster was yet another mishap—"…an industry accident," as BP CEO Tony Hayward explained shortly before he stepped down.[2] Oil spills happen all around the world and, as Hayward implied, are an inevitable part of doing business. According to the Oil Spill Intelligence Report, spills in the size range of at least 10,000 gallons have occurred in the waters of 112 nations since 1960.[3] The Deepwater Horizon spill was a very large one, releasing 205.8 million gallons, but still ranks second to the deliberate release of about 240 million gallons of crude oil into the Persian Gulf during the 1991 Gulf War.[4]

Accidents involving oil tankers, pipelines, and offshore platforms have caused a number of very large oil spills. Platforms have several failsafe systems to reduce accidental spills. The weight of the drilling fluid/drilling mud acts as the first line of well control. If an influx of pressurized oil or gas breaks through the mud, well-control is maintained through the rig's emergency-closure devices (rams) that seal off the well and route the wellbore fluids to specialized pressure controlling equipment.[4] Both systems failed the Deepwater Horizon in April 2010.

Chapter 2 picks up the BP story and explains why the Deepwater Horizon spill was more than an accident. But to provide context for this and the many other case studies that follow, it is important first to introduce the variables that can transform a business operational event into a reputational event:

- The event affects a large number of stakeholders comprising many different interests.

- Reputation-impacting business processes are at the heart of the event.

Reputation, Stock Price, and You   5

- 24/7 news coverage and incessant exposure through social media promote awareness of the event.

- The company's antecedent PR campaign(s) is dissonant with the unfolding facts of the event.

- The company's inept crisis communications exacerbate the ill-will triggered by the event.

Because all these key variables were present, BP's accident was a modern reputational perfect storm. Deepwater Horizon is the poster child for a reputational event in which the market punishes a company.

Reputational Stakeholders

The stakeholders who impact directly the profit and loss statement are customers, employees, vendors and suppliers, and creditors. Investors set the earnings multiple. The special stakeholders, by virtue of their enterprise-wide as well as industry-wide influence, include corporate directors, analysts, and regulators.

Though the perspectives and values of stakeholders vary, each of them forms *expectations* of how a corporation will behave. In chapters devoted to each of the stakeholders, Parts 2 and 3 of this book show how expectations stakeholders hold about a company help shape a company's reputation and its stock price.

Reputation-Impacting Corporate Behaviors

Behaviors in six key areas of business performance underpin reputation: ethics, innovation, quality, safety, sustainability, and security (Table 1-1). Reputation is the summation of stakeholder *expectations* in these six areas of behavior.

Table 1-1. The Six Key Business Processes Underpinning Reputation[5]

Business Process	Definitions
Ethics	The moral principles by which a company operates; integrity is the act of adhering to those moral principles. Ethics are an integral part of governance that, along with integrity, affect the reputation value of all other intangible assets. Ethics are also the keystone intangible asset because they form the basis for trust and confidence.

Chapter 1 | Avoiding Hara-Kiri

Innovation	The design, invention, development, and/or implementation of new or altered products, services, processes, systems, organizational structures, or business models for the purpose of creating new value for customers and financial returns for the firm. Intellectual Property is part of this.
Quality	The extent to which a product is free from defects or deficiencies. The extent to which a service meets or exceeds the expectations of customers or clients, especially in comparison to peers. The extent to which products and services conform to measurable and verifiable criteria.
Safety	The state of being reasonably certain that a set of conditions will not accidentally cause adverse effects on the well-being of employees, the public, or the environment.
Sustainability	The making, using, offering for sale, or selling of products and services that meet the needs of the present without compromising the ability of future generations to meet their own needs.
Security	The degree of protection a company offers against events undertaken by actors intentionally, criminally, or maliciously for purposes that adversely affect the firm. Because fear is the great disruptor of life and commerce, it is useful to think of security, the most ethereal of the intangible assets, as "absence of fear."

The chapters that follow show how companies' cultures lead to choices in managing ethics, innovation, quality, safety, sustainability, and security that shape stakeholders' expectations. They show how companies' reputations affect stakeholders' economic behaviors and, in turn, how those behaviors create reputational value shaping companies' profit and loss statements and stock prices. The book builds the business case for reputation awareness by operating executives, reputational management by senior executives, and reputation oversight by the board of directors. We conclude that since measurements facilitate management, reputational value metrics can help companies do the right thing by their stakeholders.

Reputation, Marketing, and Crisis Communications

Reputation is an expectation of behavior shaped by direct personal experience and by information from diverse secondary sources.[6,7] The cacophony of secondary sources has increased in step with the growth in the democratic capabilities of the Internet: every individual armed with a keyboard, camera, and Web access or even just a smartphone can be an investigative journalist. While it remains true that communications professionals can help disseminate information and shape a story with authentic content, they have less impact on reputation creation than in the past.

Many businesses are still somewhat uncertain about whether to perceive reputation as the outcome of actual business practices or as an image created through company-generated communications. This book shows that it is both. It is a diversity of communications channels and third-party signals, reflecting authentic corporate behavior, that can help shape the expectations of stakeholders. It also shows that when image-making is not grounded in substance, it can produce highly counterproductive results.

Reputation and Risk Management

Executives are seeking reputation management advice, even if they're not sure where to look for it.[8] They intuit a link between reputation and intangible asset value and recognize that intangible assets comprise more than 65% of the value of the average traded firm. Many have heard that improving a firm's reputation can add on average 6% to its enterprise value,[9] and that the average major crisis will shave 7% of a firm's market capitalization. Growing awareness of the importance of reputation is also showing up in corporate annual reports. As of June 2012, 355 of the annual reports of the S&P 500 constituent companies were disclosing the significance of reputation risk, up from only 40 firms in 2009.

This book considers the subject of reputation from the perspective of a risk underwriter of reputational value. Most case studies conclude with action points, and each chapter provides an actionable summary. The content is geared toward improving readers' understanding of the links between corporate culture, behaviors, reputation, and value. The single most important management lesson is that managing reputation means managing the business processes underpinning reputation. Consider this:

Reputation is a consequence of corporate behavior that motivates stakeholders to behave in ways that either reward or punish the corporation.

Organization of the Book

Chapter 2 is an overture that fleshes out the BP reputation story and details the failure of reputation-linked business processes. It describes how the reputation of BP evolved within each stakeholder group, how that evolution changed each stakeholder's expectations of BP, and how those changes triggered economic consequences.

Chapter 1 | Avoiding Hara-Kiri

Part 2 of this book, comprising Chapters 3 through 6, focuses successively on the classes of stakeholders whose actions directly drive revenues and the costs of operations thereby creating measurable reputational value. *Customers* will reward companies with superior reputations by accepting higher prices, consuming greater volumes, and compressing purchase cycle times. In the setting of a superior reputation, *employees* generally will work for lower wages and create less operating friction; *vendors and suppliers* will provide superior service at lower cost; and *creditors* will provide capital on better terms.

Part 3 looks at the groups of stakeholders with outsized influence on corporate reputational value: equity investors through their voting rights in Chapter 7, corporate boards in Chapter 8, analysts in Chapter 9, and regulators in Chapter 10.

Part 4 offers perspectives. The book overall is objective—just as risk is an objective probabilistic *expectation* of frequency and severity. In the spirit of American pragmatism, this book observes and explains without moralizing.[10]

For example, we make no judgment on what ethical behavior is. A vast literature exists on that subject dating to ancient civilizations. We don't define it. Rather, we measure the results of behaviors associated with it.

Andrew Carnegie once said, "I used to listen to what people say; I now pay attention to what people do." We too look at behaviors: specifically, how each class of stakeholders behaves in response to the organization's reputation. Those behaviors constitute observable, empirical evidence—not judgments and not speculative opinions. Those stakeholder behavior response patterns are the pillars of reputational value metrics calculated by Steel City Re, employer of this book's author.

But since the drivers of reputation are corporate behaviors, and behaviors are subject to moral hazard, Chapter 11 focuses on reputation as a human construct in the context of liberal and conservative politics. It suggests that reputation can provide a mechanism for merging human values and the profit-making imperative of corporations.

Chapter 12 returns to form and introduces algorithmically generated reputational value metrics on seven of the companies presented in the preceding studies. These mathematical formulations objectively link reputation to the actual public record of *expected* stakeholder behaviors in the market. These algorithms generate dependable metrics that can offer guidance to stakeholders interested in recognizing, shaping, and valuing the behaviors that create corporate reputation.

Chapter 13 reviews central lessons in the volume and restates the business case for reputation management on the premise that executives at all levels of an organization can manage best that which they measure. The book wraps up with a diversity of strategies to increase, protect, and restore reputational value. And that's the essence of *Reputation, Stock Price, and You.*

Endnotes

1 Broder JM. Oil Executives break ranks in testimony. *New York Times.* 15 June 2010. Available at: http://www.nytimes.com/2010/06/16/business/16oil.html. Accessed 14 June 2012.

2 Elkind P, Whitford D, Burke D. BP: 'An accident waiting to happen'. *Fortune.* 24 January 2011. Available at: http://features.blogs.fortune.cnn.com/2011/01/24/bp-an-accident-waiting-to-happen/ Accessed 22 July 2012.

3 Accidental discharges of oil. *Global Marine Oil Pollution Information Gateway.* Available at: http://oils.gpa.unep.org/facts/oilspills.htm Accessed 21 July 2012.

4 Repanich J. The Deepwater Horizon spill by the numbers. *Popular Mechanics.* 10 August 2010. Available at: http://www.popularmechanics.com/science/energy/coal-oil-gas/bp-oil-spill-statistics. Accessed 21 July 2012.

5 Kossovsky N, Miller TA. *Mission: Intangible. Managing risk and reputation to create enterprise value.* Pittsburgh/Vancouver: Intangible Asset Finance Society/Trafford, 2010.

6 Abdul-Rahman A, Hailes S. Supporting trust in virtual communities. In: *Proceedings of the Hawaii International Conference on System Sciences*, Maui, Hawaii, 4–7 January 2000.

7 Sheehan NT, Stabell CB. Reputation as a driver in activity level analysis: reputation and competitive advantage in knowledge intensive firms. *Corp Reput Rev.* 2010;13:198–208.

8 Schumpeter. What's in a name? *Economist,.* 21 April 2012. http://www.economist.com/node/21553033. Accessed 22 July 2012.

9 Greenberg MD. On breaking the log jam: The how and why of corporate reputation leadership. *Corp Finance Rev.* 2012; 17(1):11–17.

10 Pfeiffer R. An introduction to classic American pragmatism. *Philosophy Now,* October/November 2003 (43). Available at: http://philosophynow.org/issues/43/An_Introduction_to_Classic_American_Pragmatism. Accessed 29 July 2012.

CHAPTER

2

A $54 Billion Reputation

BP plc delivered the worst of a poor set of quarterly results among top oil companies on Tuesday, slashing $US5 billion off the value of US assets and undershooting expectations with its operating result. The British oil company is struggling under the weight of litigation over the 2010 US Gulf oil spill... bringing the total set aside for the disaster to $US38 billion or well over two years worth of profits at current prices.[1]

—Canberra Times (31 July 2012)

For more than a century, BP (NYSE: BP) has been one of the world's giant oil producers. The company was founded in 1901 when a lawyer-turned-mining-and-mineral-tycoon named William Knox D'Arcy negotiated with the Persian Shah for a 60-year concession to explore for oil on property covering 480,000 square miles. Nearly a century later, in a $50 billion deal, British Petroleum acquired Amoco Corporation, the fifth largest oil company in the United States and largest producer of natural gas in North America, forming BP Amoco plc. The "Amoco" name soon disappeared and the company has been known since as "BP plc."

Headline Risk: Reputation vs. Reality

From the mid-1990s to the early part of the new century, BP deliberately turned green—at least in its public persona. In a speech on climate change at Stanford University in March 2002, Lord John Browne, the group chief executive of the British oil giant, declared BP to be a different kind of company: "I believe the American people expect a company like BP...to offer answers

Chapter 2 | A $54 Billion Reputation

and not excuses.... Companies composed of highly skilled and trained people can't live in denial of mounting evidence gathered by hundreds of the most reputable scientists in the world." Stakeholders took Brown at his word. "BP was the first to say that climate change was a problem, the first to take responsibility, and the first to have an internal target" for reducing their emissions, said Eileen Claussen, the president of the Pew Center on Global Climate Change. "They were pretty brave."[2]

BP's reputation as a green company was solidifying in the early 2000s. Although Tony Hayward, Lord Browne's successor, dismissed the idea that the group was working to "save the world," many employees continued to take the green commitment very seriously.[3]

Time magazine framed stakeholders' expectations in 2006 this way:

> *Pull into a BP station this holiday weekend and you may notice a green and yellow starburst over the pump, an image intended to remind you, as you're emptying your wallet of $20 bills, that at least you're supporting a green company. BP, after all, was the first oil giant to publicly acknowledge the risks of global warming, back in 1997. The firm has cut its own carbon emissions 10% below 1990 levels and last year established an alternative energies division. It's investing big money—$8 billion over the next decade —on renewable fuels, such as wind and solar power. Just last week, BP announced a partnership with DuPont to develop and commercialize advanced biofuels (superior to ethanol), starting next year. Even if you're being gouged at the pump, as you might suspect, BP at least seems to be putting its profits to good use.[4]*

BP's observable actions affirming a commitment to sustainability were reinforced with an effective media campaign. Beginning in 2000, and at a cost of $200 million, Ogilvy & Mather Worldwide initiated a campaign that "aspires to a conversational, almost confidential voice that suggests, 'You know what oil companies do to the environment, and we do, too, but honestly, we're not like that at all.'"[2] Out went the old British Petroleum shield that had been in Britain for more than 70 years, and in came the green, yellow, and white sunburst that seemed to suggest warm and fuzzy feelings about Earth.

Five years after the company's successful repositioning as oil industry leader on environmental issues, a string of adverse events began chipping away at the firm's reputation. In 2005, an explosion at BP's Texas refinery in the United States resulted in 15 deaths and 170 injuries. The company was forced to settle 1,350 lawsuits related to the refinery disaster, and hundreds of civil suits are still pending. In 2006, corroded pipelines caused two BP oil spills in Prudhoe Bay, Alaska, and 267,000 gallons of thick crude oil spread over two acres on the Tundra of Alaska's North Slope. In 2007, BP agreed to pay $373

Reputation, Stock Price, and You | 13

million in restitution and fines to settle illegal propane trading allegations, including alleged environmental violations centering on the Alaskan pipeline leaks and Texas refinery explosion.

BP welcomed some good news in 2007 when the company inked an agreement with Libya providing for access to deepwater blocks for exploration. Even that news, however, was tainted by allegations that the deal was conditioned on the United Kingdom's release of the Libyan intelligence agent, Abdel Baset al Megrahi, the man responsible for the destruction of Pan Am Flight 103 and the loss of 270 lives over Lockerbie, Scotland.

The list of adverse events continued to lengthen. In early 2009, the State of Alaska, the U.S. Department of Justice, and the U.S. Department of Transportation all filed civil lawsuits against BP's exploration business relating to the 2006 Prudhoe Bay spill.

Stakeholders' expectations, and the reputation that BP had established for its unique concern for Earth, initially helped minimize the adverse effects of these events. BP had created some degree of reputational resilience, exemplified by this observation from *Time* magazine: "It's also worth putting BP's transgressions, alleged or otherwise, in context. No other integrated oil company—certainly none with $285 billion in sales—has made a bigger commitment to alternative energy, cutting greenhouse gases and educating the public about conservation."[4] A January 2007 issue of *Business Week* reinforced a positive perception of BP with the cover story, "Beyond the Green Corporation." Pondering whether socially responsible policy could also add to a company's bottom line, the article contended that Innovest's better-than-Exxon AA risk rating for BP was derived from its $8 billion commitment to alternative energy.[5]

But BP was under financial pressure. When Tony Hayward assumed the helm of BP in 2007, he received a mandate from the board: no more safety disasters. He committed to increase the company's attentiveness to safety. Just a few months later, Hayward made a second pledge to boost BP's "dreadful" bottom line, promising to close an "$8 billion 'profit gap' with Shell. That, of course, meant cutting budgets."[6]

Hayward was aware of the tension between the costs of safety processes and profits. The U.S. Chemical Safety Board's 341-page report after the 2005 Texas City refinery fire identified one major cause to be corporate cost-cutting.

Furthermore, the company was aware of the importance of key business processes to its value and proudly disclosed its safety management processes to its shareholders. The company's 2009 Annual Report disclosed that a key enabler for safe, reliable, and compliant operations was the BP Operating

Chapter 2 | A $54 Billion Reputation

Management System, which "provides a common framework for all BP operations, designed to achieve consistency and continuous improvement in safety and efficiency. BP's operating management system includes mandatory practices, such as integrity management and incident investigation, which are designed to address particular risks."

BP also asserted that these processes created value when deployed by the right people with the right skills and capabilities. But given the relative underperformance of equity, the company also acknowledged that it needed to improve performance. They stated that incentives were in place to create value for shareholders. "Our people strategy has already resulted in refreshed group leadership and senior management teams, recruitment focused on individuals with strong operational and technical expertise, and *appropriate reward for performance at all levels*" (italics ours).

Notwithstanding those incentives, the federal Occupational Safety and Health Administration (OSHA) proposed in 2009 a record fine against BP for "failure to abate" previously cited hazards at Texas City.[7] OSHA also cited BP for hundreds of new "willful" safety violations, which, according to the Center for Public Integrity, totaled 829 from June 2007 to February 2010—97% of the violations for the entire industry.[6] In short, as the chairman of the federal Chemical Safety Board observed, BP had "yet to achieve an effective safety culture with regard to process safety management."[8]

The BP Regional Oil Spill Response Plan—Gulf of Mexico, dated June 30, 2009, covers all of the giant oil company's offshore operations in the Gulf and is one more example of a work product developed in an environment that had yet to develop an effective safety culture.[9]

BP mentioned sea lions, seals, sea otters, and walruses in its plan—Arctic animals that had not been seen in the Gulf for millions of years.

The BP plan offered a Japanese home shopping site as the link to one of its "primary equipment providers for BP in the Gulf of Mexico Region [for] rapid deployment of spill response resources on a 24 hour, 7 days a week basis."

In due course, lawmakers and TV comics would find fodder for incredulity and humor throughout.[10] Three omissions were less laughable:

- The plan included no information about tracking subsurface oil plumes from deepwater blowouts, although more oil might spread below the surface than at the top.

Reputation, Stock Price, and You

- The plan included no oceanic or meteorologic data, despite the ocean-floor site being in a hurricane-prone region.

- The plan included no measures for preventing viral and bacterial disease transmission to captured animals in rehab facilities. This had been found to be a major risk after the Exxon Valdez spill.

When metrics and control systems go awry and cost-cutting happens, morale among employees tends to decline quickly. One indication of morale decline at BP was an increase in complaints filed under BP's code of conduct. This code is designed to ensure that all employees comply with legal requirements and company standards in key areas such as safety, workplace behavior, bribery and corruption, and financial integrity. A second indication of morale decline was an uptick in employee complaints under Open Talk, a BP program that enables employees and contractors to report confidentially safety concerns or any suspected breach of compliance, ethics, or the code of conduct. When complaints under the *Open Talk* program decreased from 1,064 in 2006 to 874 in 2009, BP inferred that the risk controls in their operating management system were working. In fact, when normalized against a shrinking employee pool, the reporting rate was actually increasing. On the other hand, dismissals for violations fell off sharply. Slipping morale began to show elsewhere. In 2008, for example, only 42% of employees even bothered to respond to the survey on employee engagement.

Reputationally Linked Process Failure

Safety is a reputationally linked process. In the energy business, process safety generally comes down to a single issue: keeping hydrocarbons contained inside a steel pipe or tank.[6] An early chapter of the official U.S. government report, issued less than eight months after the explosion, explains that the disaster was not fortuitous but institutional. The January 2011 report, *Deepwater: The Gulf Oil Disaster and the Future of Offshore Drilling*, observed that "most of the mistakes and oversights at [the] Macondo [well] can be traced back to a single overarching failure—a failure of management."[11,12] All stakeholders were affected by the failure.

The 24/7 news cycle brought stories that outraged stakeholders of every variety. Many vented through various social media channels. The media saw that adverse BP news sold content and advertising and they produced more of the same. "The ink in the drink," as the disaster was soon called, generated predictable reactions among every stakeholder group: customers, employees, suppliers, creditors, equity investors, the board, analysts, and regulators.

Chapter 2 | A $54 Billion Reputation

Customers

Both customers and potential customers of BP were shocked. Initially most customers seemed to withhold negative reactions.[13] But three months into the crisis, the average consumer—and how many individuals of driving age are not potential consumers of BP-branded fuel products?—began to look at BP differently. Many had seen the logo's yellow sun and green leaves as evidence that the company was "beyond petroleum" and different from other oil companies and expected different behavior from the firm. They were profoundly disappointed and felt deceived.

In 1998, Ernest Lowe and Robert Harris published a paper in *Corporate Environmental Strategy* lauding BP for "Taking Climate Change Seriously: British Petroleum's Business Strategy." Twelve years later, they added a red-letter banner to their website:

> BP's Deep Horizon Blowout demonstrates that the company culture reported on in this [1998] paper has drowned in deeply polluted water. BP's own employees are reporting pre-blow out decisions made on a least cost rather than lowest risk basis, decisions leading to the deadly explosion of the oil platform. This disaster is already at the scale of the Exxon Valdez oil spill, with oil and toxic dispersants soaking Gulf wetlands, killing birds and marine life, and threatening the livelihood of tens of thousands of fisherman, processors, and tourist industry employees. Perhaps BP and the rest of the petro-industry can learn from the "golden era" described here.[14]

In the aftermath of the spill, BP-branded gas stations reported sales declines of 10%–40% from Florida to Illinois.[15] But BP owned just a fraction of the more than 11,000 stations across the United States that sold fuel under the BP banner. In an unfortunate demonstration of unintended consequences, the boycotts hurt mostly independent business owners who licensed the BP brand, and the net effect on BP's revenue line was negligible because the drop in BP's branded-fuel sales was offset by an almost equal jump in its unbranded-fuel sales.

Brand licenses eventually come up for renewal, and a BP-branded service station can just as easily offer fuel and convenience products under alternative brands. In 2011, BP reported 2.6% fewer BP, ARCO, and Aral retail brand licensees and 7% lower branded-fuel sales globally than in 2009.[29]

Fuel is fungible. Notwithstanding a damaged brand, BP can just as easily distribute fuel through resellers who will then bring white-label products to market. In 2011, BP reported 5.9% higher unbranded-fuel sales globally than in 2009.

Employees

Employees, including the CEO, suffered in the usual way: loss of morale and turnovers. Five weeks after the explosion, CEO Tony Hayward wrote an e-mail to all BP employees apprising them of the particulars of the event and response. He closed with a direct appeal: "[My]...request of you all remains the same—to stay focused, and do all that you can to ensure we have safe, reliable and efficient operations, wherever you are working."[16] Meanwhile, the company was shedding 800 more employees from its U.S. operations—a net of 3.5%, mostly from the corporate unit.

"Everybody is really angry," said an employee at the London headquarters in St. James's Square to the *Financial Times*. "There is some sympathy that this may be down to bad luck. But [chief executive] Tony Hayward has made the situation a million times worse." The reaction of staff mirrored that of the outside world. The question they were asking is: Am I working for the company I thought I was working for, with the right values?"[17]

Internally, there were two major worries. The first was whether concerns about BP's potential liabilities would hold back crucial investments in other parts of the business. But the bigger internal worry was how both the widespread disillusionment and potential cash crunch would impair the ability of BP to pay enough to retain and recruit talent.

The stress of four months of relentless crisis management took its toll on the CEO. When he closed an apology for the disruption to the lives of Gulf of Mexico area residents, he added for emphasis, "There's no one who wants this over more than I do. I'd like my life back."[3] Against memories of videos of Hayward at polo matches and of Deepwater deaths, it was a gaffe heard round the world. The company gave him his life back in July, replacing him with new CEO Bob Dudley.

Suppliers

As one of many cost-cutting strategies in 2009, BP began to simplify supplier relationships. Mr. Hayward spoke of his commitment to "driving deflation into the supply chain"[18] and reduced the number of IT suppliers from 40 to 5.[19] In the Gulf of Mexico, the company was drilling in cooperation with suppliers Halliburton and Transocean. Strategic partnerships with a few key suppliers is clearly better than managing many, but to succeed in any strategic multisourcing, governance becomes critical. With BP, merely shrinking the number of suppliers was inadequate when both supply-chain visibility and governance fell far short of the task.[20] Transocean, Halliburton, and other partners made

Chapter 2 | A $54 Billion Reputation

small safety tradeoffs that combined to create a much higher overall risk profile for the ultimate provider of goods to the end-customer, BP.

After the explosion, supplier-associated costs jumped as companies discovered that doing business with BP was riskier than previously imagined. Credit risk was an obvious consideration as BP's cash flows began being channeled in a variety of unexpected directions (see Chapter 9). Vendors also discovered that BP was attempting to spread some of the costs of the fallout. After adjusting for declines in the wider stock market, BP's two minority partners, Anadarko and Mitsui, and the rig's owner, Transocean, lost about $35 billion in combined value.[21] BP also sued its vendors: On April 21, BP sued Halliburton and Cameron International over the Gulf disaster, aiming to hold Halliburton accountable for "improper conduct, errors and omissions, including fraud and concealment." Halliburton said it would "vigorously deny these claims." BP also filed suit against Transocean Ltd., the Deepwater Horizon's owner and operator. According to BP's complaint, the former "breached its contractual duties, including failing to adequately maintain the rig and fix earlier engine problems and failing to train its crew and properly coordinate efforts to fight fires on the vessel." They also sued Cameron International over allegations that the blowout-prevention equipment they had supplied was a cause "in whole or in part" of the blowout and ensuing oil spill in the Gulf.[22]

The increased risk of doing business with BP ballooned production and manufacturing expenses. From 2008 to 2009, BP had cut its expenses from $26 billion to $23 billion, and cut purchases from $266 billion to $163 billion. In 2010, among the consequences of the explosion were jumps in expenses by $41 billion to $64 billion and in purchases by $53 billion to $216 billion.[10] Included in these additional $94 billion in costs were $40 billion BP set aside for various claims. As of April 2012, vendors conducting cleanup operations pocketed around $14 billion of BP money.

Creditors

Though BP was asset-rich, its liquidity position was challenged before the spill. After the spill, its credit costs rose dramatically as its credit-spread movements, usually measured in hundredths of a percentage point, rose to six percentage points over government rates. *The Economist* noted at the time that such dramatic deterioration in perceived creditworthiness can create a vicious and unpredictable spiral. There was a fear that counterparties to BP's giant and poorly disclosed derivatives book might demand extra collateral from it, leading to big cash calls.[20] Or not lend at all.

Tony Hayward spoke of how capital markets were "effectively closed" to BP at the height of the crisis. "We were not able to borrow in the capital markets

Reputation, Stock Price, and You

either short or medium-term debt at all," he said.[23] Bob Dudley called it a "near-death experience."

The regulatory arms of the executive branch and the oversight arms of the legislative branch of the U.S. government, as described below, pummeled BP. A meeting with U.S. President Barack Obama on 16 June 2010 gave BP what it desperately needed to calm the credit markets, starting with a limit on its damages outlay. "Obama … promised to end his market-rattling assault, telling the world, 'BP is a strong and viable company, and it is in all of our interests that it remain so.' Said Hayward: 'We needed political calmness. We needed to stop being attacked by the most powerful government in the world.'"[6]

The reputational benefits of this about-face by the United States were desperately needed. BP was not so lucky enlisting help from its home government. Much-needed relief from financial pressure through a parallel strategy involving investment by a sovereign wealth fund was thwarted by concurrent suggestions that BP had pressured the British government into commercially beneficial but ethically questionable actions.

Nineteen days after the BP executives' meeting with the U.S. president, on 5 July 2010, the chairman of Libya's national oil company disclosed that he was encouraging Libya's sovereign wealth fund to take a strategic stake in BP. The announcement came shortly after news that Libya had agreed to allow BP to start drilling off shore in accordance with a 2007 agreement. While these two pieces of news might have opened capital markets, they were instead met by howls of outrage when the physician who had diagnosed former Libyan agent Megrahi's terminal prostate cancer and given him three months to live—the grounds given for his compassionate release by the United Kingdom the year before—stated that on further reflection he "could survive for 10 years or more."[24] In fact, Megrahi succumbed to his cancer nearly 6 years later in May 2012.

Equity Investors

In 2009, BP profits fell by 45% as Tony Hayward received a 41% increase in his remuneration package comprising about £4 million ($6 million) in salary, bonus, and share awards. Four days before the Deepwater Horizon explosion, BP appeared to have shrugged off fears of a shareholder revolt over its executive pay policy after preliminary results showed that notwithstanding the lobbying of PIRC, the investor body, 84% of shareholders voted in favor of its remuneration plans.[25]

Chapter 2 | A $54 Billion Reputation

After adjusting for declines in the wider stock market, about $65 billion was wiped off the value of BP in the first eight weeks following the crisis. Shareholders reacted through both their votes and their lawyers.

At the 2010 annual general meeting, Sir William Castell—BP's senior independent director and chairman of the safety committee—saw 43% of shareholders vote against his re-election. He stepped down from the board. BP Chairman Carl-Henric Svanberg saw 15% of shareholders vote against him, but he managed to retain the confidence of the majority of investors.[26]

In the aftermath of the event and the loss in equity value, shareholders filed three derivative lawsuits in the United States against the directors and officers of BP.[27] The lawsuits allege that the blowout, fire, and oil spill could have been prevented if the directors and officers of BP had paid more attention to safety issues. The plaintiffs allege that the directors and officers have a fiduciary duty to put in place and monitor systems that will detect and address those problems, but the defendant BP officials only "went through the motions." They further allege a pattern of accidents and other close calls should have alerted BP CEO Tony Hayward and other high-level employees that their cost-cutting measures left the company vulnerable, but they still ignored the red flags. Last, the suits allege breach of fiduciary duty and waste of corporate assets.

The plaintiffs sought more than monetary damages. They also asked the court to force BP's board to institute a long list of corporate governance changes aimed at improving accountability and transparency at BP.

In September 2011, Judge Keith Ellison of the Southern District of Texas dismissed the cases, "as the English High Court is the more appropriate forum for this case."[28] Yet, as recently as July 2012, investors were still trying to revive the cases in the United States Fifth Circuit.

BP Executives and Board of Directors

After replacing CEO Tony Hayward with Bob Dudley in July 2010, the embarrassed board took an active interest in safety oversight. On safety, the board supported and challenged Bob Dudley and his executive team as they restructured and enhanced BP's processes, systems, and culture. They also initiated a review of the way BP manages, reports, and acts on risk, including board oversight.[29]

Capital Market Analysts

Nine weeks into the crisis, Moody's slashed BP's credit rating by three notches, saying its downgrade "reflects the worsening impact expected from the oil pouring into the Gulf of Mexico." Fitch, another rating agency, downgraded the company to close to junk levels.

Regulators

Over a 12-week span following the explosion, Congress held more than 50 hearings and examined more than 80 bills related to the spill, including some that would limit BP's future business opportunities.[30] Investigations continued, with U.S. Attorney General Eric Holder stating on April 24, 2012, "The Deepwater Horizon Task Force is continuing its investigation into the explosion and will hold accountable those who violated the law in connection with the largest environmental disaster in U.S. history." The first arrest related to the spill was in April 2012; an engineer was charged with obstruction of justice for allegedly deleting 300 text messages showing BP knew the flow rate was three times higher than initial claims by the company, and for knowing that the Top Kill effort to cap the well was unlikely to succeed, but claiming otherwise.[31,32,33]

Health, safety, and environment fines and penalties levied by regulators totaled only $77.4 million in 2011—not much more than several past years had cost.[34] Penalties and fines, however, are lagging indicators. Under the Clean Water Act, depending on whether the company is found grossly negligent, BP plc could be fined between $5.4 billion and $21.1 billion.[35] The Department of Justice signaled that it was looking for an out-of-court settlement of $25 billion. BP is hoping to settle for under $15 billion. As of June 2012, $11 billion remained in the fund BP set aside in 2010 for all Gulf-related claims,[36] but only $3.5 billion of that fund was allocated for penalties under the Clean Water Act. Those could balloon to $21 billion if the Justice Department proves gross negligence. The *Financial Times* concluded that "a gross negligence finding would seriously—perhaps fatally—damage" BP's reputation.[37]

Reputational Value Lost: Summary

The economic consequences of BP's reputational fall after April 2010 underscore how much value BP had created in its reputation and how much it had placed at risk by not instituting the oversight or operational controls needed to effect a thorough cultural transformation. Relative to 2009 on a per-barrel basis,[38] in 2011 BP spent 81% more on goods and services, 8% more to produce and manufacture, 41% more to explore, and 16% more to

Chapter 2 | A $54 Billion Reputation

finance its operations (Table 2-1). In total, a reasonable estimate of the dollar value lost by BP amounts to $91 billion in direct and increased costs in 2010 and $124 billion in inflation-adjusted costs in 2011 for a total of $215 billion of additional costs over two years relative to 2009. With respect to enterprise value, between 10 March 2010, and 1 June 2012, while the S&P 500 composite equity index climbed 9.3%, BP's stock price dropped 35.4%. The 44% difference would add around $54 billion to BP's enterprise value. It is one of the most dramatic examples on record of a failure of oversight and management of the elements of reputation.

Table 2-1. Proportional Cost Increases (Decreases) over the 2009 Pre-Disaster BP Group P&L Statement

Cost Item per Barrel	2010 (%)	2011 (%)
Purchases (expense)	41.57	80.86
Production and manufacturing expense	198.63	7.92
Exploration expense	(19.00)	41.24
Finance costs	13.03	16.41

Retrospective

Following the Deepwater Horizon accident, BP entered 2011 facing a range of uncertainties. These included concerns about its ability to operate safely in deepwater; meet its financial commitments in the Gulf of Mexico; and, more broadly, how to recover the trust and reputational value it had lost. The 2011 annual report reflects these concerns and presents a company that is focused on safety, trust, and risk management at the highest levels of the organization. These intangible assets are presented in an integrated operational framework. Innovation, safety, security, and sustainability receive joint mention under the heading of "Reputation and Competitive Advantage":

> Our development and application of technology represents [sic] a distinctive capability that is central to our reputation and competitive advantage. For us, technology is the practical application of scientific knowledge to manage risks, capture business value and inform strategy development. This includes the research, development, demonstration and acquisition of new technical capabilities and support for the deployment of BP's know-how.

Reputation, Stock Price, and You | 23

We monitor the potential opportunities and risks presented by emerging science, interdisciplinary innovation and new players; natural resource issues and climate concerns; and evolving policy concerns, including the current emphasis on energy security and efficiency.

In 2011, the company deployed a "multi-tiered risk-management solution" to manage three types of risks: strategic, safety and operational, and compliance and control. Under the heading of safety and operational risks came process safety, environmental risk, physical security, product quality, cyber security, and crisis management and business continuity. The purposes of the "integrated solution" were to reduce costs, mitigate overall risks, and protect the company's reputation.

At the group level, the safety and risk management component included targets for recordable injury frequency, loss of primary containment, and implementation of change programs. Significantly, safety was now a factor in the executive bonus plan. This underlined the company's strategic priorities of reinforcing safety and risk management at the highest executive and board levels.

BP's board considered reputation from two perspectives: the reputational risks to the group and the processes the company has in place to manage these risks. In 2011, the board reviewed external reputation data that looked at BP's reputation in the United Kingdom and United States. It also discussed the group's communications strategy and its reputation-management plan.

To underscore how serious BP was about reputation and its risk management, the annual report employed the term twenty times in the "Item 1A. Risk Factors" section of Form 10-K. The term also appeared liberally throughout the balance of the document (a total of 45 mentions over 20 different pages in the 300-page document). The processes of rebuilding trust and reinforcing value creation were now focused on external reputation measured by external surveys and internal morale measured by internal surveys.

All these changes reflected what BP argued was an improvement in its culture for safety. It was a challenging argument to make in the face on ongoing regulatory pressures, for, as the *Financial Times* noted: "If the U.S. Department of Justice does push its accusations of gross negligence against BP to trial, disinterested observers can look forward to a detailed exploration of the oil company's culture and management."[39]

Consider This

- Authenticity is important. BP aggressively promoted an image of the firm that, while aspirational, was at odds with reality. If you tell the world how great you are, you had better live up to your hype. Jerry Della Femina, reputedly an inspiration for the TV series *Mad Men*,[40] observed, "Nothing kills a bad product faster than good advertising."[41]

- Restoring a reputation entails more than marketing. Implementing authentic operational controls and linking them to reputation risk and value, as BP reported in their 2011 annual report, was an exemplary demonstration of evolution in process control and risk management to reduce reputational volatility and stabilize enterprise value.

- When trust is violated, authenticity may require a third party's validation. BP's long history of reputational crises will doubtless color its reputational metrics for some time to come. Stakeholders remain cautious about revaluing the company until such time as credible third parties or insurers validate real behavior changes from BP's reputation restoration efforts.

By the Numbers

BP's story dramatizes the measurability and magnitude of reputational value, and how each stakeholder impacts that value. In keeping with this book's mission of showing the relationship among reputation, stakeholder behaviors that are reflected in measures of profit and loss, and stock price, Table 2-2 and all similarly placed tables at the end of each future chapter recap quantitative measures introduced in the preceding materials.

Table 2-2. Reputational Value Losses: Additional and Extraordinary Costs of BP's Reputational Crisis Arising from Stakeholder Behaviors

Stakeholder	Effects on BP plc
Customers	2.6% fewer BP, ARCO, and Aral retail brand licensees and 7% lower branded fuel sales globally than in 2009
Employees	Morale: overall employee satisfaction index score (BP internal metric) for 2011 (62%) was below the score from 2009 (65%); CEO fired.

Vendors and suppliers	$94 billion in additional expenses Production: 8% increase over 2009 Exploration: 41% increase over 2009
Creditors	Liquidity crisis; net cost of credit 16% increase over 2009; credit default swap spreads August 2012 about 35 basis points higher (70% higher) than March 2010
Investors	Two board members not re-elected; three derivative lawsuits; and friction over future CEO compensation
Board of Directors	Additional responsibilities; new compensation plans with reputation and safety-linked bonus
Analysts	Credit downgrade: S&P AA (stable outlook) before the event to A (stable outlook) by December 2011
Regulators	50 hearings; 80 bills; and $15–$25 billion in fines and penalties
All stakeholders combined	Net $54 billion in lost market capitalization

Endnotes

1   BP results hit by $US5b US writedown. *Canberra Times*. 31 July 2012. Available at: http://www.canberratimes.com.au/business/mining-and-resources/bp-results-hit-by-us5b-us-writedown-20120731-23cos.html. Accessed 4 September 2012.

2   Frey D. How green is BP? *New York Times*. 8 December 2002. Available at: http://www.nytimes.com/2002/12/08/magazine/how-green-is-bp.html?pagewanted=all&src=pm. Accessed 17 June 2012.

3   BP CEO Tony Hayward (VIDEO): 'I'd like my life back.' *Huffington Post*. 1 June 2010. Available at: http://www.huffingtonpost.com/2010/06/01/bp-ceo-tony-hayward-video_n_595906.html. Accessed 14 June 2012.

4   Fonda D. Is BP really that green? *Time*. 29 June 2006. Available at: http://www.time.com/time/business/article/0,8599,1209454,00.html. Accessed 17 June 2012.

5   Solman G. BP: coloring public opinion? *Adweek*. 14 January 2008. Available at: http://www.adweek.com/news/advertising/bp-coloring-public-opinion-91662. Accessed 17 June 2012.

6   Elkind P, Whitford D, Burke D. BP: 'An accident waiting to happen.' *Fortune*. 24 January 2011. Available at: http://features.blogs.fortune.cnn.com/2011/01/24/bp-an-accident-waiting-to-happen/. Accessed 22 July 2012.

7   Aulds TJ. OSHA slaps BP with record $87M fine. *The Galveston Daily News*. 31 October 2009. Available at: http://galvestondailynews.com/story.lasso?ewcd=3a8ab45c2e06da20 Accessed 22 July 2012.

Chapter 2 | A $54 Billion Reputation

8 Greenhouse S. BP to challenge fine for refinery blast. *New York Times*. 30 October 2009. Available at: http://www.nytimes.com/2009/10/31/business/31labor.html. Accessed 22 July 2012.

9 Regional oil spill response plan – Gulf of Mexico. *Public Intelligence*. 20 May 2010. Available at: http://publicintelligence.net/bp-gulf-of-mexico-regional-oil-spill-response-plan/ Accessed 15 September 2012.

10 Mohr H, Pritchard J, Lush T. BP spill response plans severely flawed. *Associated Press*. 9 June 2010. Available at: http://www.msnbc.msn.com/id/37599810/ns/disaster_in_the_gulf/t/bp-spill-response-plans-severely-flawed/#.T9pJzvGN9qI. Accessed 14 June 2012.

11 An oil spill born of complacency. *Financial Times*. 6 January 2011. Available at: http://www.ft.com/intl/cms/s/0/2159e888-19cd-11e0-b921-00144feab49a.html#axzz1xzO61Xtp. Accessed 17 June 2012.

12 National Commission on the BP Deepwater Horizon Oil Spill and Offshore Drilling. Deepwater: the Gulf Oil disaster and the future of offshore drilling. 11 January 2011. Available at: http://www.oilspillcommission.gov/final-report. Accessed 15 September 2012.

13 Antczak J. Gulf oil spill yet to affect consumers' gas choice. *Associated Press*. 5 May 2010. Available at: http://www.newsvine.com/_news/2010/05/05/4243815-gulf-oil-spill-yet-to-affect-consumers-gas-choice. Accessed 14 June 2012.

14 Lowe EA, Harris RJ. *Taking Climate Change Seriously: British Petroleum's Business Strategy*. Ph. D thesis published in *Corporate Environmental Strategy*. Winter 1998. Available at: http://www.indigodev.com/BPclim.html. Accessed 15 June 2012.

15 Some BP gas station owners believe name change to Amoco might bring back angry customers. *Associated Press*. 30 July 2010. Available at: http://www.cleveland.com/nation/index.ssf/2010/07/some_bp_gas_station_owners_bel.html. Accessed 14 June 2012.

16 Gulf of Mexico oil spill: Tony Hayward's email to BP staff. *The Telegraph*. 19 May 2010. Available at: http://www.telegraph.co.uk/finance/newsbysector/energy/oilandgas/7743054/Gulf-of-Mexico-oil-spill-Tony-Haywards-email-to-BP-staff.html. Accessed 14 June 2012.

17 Boxell J, Crooks E. Inside BP: a giant wounded. *Financial Times*. 15 July 2010. Available at: http://www.ft.com/intl/cms/s/0/bded3254-9048-11df-ad26-00144feab49a.html#axzz1xp9rjZl0. Accessed 15 June 2012.

18 Crooks E. BP pledges to keep spending plans. *Financial Times*. 4 February 2009. Available at: http://www.ft.com/intl/cms/s/0/4f3fa228-f25c-11dd-9678-0000779fd2ac.html#axzz1xzO61Xtp. Accessed 16 June 2012.

19 BP: the challenges of strategic multi-sourcing. *Computer Weekly*. 28 August 2009. Available at: http://www.computerweekly.com/news/1280096992/BP-the-challenges-of-strategic-multi-sourcing. Accessed 16 June 2012.

20 Operations lessons from BP. *Corp Exec Board Views*. September 12, 2010. Available at: http://cebviews.com/2010/09/12/operations-lessons-from-bp/. Accessed 16 June 2012.

21 BP counts the political and financial cost of Deepwater Horizon. *The Economist*. 17 June 2010. Available at: http://www.economist.com/node/16381032. Accessed 16 June 2012.

22 BP: Finger pointing. Mission Intangible blog of the Intangible Asset Finance Society. 29 April 2011. Available at: http://www.iafinance.org/_blog/MISSION_INTANGIBLE/post/BP_Finger_pointing/. Accessed 17 June 2012.

Reputation, Stock Price, and You | 27

23 Crooks E. 'Bad calls' preceded Gulf of Mexico blast. *Financial Times*. 9 November 2010. Available at: http://www.ft.com/intl/cms/s/0/a51cfcbc-ec0c-11df-b50f-00144feab49a. html#axzz1AlvCT9ip. Accessed 17 June 2012.

24 Jamieson A. Dying Lockerbie bomber 'could survive for 10 years or more.' *The Telegraph*. 4 July 2010. Available at: http://www.telegraph.co.uk/news/worldnews/africaandindianocean/ libya/7871234/Dying-Lockerbie-bomber-could-survive-for-10-years-or-more.html. Accessed 14 June 2012.

25 BP shareholder revolt over executive pay plans shrugged off. *Personnel Today*. 16 April 2010. Available at: http://www.personneltoday.com/Articles/16/04/2010/55255/bp-shareholder-revolt-over-executive-pay-plans-shrugged-off.htm#.UAxRskS1_-k. Accessed 22 July 2012.

26 Macallster T. BP faces shareholder revolt over Bob Dudley's pay. *The Guardian*. 11 April 2012. Available at: http://www.guardian.co.uk/business/2012/apr/11/bp-shareholder-revolt-bob-dudley-pay. Accessed 22 July 2012.

27 Grimm MR, Herman HR, Herman TR. Director and Officer Insurance and the Gulf Oil Spill. *Clausen Miller*. August 2010. Available at: http://www.clausen.com/index.cfm/fa/firm_pub. article/article/1abaff03-46ad-4092-a974-7ce99b7bab0a/Director_And_Officer_Insurance_And_The_Gulf_Oil_Spill.cfm. Accessed 22 July 2012.

28 LaCroix, K. BP Deepwater Horizon derivative suit dismissed in favor of English forum. *The D&O Diary*. 19 September 2011. Available at: http://www.dandodiary.com/2011/09/ articles/shareholders-derivative-litiga/bp-deepwater-horizon-derivative-suit-dismissed-in-favor-of-english-forum/. Accessed 22 July 2012.

29 BP Annual Report and Form 20-F 2011 p10.

30 Werdigier J, Mouawad J. Road to new confidence at BP runs through U.S. *The New York Times*. 26 July 2010. Available at: http://www.nytimes.com/2010/07/27/business/27dudley. html?pagewanted=all. Accessed 14 June 2012.

31 Rudolf J. Kurt Mix, BP engineer, faces first oil spill charges (UPDATES). Available at: Huffingtonpost.com. Accessed 14 June 2012.

32 Johnson K, Jervis R. Former BP engineer charged in oil spill probe. *USA Today*. 24 April 2012. Available at: http://www.usatoday.com/money/industries/energy/story/2012-04-24/ bp-oil-spill-arrest-justice-department/54504158/1. Accessed 14 June 2012

33 Lustgarten A. Feds file first criminal charges related to BP Gulf spill. *ProPublica* 24 April 2012. Available at: http://www.propublica.org/article/feds-file-first-criminal-charges-related-to-bp-gulf-spill. Accessed 14 June 2012.

34 BP Global HSE fines and penalties. Available at: http://www.bp.com/ sectiongenericarticle800.do?categoryId=9036151&contentId=7066887. Accessed 17 June 2012.

35 Burdeau C. BP oil spill: fines from Clean Water Act will go to restoration. *Associated Press*. 8 March 2012. Available at: http://www.huffingtonpost.com/2012/03/09/bp-oil-spill-fines-restoration_n_1333019.html. Accessed 17 June 2012.

36 Hammer D. BP wants to pay less than $15 billion to settle government spill claims, London paper says. *Times-Picayune*. 8 June 2012. Available at: http://www.nola com

Chapter 2 | A $54 Billion Reputation

/news/gulf-oil-spill/index.ssf/2012/06/bp_wants_to_pay_less_than_15_b.html. Accessed 17 June 2012.

37 Lex. BP–still in deep water. *Financial Times*. 5 September 2012. Available at: http://www.ft.com/intl/cms/s/3/b30160b0-f75a-11e1-8e9e-00144feabdc0.html#axzz25h3VSeTG. Accessed 6 September 2012.

38 Historical crude oil prices (table). Available at: http://inflationdata.com/inflation/inflation_rate/historical_oil_prices_table.asp. Updated June 14, 2012. Accessed 23 June 2012.

39 Hill A. DoJ's plan to put BP's culture on trial. *Financial Times*. 5 September 2012. Available at: http://blogs.ft.com/businessblog/2012/09/dojs-plan-to-put-bps-culture-on-trial/#axzz26YjLMWYP. Accessed 15 September 2012.

40 Wikepedia. Jerry Della Famina. Available at: http://en.wikipedia.org/wiki/Jerry_Della_Femina. Accessed 22 June 2102.

41 Famous quotes on advertising and copywriting. Available at: http://www.zagstudios.com/ZagStudios/famous_quotes_on_advertising.html. Accessed 22 June 2012.

PART II

Profit and Loss

CHAPTER

3

Customers

Repetition makes reputation and reputation makes customers.

—Elizabeth Arden

Customers are thoughtful people. They have choices. Customers may act on behalf of themselves or their households, businesses, or government offices. But regardless of who foots the bill, customers are intelligent decision makers. When they make a decision, three major factors are in play: price, quality, and reputation.[1,2,3] Moreover, unless price is the only consideration by virtue of a "lowest bid" mandate, reputation will reduce customers' sensitivity to price, increase sales volume, and accelerate the speed with which purchase decisions are made.

This chapter builds on the BP case that illustrated a complex relationship between customer and company and an evolving reputation. The focus is on how reputations are formed in the minds of customers; how reputation value—the economically relevant actions triggered by reputation—impacts the revenue line of the Profit and Loss statement; and, ultimately, how these customers' behaviors impact stock price.

The BP case showed how customers responded to a lost reputation. Even though petroleum products are fungible commodities—automobile engines will shamelessly burn 89 octane gasoline drawn from any pump—with no obviously discernible features from competitive products, the costs of BP's reputational crisis were that brand licenses fell off 2.7% and branded fuel sales fell off 7%. To illustrate the points with noncommodities, we turn to case studies on several key drivers of reputation. For Rolls-Royce Holdings plc, the dominant concern for stakeholders is safety—in this case the unerring performance of the Rolls-Royce aircraft engines. For Zale Corporation, the dominant concern for stakeholders is quality of service. For Research In Motion Limited, innovation is the critical dimension of reputation.

Chapter 3 | Customers

Safety

[Safety is] the state of being certain that a set of conditions will not accidentally cause adverse effects on the well-being of employees, the public, or the environment. (Table 1-1)

On 4 January 2011, an anonymous poster left an ominous query on Answers. com: "Is the Rolls-Royce Trent 900 engine safe?" Nine weeks earlier, Qantas flight QF32 from Singapore and Sydney was forced to turn back and make an emergency landing after an explosion in one of the aircraft's Rolls-Royce engines—a Trent 900. The force of the blowout damaged the body of the plane, an Airbus A380, and, to put it mildly, heightened the awareness of 433 passengers and 26 crew members. It also rained debris on the Indonesian island of Batam below.[4] A second Qantas flight, a Boeing 747 with the same type of Rolls-Royce Trent 900 engine, had to return to Singapore a day later, and shortly thereafter, Qantas reported that it found oil leaks that were "beyond normal tolerances" in Trent 900 engines on three additional aircraft. In a story headlined "Rolls-Royce's reputation is most of its value," Robert Cole, writing for Reuters' *Breakingview*, noted that day: "Rolls is a business built upon its ability to forge awe-inspiring technology from plain metals. But it trades to a large extent on its reputation for the reliability of that technology and the sturdiness of the metals it uses."[5]

Rolls-Royce

In a business in which safety is a life-and-death issue, systems for ensuring safety through quality are the core of reputational value creation and maintenance. Rolls-Royce Group plc is such a business. Rolls-Royce is iconic. This $19-billion integrated-power-systems company delivers reliable power that is "mission-critical" to its customers. Operating in civil and defense aerospace, marine, and energy markets, the company serves customers in more than 120 countries. It is a global provider of defense aero-engine products and services, with 18,000 engines in service for 160 customers in 103 countries. Its marine business has equipment installed on more than 30,000 vessels worldwide among more than 2,000 customers including 70 navies. The company's energy business is a supplier of power systems for onshore and offshore oil and gas applications.

Reputation Management

Delivering "mission-critical" power to keep commercial aircraft aloft is an awesome responsibility. Loss of power in an A380 super carrier places at risk

Reputation, Stock Price, and You

the lives of 525 passengers in a typical three-class configuration or up to 853 passengers in an all-economy class configuration, plus crew.

Rolls-Royce both understands this responsibility and has developed systems to address relevant risks. Its asset preservation policy prioritizes the three greatest things it is protecting: reputation, profitability, and viability.[6]

The distinction here is Rolls-Royce's recognition of reputational benefits of safety above all else—safety is the industry's central obsession. In 1985, a Japan Airlines (JAL) jet plowed into Osutaka Ridge, about a three-hour distance by car north of Tokyo, marking what is still the world's deadliest single-plane disaster. JAL executives have visited the crash site every year since then to remind themselves of the importance of safety to their industry.[7]

Process Controls

Rolls-Royce, the second largest maker of aerospace engines behind General Electric, is an engineering firm. Revered by many in the community for its technical acumen, Rolls-Royce has long had a reputation for innovation, quality, safety, and overall engineering excellence. It maintains strong controls both internally and over its supply chain. The head of one long-term supplier put it this way to the *Financial Times*, "I think of Rolls-Royce (as) a rather fussy mother hen."[8]

Global supply chains are complex, with multiple interrelationships across a wide network of organizations. While the company's strategy is to simplify internal and external elements of its supply chain by building long-term strategic links with fewer, stronger suppliers, risk of disruption remains from financial or physical causes such as bankruptcy, natural disaster, armed conflict, or pandemic. Intangible asset risks (ethical, quality, safety, etc.) also arise from the supply chain, which inevitably flow downstream to Rolls-Royce.

All of Rolls-Royce's procedures have teeth: the company has a reputation for being tough on suppliers whose performance falls below standard. On the Trent 900 explosion, the *Financial Times* reported, "If this [the perpetrator of the fault] turns out to be a supplier, it will be crucified."[9]

In its preliminary investigation into the QF32 engine explosion, Australian investigators, working with Rolls-Royce, Qantas, and Airbus engineers, traced the likely cause to a badly manufactured oil pipe that cracked, causing oil to leak and catch fire, leading to the engine over-revving and the turbine disc being flung through the side of the engine.

While the company worked flat out to rectify the faults and to understand why the faults were not identified during inspections, it remained remarkably

Chapter 3 | Customers

tight-lipped about crisis management. Aside from noting the existence of a crisis management plan for supply chain interruption, the 2009 annual report is silent on the subject. "It's as though your maiden aunt has suffered a trauma but is trying desperately to preserve an air of Victorian composure" said the *Financial Times*.[9] The company refused to expand on a short statement on 12 November 2010 in which Rolls-Royce said it had isolated the problem to a "component"—believed to be the pipe coupling—and had a program in hand to rectify the faults across all Trent 900 engines.

Few familiar with its culture were surprised by the aero-engine maker's unwillingness to divulge details about the investigation. First, the company is justifiably worried about others gaining access to its technical secrets. Second, with its deep engineering heritage, the predominant culture at the company is against making "snap judgments and early pronouncements, preferring to carefully establish the facts."[9]

Trent 900 Explosion-and-Aftermath Timeline

By the close of markets 4 November 2010, shares in the engine's manufacturer, Rolls-Royce plc, fell 5.5% to 618.5 pence on the London Stock Exchange—their sharpest fall in 18 months[9] and the lowest price since mid-September 2010. Shares in the European Aeronautic Defence and Space Company (EADS), which owns Airbus, also fell.[10]

In the spirit of "kicking 'em while they're down," the day after the incident, United Technologies Corp.'s Pratt & Whitney jet-engine unit and the third largest aerospace engine manufacturer, filed patent-infringement complaints against Rolls-Royce claiming the Trent 900 infringed a patent for a swept-fan blade.[11]

The suit was, at a minimum, strategic and designed to capture the attention of Boeing 787 customers. In the market for engines for the Boeing aircraft, the apparent low risk of the Trent was competitively advantageous. Both the recent history of a catastrophic failure and a pending intellectual property lawsuit posed new risks for a potential customer.

That same day, Qantas reported that 10 affected planes would be out of service for "as long as it takes," Chief Executive Officer Alan Joyce said at a press briefing in Sydney. "At Qantas we are proud to put passenger safety before profit," he said.[12] With its fleet of A830s grounded for several weeks, Qantas substituted Boeing 747 aircraft.

Reputational crises attract lawyers for a wide range of issues. On 2 December, Qantas filed a claim to ensure it could take legal action against Rolls-Royce to recover passenger traffic losses caused by the explosion and the additional

Reputation, Stock Price, and You 35

costs due to aircraft substitution. (Rolls-Royce paid Qantas $100 million within 6 months to settle those claims.[13])

That same day, Rolls-Royce informed the general public that it seemed to have gotten its arms around the accident's cause. The company determined that the direct cause of the oil fire and resulting engine failure was a misaligned counter bore within a stub oil pipe leading to a fatigue fracture.[14] On 10 December, Rolls-Royce disclosed that it would cost $500 million to repair the defects in a series of small metal couplings that feed oil to bearings in the Trent 900 engine.

Although the engineering problem may have been solved, the growing reputation crisis was in full swing. On 23 December, BBC business news reporter Shanaz Musafer opened a discussion with, "Have you ever played that game where someone says a word to you and you say the first thing that you associate with it? If not, try these: Toyota, BP, Rolls-Royce, or perhaps even Heathrow Airport."[15]

Rolls-Royce Customers

"Trent 900" was unknown to those outside of a select few in the industry and had not been a household word until late 2010. That's when customers of Rolls-Royce's customers—potential airline passengers—took an extraordinary interest and turned to the modern-day oracle: Google Search. A Google Trends chart (Figure 3-1) shows a progressive decline over the years in Web searches for Rolls-Royce and immediately following the crisis, a marked spike in searches for the esoteric term, "Trent 900."

Within days, equity investors had their say. Indirect stakeholders, airline passengers, had their say. And the media pundits had theirs. But notwithstanding Qantas's litigation for damages, the engine manufacturer's customers had been silent.

On 6 January 2011, the first customer spoke. In a compelling vote of confidence from British Airways plc, Europe's third-biggest airline, CEO Willie Walsh agreed to buy Trent 900s for 12 A380s to be delivered starting 2013. "British Airways signed the A380 contract, first flagged in 2007, after Chief Executive Officer Willie Walsh affirmed his 'absolute confidence' in the Trent 900…The deal took years to seal because of talks over through-life servicing, a BA spokesman said, declining to reveal if the carrier got a discount on the order's list price of $5 billion, including seven A380s and 18 787 Dreamliners it has options to buy."[16]

Rolls-Royce's reputation for engineering safety had produced a miracle. "Rolls-Royce, the world's largest engine maker after General Electric Co., is pleased

Chapter 3 | Customers

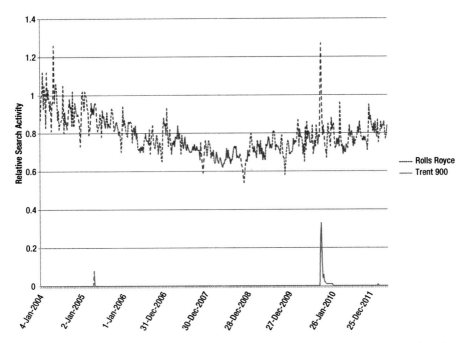

Figure 3-1. Google trends plot illustrating the November 2010 spike in Web searches for the terms "Rolls-Royce" and "Trent 900." Data source: *Google Trends*.

that one of its biggest airline clients continues to 'trust' in its products, CEO John Rose said." In its 2011 Annual Report, Rose emphasized that no customers dropped Trent 900 orders, while some had reconfirmed business since November 2010.[17] In 2006, Rolls-Royce had become the sole engine supplier to Airbus for the 350 series.[18] And it still held that coveted distinction[19] in June 2011, when Airbus affirmed that Rolls-Royce remained the sole supplier to the A350 series.[20]

As to reputational matters, customers tend to act fast. Surprisingly, so can regulators. On 5 March 2011, Europe's air safety regulator lifted the requirement for frequent, repetitive engine inspections of Rolls-Royce engines fitted to the Airbus A380 superjumbo, partly out of concern the inspections could now be doing more harm than good. "The root cause of the [QF32] incident having been addressed through other adequate measures, it is considered prudent to cancel these inspections," the agency said.[21]

Retrospective

Eight weeks out from the catastrophic failure of a mission-critical product, Rolls-Royce showed the reputational and economic profile of a company with significant reputation resilience. The media backed off, and the general public

Reputation, Stock Price, and You | 37

lost interest. Much of the credit for this display of enterprise value preservation goes to the company's reputation for engineering excellence and its outstanding intangible asset risk management program.

If one criticism may be levied, it is about weak crisis-communications efforts. Many communications pundits peppered the blogosphere with the central message that CEO Sir John Rose should have been much more visible and forthcoming.

"I'm not surprised," explained Jonathan Salem Baskin, noted brand marketer and author of the *Histories of Social Media* and *Tell the Truth*. "Rolls-Royce focused on analyzing and fixing the problem, and was likely having conversations with numerous stakeholder groups involved in that operational reality. The world wanted the business focused on business, some outlier bloggers notwithstanding, and Rolls-Royce's successes in its efforts were obviously recognized and valued."

Eighteen months later, all was going well. In April 2012, the Reputation Institute reported that the three most reputable companies in Britain were Rolls-Royce (jet engines), Dyson (vacuum cleaners), and Alliance Boots (drugs and prawn sandwiches).[22] And customers were buying product. The commercial aviation section that sold Trent 900 engines, among others, reported strong sales in 2011. Although the costs of the repairs and indemnifications cut deeply into profits, future sales, deliveries, and revenues were all up substantially in the year following the explosion, with growth over 2009 of 10.4%, 14.0%, and 24.3% respectively (Table 3-1).[23]

Notwithstanding great sales and engineering power, Rolls-Royce had not lost track of what its customers value. Rolls-Royce cited "reputation" 15 times in its 2011 annual report; the company disclosed that its sources of reputational risk include failures in sustainability practices, regulatory compliance, innovation effectiveness, ethical practices, oversight, operational controls (quality and safety), and IT security. The company also explained its strategy for managing each of the reputational risks it disclosed.

Table 3-1. Percentage Changes in Rolls-Royce Commercial Aviation Section's Orders, Deliveries, Revenue, and Profits for 2010 and 2011 Relative to 2009

(Relative to 2009 values)	2010 (%)	2011 (%)
Order book	3.2	10.4
Engine deliveries	0.2	14.0
Revenue	9.8	24.3
Profits	−20.5	1.2

Chapter 3 | Customers

Consider This

- In the aircraft power plant business, a reputation for safety is a critical asset.

- In a globally integrated manufacturing operation, such a reputation is the product of superior engineering design and risk management, which includes top-notch supply chain oversight and operational control.

- Notwithstanding other costs associated with a reputational crisis, a superior reputation can preserve a company's relationship with customers and protect revenues against "headline risks."

Quality: Zale Corporation

[Quality is] the extent to which a product is free from defects or deficiencies; a service meets or exceeds the expectations of customers or clients, and both products and services conform to measurable and verifiable criteria. (Table 1-1)

In 2009, Zale Corporation was one of North America's largest specialty jewelry retailers.[24] With about 50,000 jewelry retail stores in 2009, the jewelry industry employed approximately 200,000 individuals. Wal-Mart was the largest U.S. retailer and the next largest was Zale, with more than 2,000 stores and kiosks.

Zale sells diamond fashion rings, semiprecious stones, earrings, and gold jewelry, as well as watches and gift items. It operates under three business segments: Fine Jewelry, Kiosk Jewelry, and All Other. During the fiscal year ending 31 July 2008, the Fine Jewelry segment generated approximately 88% of the company's net revenues and the Kiosk 12% of total revenues. Total sales were $2.1 billion, with earnings of $10.8 million. In September 2008, its share price peaked at almost $31. Just over a year later, in December, 2009, its share price had plunged to $3.25 and its market cap to levels as low at $100 million. What happened?

In Jewelry, Reputation Is Crucial

Fine jewelers sell precious stones and metals that are worked to produce a product with both emotional and resale value. Since jewelry is seldom branded and varies widely in design and quality in the mid-market segment, purchasers require some form of "trusted expertise" in retail environments. The jeweler's

Reputation, Stock Price, and You | 39

name is the brand: retailers with strong reputations for knowledge, integrity, and trust attract the most consumers.

In the fine jewelry business, the last 18 inches is crucial. That's the space between a salesperson and a customer, just enough room to place the product (and what it represents) between two human beings and build a trusting relationship focused on the consumer's aspirations, hopes, and dreams. Because jewelry's intrinsic value is based on a significant amount of knowledge about how to evaluate quality, most customers must rely on the salespeople across the 18-inch countertop in front of them. In the middle market, the customer must trust that the price is fair, a factor that includes recoverable or liquidation value as well. These elements are the essence of quality in fine jewelry.

Damaging Zale's Reputation for Quality

The first Zale Jewelers opened in 1924 in Wichita Falls, Texas, founded by Morris Zale, William Zale, and Ben Lipshy. Their winning strategy was to provide quality merchandise at the lowest price in its market segment. By 2004, Zale enjoyed a $2.5 billion market cap. For decades Zale was known for offering fine jewelry assortments through convenient locations at fair prices. Their employees were friendly and knowledgeable. The leadership of the company signaled that it valued its staff by training, development, recognition, and compensation. The company had also signaled that it valued its customers by extending credit and standing behind its products through exemplary service. The company understood the intrinsic value of reputation. It understood why suppliers supply, why employees perform, and why customers buy. Customers' expectations for a reliable repeatable experience in those last 18 inches were met with admirable regularity.

In mid-2002, after eight years at the helm, CEO Bob Dinicola stepped down. He had taken Zale to what turns out to have been the apex of its financial success. Over the next five years, three CEOs each had his or her own different strategy for the business. Sadly for Zale, each strategic change diminished the customer experience and the company's financial performance, and each deterioration in financial performance paved the way for the next CEO and more decline.

The fourth new CEO, Neal Goldberg, appointed in February 2008, set out to leave his own mark on Zale and more broadly the jewelry business. He was quoted as stating, "What I see in this business [jewelry] is a sea of sameness. It's all about price and there is no romance to it. The way the goods are presented is very flat. I was never inspired walking into any jewelry store to say: 'Wow. Look at this presentation.' You go into other retailers, other commodities and you do go, 'Wow.' Apple is probably the pinnacle of that."[25]

Chapter 3 | Customers

It appears that Goldberg sought to transform both Zale and the business of selling fine jewelry. He felt that "romance"—an emotional connection typically associated with the psychological construct of a brand—was the critical element linking the product to a customer, and that successfully romancing the product in a store would increase the appeal of products and ultimately sales. It also appears that he did not understand Apple's retail model (discussed in Chapter 4).

His paradigm of "romance" affected all aspects of the business: product assortments, advertising, store layouts/design, staffing, etc. It also impacted quality—not of the merchandise itself, but rather of the customer experience.

Goldberg's strategy change to enhance the romance between the product and the customer took precedence over the 18-inch experience between the salesperson and the customer. Where Zale historically had offered a customer a "trusted" person in the store to help him or her make the right choice, these knowledgeable salespeople were replaced by part-time employees to cut labor costs and pay for the new store designs.

Result: customers started grumbling (Figure 3-2), stopped shopping at Zale, and had their needs met at their arch competitor, Signet Jewelers. When Zale then tried to lure them back by reducing prices, they compounded the confusion. Heavy discounting with no other rationale for it, such as a store going-out-of-business sale, cheapens the perceived value of the products offered.

Retrospective

In disappointing customers with a new branding strategy, Goldberg reaffirmed the lessons learned by The Coca Cola Company when it rolled out New Coke and enraged its loyal customer base, who defected in droves to Pepsi. Zale followed the script for ensuring humiliating failure: the company eviscerated its golden goose and Signet cleaned up.[27]

The revenue deterioration trend ended with the 2011 fiscal year (Figure 3-3) as Zale CEO Theo Killion, hired in February 2010, began to make his mark. "Under Killion's guidance over the past two years, Zale's bottom line improved $141 million and its reputation has improved." His focus: making the customers, i.e., guests, feel valued.[28]

The message: while brand and reputation are cousins, they are not the same and should not be conflated. Reputation is a cognitive expectation of behavior held by stakeholders; brand is an emotional relationship. Unfortunately, Zale apparently has not yet recognized this difference. Although its annual report cites "reputation" four times, the company formally acknowledges IT security

Reputation, Stock Price, and You 41

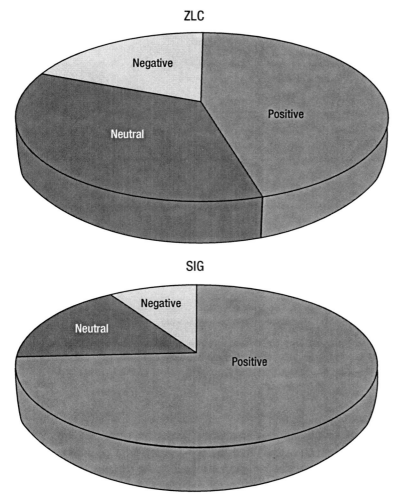

Figure 3-2. Customer sentiments of Zale (ZLC) and Signet (SIG) in 2009 (Newssift).[26]

breaches as the only source of reputational risk. Future reports afford potential for expanded institutional self-awareness.

Consider This

- Zale's changed its strategic direction when it sought to engage the customer through an emotional relationship based on romance rather than a cognitive relationship based on the company's reputation for quality.

Chapter 3 | Customers

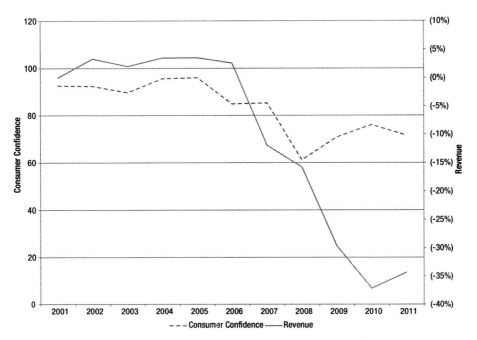

Figure 3-3. Stagnation followed by a rapid deterioration in revenue at Zale Corporation. Values are reported in relation to 2001 sales revenue and adjusted for annual inflation. Consumer confidence data are drawn from the June 2011 values of the University of Michigan Index of Consumer Sentiment.[29]

- The actions to accomplish the transformation siphoned off resources from those that had for the better part of a century supported Zale's reputation for quality. At the end, they subverted retail experiences and wreaked havoc on the company's reputation among its customers.

- The Zale's tale underscores the fact that brand *promise* and reputation *expectation* are not the same. Zale's invested in the former at the expense of the latter. By damaging a reputation for quality valued by the customer, it lost both pricing power and sales volume.

Innovation

[Innovation is] the design, invention, development and/or implementation of new or altered products, services, processes, systems, organizational structures or business models for the purpose of creating new value for customers and financial returns for the firm. Intellectual Property is part of this. (Table 1-1)

"A reputation once broken may possibly be repaired," observed Bishop Joseph Hall. "But the world will always keep their eyes on the spot where the crack was."[30] As the world focuses on the cracked reputation for innovation that is plaguing Research In Motion, their culture for value creation is called into question.

Research In Motion

Buried among the headlines during the first week of November 2011 was this eye catcher: "RIM as 'wounded puppy' trails book value with faith fading."[31] The Chief Investment Officer of a New York fund explained, "They've been losing business, there've been operating technology problems. There isn't a lot of customer loyalty anymore." That day, for the first time in nine years, the company's market value dipped below book value.

It's not as if Research In Motion isn't trying. The 2010 fiscal year was the second year in a row the Waterloo-based BlackBerry-maker headed the list of the top 100 corporations in Canada for research and development spending. In 2010, RIM actually boosted its spending on research and development by 26% to $1.3 billion, or about 6.8% of its revenue.

But while the innovation process is well financed, the process itself has failed to produce value. John Goldsmith, a money manager with Montrusco in Toronto, said the pricing collapse shows RIM has lost its competitive advantage. "RIM was a market leader in terms of smartphones," he said. "There are a lot of guys out there able to commercialize a product at a significantly lower cost."[32]

What about the patents? In addition to its organically grown patent portfolio, RIM has also been actively acquiring them. When the auction of the patent portfolio of Canada's previous technology giant, Nortel, ended on 30 June 2011, the winning bid was an eye-popping $4.5 billion. Research In Motion was among the consortium of winning bidders comprising Apple, EMC, Ericsson, Microsoft, and Sony.

Goldsmith was not impressed. "The book value, is it well stated? A lot of stuff has happened over the past five to ten years," he said. The technology patents might not be worth as much as the now-inflated book value.[48]

Research In Motion was a superstar as it started the hand-held computing revolution. In 1984, Mike Lazaridis and his co-CEO, James Balsillie, led RIM as it produced its first BlackBerry in 1998. With a six-line display that let users send and receive basic e-mail, the device changed business communications forever. By 2002, the BlackBerry had added voice and data capabilities, and RIM stood virtually alone in the nascent smartphone industry.

44 *Chapter 3 | Customers*

A 2002 press release said it best: "RIM pioneered the market for enterprise wireless email in 1999 and has propelled adoption and innovation since that time. With over 14,000 organizations already using BlackBerry, RIM is now delivering the next generation of wireless enterprise solutions with converged voice and data services. RIM has maintained its industry leadership with the only complete 2.5G wireless enterprise solution ready to address the needs of both users and IT departments."[33]

And therein lies the rub. RIM targeted the corporate IT department as its customer. By 2008, no less a figure than Barack Obama was musing about his BlackBerry addiction, and whether he could break it upon entering the presidential security bubble. But the U.S. government did not issue the president a mobile device, so he got one for himself. Like many other companies, and governments, RIM missed the power shift from the corporate IT department to the individual worker. Today, most workers do not want company-issued BlackBerrys: they want iPhones and the like.

Amitabh Passi, who covered the smartphone sector for UBS, said RIM stumbled. "They need to introduce exciting products. They're not there. They need to hit the time-to-market windows. They're not there," he said. "They need to rejuvenate and reenergize the brand. They're not there. I think it's partially a management issue. Partially it's a culture issue. Partially it's really getting a better sense of consumer psychology and what drives consumer decisions."[34]

Can a well-funded innovation process that creates and buys many patents be "not there?" If you define innovation along the lines of the 2008 *Report to the Secretary of Commerce by the Advisory Committee on Measuring Innovation in the 21st Century Economy*, cited at the head of this section, the answer is "yes." Patents are but an artifact of innovation, and their value is suspect if they do not create "new value for customers, and financial returns for the firm." By that definition, RIM's innovation process is failing.

"RIM is facing three major challenges," said Pierre Ferragu of Sanford Bernstein. "On its historic customer base, BlackBerry is a broken brand; RIM's business with corporate clients is ex-growth and under attack; and RIM's premium profitability is at risk." In other words, BlackBerrys are not generally seen as being "cool."[35]

Retrospective

RIM's deteriorating reputation for innovation was something many of its corporate customers were prepared to tolerate, if not value. Incompetence was another story. To stumble the day before RIM's then-top competitor, Apple,

Reputation, Stock Price, and You | 45

rolled out a new product—the iPhone 4s—was even worse. Apple CEO Steve Jobs had died the day before and the iPhone quickly became known as "4Steve."

The headlines hurt: "Is Steve Jobs crowing in heaven over RIM's week from hell?"[36] Continuing the story, The *Toronto Globe and Mail* noted: "RIM is in what charitably might be called a rough patch. Its quarterly results disappointed investors, to put it mildly, the launch of its PlayBook tablet was weak, and there are questions dogging the Waterloo, Ont., group about its management structure." In the midst of the product and management crises, RIM had a major operational failure, what Queen's University marketing professor John Pliniussen dubbed the "Blackout-Berry" as the company publicly struggled for "three days the same week to get its broken e-mail, instant message, and Internet services back up and running for millions of BlackBerry users around the world."[37]

Never mind the millions of unhappy customers. The investors with clout were taking notice. "Fast-moving Jaguar Financial is breathing down the neck of Research In Motion (Nasdaq: RIMM), and if the BlackBerry maker isn't careful, it could see a dramatic change in its board of directors and potentially management as early as three months from now." Canadian securities laws give investors significant power: "Investors holding a 5% stake in a company—either individually or as a group—are allowed to call a special meeting, says Chris Makuch, vice president at the Canadian office of proxy solicitation firm Georgeson."[38]

It's said of war that there are no winners, only survivors. Yes, Research In Motion out-survived Steve Jobs. But it sure isn't winning. As of the end of 2011, its revenue was falling faster that the decrease in product sales, indicating a simultaneous loss in pricing power (Figure 3-4).

RIM doesn't appreciate the value a reputation for innovation confers upon its enterprise. It mentions "reputation" 27 times in its 2012 annual report. It discloses reputational risks with respect to failures in IT security, sustainability or ethical behaviors, service or product quality, and regulatory compliance. Inexplicably, the company did not link innovation failure with reputational risk.

Consider This

- RIM failed to recognize that the identity and needs of its customers were evolving, and therefore failed to innovate to meet emerging customer expectations.

Chapter 3 | Customers

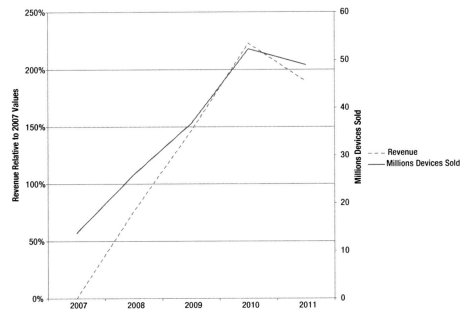

Figure 3-4. Growth in RIM's revenue, normalized to 2007 revenue and adjusted for inflation, and the number of devices sold each year. With damage to its reputation for innovation, its revenue is decreasing faster than its sales volume, indicating a simultaneous erosion of pricing power.[39]

- A reputation for innovation is a source of revenue-driven value. For RIM, it brought greater volumes of sales and increased pricing power.

- When a broad range of stakeholders perceive failure, a firm's once stellar reputation for innovation may be permanently damaged, with a resulting impact on enterprise value, if not overall company viability.

Guidance

Companies typically invest many years and significant capital to develop a reputation that is recognized and valued by customers. Reputations are formed in part by what customers experience as consumers of products and services, and in part by what customers *expect* to experience based on prior messaging—word of mouth, advertising, etc. What companies do on a tactical level is generally specific to the industry sector; what they do strategically to build a reputation can be generalized to a few principles.

Rolls-Royce built a reputation for safety through engineering controls that provided the company both oversight and operational control of its supply chain. The company's culture reflects a deep appreciation for both the importance of its engineering and the value of its reputation. As a result, customers both *expect* and receive engineering excellence and safe products. It appears that much of what Rolls-Royce does, and the way it does it, are guided by its deep respect for engineering excellence and reputation protection.

Zale built its reputation for quality by delivering a trusted service that mitigated consumer risk for the middle-market customers of fine jewelry. In their own words, "Zale's reputation for customer service for over 85 years fosters an image of product expertise, quality and trust among consumers." By confusing "image" with actual operations and service delivery, Zale risked that reputation to deliver a different type of experience to its customer—one that customers neither appreciated nor valued.

Last, RIM built a reputation for innovation that it exploited into a near-monopoly. Believing it had a lock on its customers, the company found itself struggling after three major stumbles. First, it had put all its marbles on the corporate IT customer and failed to appreciate that corporate IT was being disintermediated. Second, it failed to appreciate the speed at which its market was evolving technologically—it wasn't getting new products to market quickly. Third, notwithstanding ample evidence and prior examples of sudden corporate death, it did not appreciate that a failure to deliver critical IT services was a potential death sentence.

Each of these exemplary companies established reputations that customers appreciated and valued. That appreciation, often comprising an *expectation* of a benefit to come, translated into extraordinary sales, pricing power, near-monopoly status, and fast sales cycles. Awareness of the importance of its reputation—and how it was established—helped Rolls-Royce rebound from a crisis; conversely, both Zale and RIM stumbled badly when they failed to understand and exploit the cultural sources of prior success.

By the Numbers

The case studies illustrate how reputation can affect value-creating and value-destroying actions by customers and how that reputational value is ultimately recognized and appreciated by stockholders (Table 3-2).

Chapter 3 | Customers

Table 3-2. Reputation Effects on Customer-Driven Revenue

	P&L Effect	Stock Price Effect—Interval Gains (Losses)		
Rolls-Royce	*Sustained* sales volume and pricing power		**Rolls-Royce**	**S&P500**
		01-Nov-10	0	0
		15-Nov-10	(–8.7%)	1.1%
		28-Sep-12	41.2%	20.3%
Zale	Precipitous *decline* in sales volume and pricing power; reversed with new leadership		**Zale**	**S&P500**
		01-Feb-08	0	0
		01-Feb-10	(–87.9%)	(–21.9%)
		28-Sep-12	227.0%	32.3%
Research In Motion	Precipitous *decline* in sales volume and pricing power		**RIM**	**S&P500**
		01-Feb-08	0	0
		01-Feb-09	(–39.4%)	(–40.8%)
		28-Sep-12	(–86.6%)	74.5%

Endnotes

1 The considered purchase decision. TriComB2B/University of Dayton School of Business. 2011. The full research report is available at http://tricomb2b.com/about-us/Our-2011-B2B-Research.

2 Li K, Geng Q, Shao B Warranty. Designs and brand reputation analysis in a duopoly. *California Journal of Operations Management.* 2011;9(1):34–42.

3 Corporate image—benefits, importance of corporate image, theory of corporate image. *Encyclopedia of Business,* 2nd ed. Available at: http://www.referenceforbusiness.com/small/Co-Di/Corporate-Image.html#ixzz20h9xZKD8. Accessed 15 July 2012.

4 Family's terror as debris from exploding Qantas superjumbo engine tears 6ft hole in wall of family home. *Daily Mail.* 5 November 2010. Available at: http://www.dailymail.co.uk/news/article-1327041/Qantas-A380-Engine-debris-tears-6ft-hole-wall-family-home.html#ixzz20hDOf13I. Accessed 15 July 2012.

5 Cole R. Rolls-Royce's reputation is most of its value. *Reuters.* 8 November 2010. Available at: http://blogs.reuters.com/breakingviews/2010/11/08/rolls-royces-reputation-is-most-of-its-value/. Accessed 27 June 2012.

6 Rolls-Royce Holdings plc Annual Report 2009, p. 62.

Reputation, Stock Price, and You   49

7 Cooper C. JAL's $8.5 billion rebirth took lessons from crash-site morgue. *Bloomberg*. 13 September 2012. Available at: http://www.bloomberg.com/news/2012-09-13/jal-s-8-5-billion-rebirth-took-lessons-from-crash-site-morgue.html. Accessed 28 September 2012.

8 Marsh P, O'Doherty J. Rolls-Royce scrambles to pin down problem. *Financial Times*. 20 December 2010. Available at: http://www.ft.com/intl/cms/s/0/3e5a2254-0c67-11e0-8408-00144feabdc0.html#axzz20bj70q2d. Accessed 15 July 2012.

9 Mustoe H, Rothman A. Rolls falls most in a year after engine failure grounds A380s. *Bloomberg*. 4 November 2010. Available at: http://www.bloomberg.com/news/2010-11-04/rolls-falls-most-in-a-year-after-engine-failure-grounds-a380s.html. Accessed 15 July 2012.

10 Madslien J. Qantas emergency points spotlight at Airbus and Rolls-Royce. *BBC News*. 4 November 2010. Available at: http://www.bbc.co.uk/news/11692362. Accessed 15 July 2012.

11 Layne R, Decker S. Pratt & Whitney sues to block Rolls-Royce engines. *Bloomberg*. 5 November 2010. Available at: http://www.bloomberg.com/news/2010-11-05/pratt-whitney-sues-to-block-rolls-royce-engines.html. Accessed 15 July 2012.

12 Easdown G. Rolls-Royce Trent 900 engine linked to three mid-air emergencies. *Herald Sun*. 5 November 2010. Available at: http://www.heraldsun.com.au/news/rolls-royce-trent-900-engine-linked-to-three-mid-air-emergencies/story-e6frf7jo-1225948178631. Accessed 27 June 2012.

13 Koranyi B, Smith M. Rolls-Royce, Qantas settle A380 engine dispute for $100 million. *Insurance Journal*. 22 June 2011. Available at: http://www.insurancejournal.com/news/international/2011/06/22/203682.htm. Accessed 15 July 2012.

14 Govindasamy S. Pipe fatigue behind Qantas A380 Trent 900 failure: ATSB. *Flightglobal*. 2 December 2010. Available at: http://www.flightglobal.com/news/articles/pipe-fatigue-behind-qantas-a380-trent-900-failure-atsb-350414/. Accessed 15 July 2012.

15 Musafer S. 2010: A year some companies would rather forget. *BBC News*. 23 December 2010. Available at: http://www.bbc.co.uk/news/business-11828093. Accessed 15 July 2012.

16 Mustoe H, Rothwell S. British Airways picks troubled Rolls engine for A380s. *Bloomberg*. 6 January 2100. Available at: http://mobile.bloomberg.com/news/2011-01-06/rolls-royce-wins-british-airways-order-for-trent-plane-engines. Accessed 15 July 2012.

17 Rolls-Royce counts cost of Trent 900 failure. *Asian Aviation*. 1 March 2011. Available at: http://www.asianaviation.com/articles/109/Rolls-Royce-counts-cost-of-Trent-900-failure. Accessed 28 June 2012.

18 Kaminski-Morrow D. Rolls-Royce becomes first engine supplier for Airbus A350, with formal development of 'Trent XWB' powerplant. *Flightglobal*. 4 December 2006. Available at: http://www.flightglobal.com/news/articles/rolls-royce-becomes-first-engine-supplier-for-airbus-a350-with-formal-development-of-trent-xwb-powerplant-210894/. Accessed 27 June 2012.

19 Michaels D, Sanders P. Rolls-Royce isn't on board with Airbus's engine plan. *Wall Street Journal*. 19 August 2010. Available at: http://online.wsj.com/article/SB10001424052748704557704575437391200860352.html. Accessed 27 June 2012.

20 O'Doherty J. Rolls-Royce to redesign Airbus A350 engine. *Financial Times*. 6 June 2011. Available at: http://www.ft.com/intl/cms/s/0/7347ad96-9057-11e0-9227-00144feab49a.html#axzz1z39pzroC. Accessed 27 June 2012.

Chapter 3 | Customers

21 Heasley A. A380 engine inspections may be doing more harm than good. *Sydney Morning Herald*. 5 March 2011. Available at: http://www.smh.com.au/travel/travel-news/a380-engine-inspections-may-be-doing-more-harm-than-good-20110305-1biip.html. Accessed 11 August 2012.

22 What's in a name? Why companies should worry less about their reputations. *Economist*. 21 April 2012. Available at: http://www.economist.com/node/21553033. Accessed 27 June 2012.

23 Rolls-Royce Holdings plc Annual Report 2011, p. 18.

24 Zale Corporation Company Description. *Hoovers*. Available at: http://www.hoovers.com/company/Zale_Corporation/rjyfri-1.html. Accessed 15 July 2012.

25 Bates R. We need a compelling shopping experience. *JCK*. November 2008. Available at: http://www.jckonline.com/article/287778-_We_Need_a_Compelling_Shopping_Experience_.php. Accessed 15 July 2012.

26 Kossovsky N. Why Zales must learn a quality lesson (case study). *Intellectual Asset Management*. 2010;40(March/April): 31–35.

27 Schumpeter. How to make a megaflop. *Economist*. 31 March 2012. Available at: http://www.economist.com/node/21551455. Accessed 15 July 2012.

28 Zale CEO accepts Visionary Merchant award. *Mays Business Online (Texas A&M)*. July 2012. Available at: http://maysbusiness.tamu.edu/index.php/Zale-ceo-accepts-visionary-merchant-award/. Accessed 29 July 2012.

29 Surveys of consumers. Thomson Reuters/University of Michigan. Available at: http://www.sca.isr.umich.edu/main.php. Accessed 28 June 2012.

30 Joseph Hall. *Wikiquote*. Available at: http://en.wikiquote.org/wiki/Joseph_Hall. Accessed 15 July 2012.

31 Miller J, Walcoff M. RIM as 'wounded puppy' trails book value with faith fading. *Bloomberg*. 3 November 2011. Available at: http://www.bloomberg.com/news/2011-11-03/rim-as-wounded-puppy-trails-book-value-with-investors-confidence-shaken.html. Accessed 15 July 2012.

32 RIM falls below book value for first time. *Profitimes*. Available at: http://profitimes.com/value-investing/rim-falls-below-book-value-for-first-time/. Accessed 15 July 2012.

33 RIM outlines BlackBerry plans at PC Expo. Press release, 25 June 2002. Available at: http://press.rim.com/newsroom/press/2002/pressrelease-816.html. Accessed 15 July 2012.

34 Goldberg A. Can Research In Motion get back in the race? *Law.com*. 27 July 2011. Available at: http://www.law.com/jsp/law/article.jsp?id=1202506522139. Accessed 15 July 2012.

35 Taylor P. RIM struggles to last the pace. *Financial Times*. 1 May 2011. Available at: http://www.ft.com/intl/cms/s/2/61e899ec-7415-11e0-b788-00144feabdc0.html#axzz20bj70q2d. Accessed 15 July 2012.

36 Is Steve Jobs crowing in heaven over RIM's week from hell? *Globe and Mail*. 14 October 2011. Available at: http://www.allvoices.com/news/10614357-is-steve-jobs-crowing-in-heaven-over-rim146s-week-from-hell. Accessed 15 July 2012.

Reputation, Stock Price, and You

37 Kossovsky N. Reputation for innovation lost: RIM and Kodak (case study). *Intellectual Asset Management*. 2012; 51:(January/February): 75–82.

38 Kawamoto D. Jaguar could bag Research In Motion soon. *Motley Fool*. 14 October 2011. Available at: http://www.fool.com/investing/general/2011/10/14/jaguar-could-bag-research-in-motion-soon-.aspx#.UAL-YHC1_-k. Accessed 15 July 2012.

39 Research In Motion Annual Reports 2007-2012, composite.

CHAPTER 4

Employees

Lose money for the firm, and I will be understanding; lose a shred of reputation for the firm, and I will be ruthless.

—Warren Buffet to his employees[1]

On or about 13 April 2009, in a small Domino's Pizza franchise in North Carolina, two employees uploaded a two-minute prank video to YouTube of the duo offensively tampering with the food they were preparing. Within a few days, the power and reach of social media triggered more than a million views on YouTube and a "viral" spread of the subject on Twitter. No surprise that a Google Trends report showing a 50% increase in searches for "Domino's Pizza" was not accompanied by a surge in orders for freshly baked pizza pies. A national study conducted by HCD Research using its Media Curves website found that 65% of respondents who would have previously visited or ordered Domino's Pizza were less likely to do so after viewing the offensive video.[2]

Employees is a term for workers and managers working for a company, organization, or community. They are the staff of the organization, hired by an employer to do a particular job, and they are critical to a company's ability to deliver its products and services to customers. Often they are also both the largest expense (payroll) and the greatest source of risk. It is usually the actions of employees that trigger failures in ethical practices, lapses in quality and safety, breaches in security, and ineptitude in innovation.

This chapter explains how the behavior of corporate employees impacts specific lines of the profit and loss (P&L) statement and helps determine a company's stock price. Working backwards from there, we explain how the expectations employees hold about their company help shape that company's reputation, how a company's actions shape its employees' expectations, and how a company's reputation affects employees' behavior. We illustrate the

Chapter 4 | Employees

points with case studies: on ethics, News Corp. and Barclays plc; on innovation, Apple Inc. and Goldman Sachs Group, Inc.; and on quality, Domino's Pizza Inc.

We'll also explore the interrelationships among a company's culture, reputation, and employees. Tony Hsieh, who sold pizza as a student[3] and is now CEO of the online shoe and clothing shop Zappos.com, observed: "Businesses often forget about the culture and, ultimately, they suffer for it because you can't deliver good service from unhappy employees."[4] Nor, as we show in this first case study, can you expect employees to protect the enterprise if they are misdirected by incentives.

Ethics

> [Ethics are] the moral principles by which a company operates; integrity is the act of adhering to those moral principles. Ethics are an integral part of governance that, along with integrity, affect the reputation value of all other intangible assets. Ethics are also the keystone intangible asset because they form the basis for trust and confidence. (Table 1-1)

For company after company, there have been rising waves of press attention that each crest in a "critical mass—the threshold" where seemingly little things trigger a major event, the "tipping point," as Malcolm Gladwell theorizes.[5] The cumulative effects of business process failures on the reputation of a corporation produce the proverbial straw on the camel's back.

Such effects from serial transgressions are nowhere greater than in a business's ethical failure. Costly ethical failures tend to have three features in common:

- Failure of ethical controls resulting from misalignment of short-term interests among employees, management, and potential regulators

- Tolerance for an ethically flawed underlying business model and the culture of an industry

- An ultimately expensive, culturally driven purification ritual, causing a pile on of litigators, regulators, and bloggers

News Corp.

Rupert Murdoch's News Corp., a U.S.-listed global media company, is the world's second largest media conglomerate behind only Walt Disney, with operations spanning film, television, and publishing. It would be unusual to find someone on the face of this planet who has not been touched by one of its products. It produces and distributes movies through Fox Filmed Entertainment,

Reputation, Stock Price, and You

and its FOX Broadcasting network boasts more than 200 affiliate stations in the United States. The company owns and operates more than 25 TV stations, as well as a portfolio of cable networks. Its publishing businesses include newspaper publisher Dow Jones (*The Wall Street Journal*) and book publisher HarperCollins. Through its U.K. news group, News International, it publishes *The Times* (of London) and the *Sun*, and published, past tense, the now-defunct tabloid, *News of the World*.

In July 2011, News Corp., through its then-subsidiary, *News of the World*, was swept into a classic Gladwell tipping point. Two events over a span of nine years were the triggers. In March 2002, schoolgirl Milly Dowler, 13, disappeared in the London suburb of Walton-on-Thames. Her remains were found in September.[6] Investigation of her murder, one of the most notorious of the decade, came to an official end on 23 June 2011 when Levi Bellfield, a convicted double killer, was found guilty.[7]

Eleven days later, on 4 July, *The Guardian* reported that a lawyer for Dowler's family, Mark Lewis, claimed that he learned from police that Milly Dowler's voicemail messages had been hacked, possibly by a *News of the World* investigator, while police were searching for her. The lawyer claimed that some of her voicemails had been deleted to make room for more messages, misleading police and her family into thinking Milly was still alive and complicating the police investigation. Lewis described the *News of the World's* activities as "heinous" and "despicable."[8] The next day, *News International* chief executive Rebekah Wade Brooks, whose organization oversaw *News of the World*, said she was "appalled and shocked" that Milly Dowler's phone was hacked. U.K. Prime Minister Cameron called it a "truly dreadful act."[6]

News of the World reporters had been accused before of illegally accessing messages from the mobile phones of celebrities and politicians. In fact, in 2006, detectives arrested the *News of the World's* royal editor Clive Goodman and private investigator Glenn Mulcaire over allegations that they hacked into the mobile phones of members of the royal household. Three years later, the Press Complaints Commission concluded that there was insufficient evidence to suggest anyone at the *News of the World* other than Goodman and Mulcaire hacked phone messages, or that the paper's executives knew what the pair was doing.

It took the conviction of the child murderer to precipitate a full-blown reputational crisis. "Bribery, illegal wiretapping, interference in a murder investigation, political blackmail, and rampant disregard for both the truth and basic decency" is the choice phrasing Elliot Spitzer used in a 12 July 2011 column.[9] "The behavior of Rupert Murdoch's News Corp. in Britain has shocked even his closest allies and cynical British journalists." Mr. Spitzer, like Captain Renault in the film *Casablanca,* well understood how unethical

Chapter 4 | Employees

behavior had the power to shock. The former NY State attorney general, whose meteoric career rested on his high-profile prosecutions of white-collar crime, had been the 54th governor of New York until exposure of his own ethical lapse—a client relationship with a high-priced prostitution ring—forced his resignation.

The Buildup of Straws

While various existing codes of journalistic ethics have some differences, most share common elements including the principles of truthfulness, accuracy, objectivity, impartiality, fairness, and public accountability as these apply to the acquisition of newsworthy information and its subsequent dissemination to the public. Phillip Crawley, Publisher and CEO of *The Globe and Mail*, describes his "core business as Canada's most trusted source of news."[10] Tony Burman, ex-editor-in-chief of *CBC News*, said it this way in 2001: "Every news organization has only its credibility and reputation to rely on."[11]

But what about a tabloid U.K. paper like the *Sun*? Mainstream media outlets, such as the *Globe* or *The Wall Street Journal*, are generally believed to be dedicated to objective reporting and to honoring the tenets of ethical journalism. In contrast, a tabloid paper is fundamentally about spilling dirt, appealing to prurient interest, stirring controversy, and digging up personal laundry that public figures would rather keep private. Christopher Hitchens wrote that *News of the World* became a "paper where the question was not how low can poor human nature sink, but rather is there anything, however depraved, that a reporter cannot be induced to do?"[12]

Everyone knew that *News of the World* had been a guilty pleasure for at least three generations of Britons. The paper operated in a muddled gray area of impropriety. Its headlines and scoops regularly challenged the truth, and its methods of discovery were questionable. Though few readers cared enough to ponder the implications, victims of its coverage did, and they regularly sued the paper. For everyone else, its muckraking was something readers tolerated because they enjoyed it.

In this environment, an ambitious executive with a lifelong passion for journalism saw the obvious path to success: superior muckraking. Rebekah Mary Wade was born in 1968 in Warrington in the north of England and grew up an only child. At age 20, the future Rebekah Brooks, who would become editor of the *News of the World* and *The Sun*, talked her way into a job with the features editor of *The Post*, a now-defunct tabloid. "I am going to come and work with you on the features desk as the features secretary or administrator."[13] Within seven years, she was the deputy editor of the *News of the World*.

Reputation, Stock Price, and You   57

By most measures an alpha female,[14] she worked hard, played carefully, and mastered the art of power politics in a male-dominated profession. "She'd get you to do things," said a former *News of the World* reporter. "She had this charisma, this magnetic attraction. She would praise to high heaven, make you feel like you were on top of the world. It was only afterwards that you realized you were manipulated."[15]

By the end of 1996, she reportedly first met Rupert Murdoch, chairman of the enterprise for which she worked. Taking a page from Nina Godiwalla's playbook, *Suits: A Woman on Wall Street,* the newly minted Rebekah Wade Kemp understood that "doing a good job (was) expected of (her), but it's the relationships that (would) help (her) succeed."[16]

"Observers believe Rebekah (Wade Kemp) Brooks's remarkably swift rise in the company was due not so much to her talents as a journalist but to her single-minded ruthlessness and her dazzling, feline ability to charm. 'Rebekah schmoozes in one direction only — up,' says one of her oldest acquaintances. 'I don't know anyone who is better at love-bombing, when it matters. I wouldn't think Rupert stood a chance.'"[17] Commented a former *News of the World* reporter, "From the way she acted, you would think she wanted to sleep with you."[13]

In 2000, Murdoch fired Phil Hall, the editor of the *News of the World,* and gave his job to Wade Kemp. At just 32 she was the youngest national newspaper editor in the country. In a vivid demonstration of the power of the press (and of Rebekah Wade Kemp), she began a campaign as muckraker-in-chief to name and shame alleged pedophiles.[6] Some alleged offenders found themselves terrorized by angry mobs. In 2003, Murdoch installed Wade as the editor of daily tabloid *The Sun,* sister paper to the *News of the World* and Britain's biggest selling daily newspaper. She told the staff on her first day it was the job she had "dreamed of" ever since she was a child.[13] In 2009, at age 41, the soon-to-be Rebekah Brooks was appointed CEO of News International, the U.K. arm of News Corp.'s Newspapers and Information Services business.

Within the span of about 24 months, she became one of the most powerful women in Britain; married the former racehorse trainer and "international playboy" Charles Patrick Evelyn Brooks; oversaw the closure of *News of the World*; resigned from her post with News International; and was arrested on suspicion of phone hacking and corruption.

An aggressive editor backed by an aggressive chairman makes for a powerful force in a business that rewards muckraking. Reuters reported that, according to a senior police officer who was asked to investigate the matter in 2009, "illegal voicemail hacking was 'standard practice' at Britain's best-selling Sunday newspaper, and then covered up by executives."[18] Accusations that journalists

Chapter 4 | Employees

working for News Corp. illegally paid police for information have also been brought to light. The *Financial Times* reported: "*The Sun* had a culture of corrupt payments to a network of public officials which was authorized at a senior level, the police testified at an inquiry into press standards. Deputy Assistant Commissioner Sue Akers said evidence showed that payments were 'frequent, regular and on occasion significant sums of money were involved.'"[19] As part of the fallout, Prime Minister David Cameron announced two inquiries relating to the scandal. One of them, led by a judge, was charged to look at the way the police investigated the allegations against *News of the World* and the relationship between newspapers and the police.

Along the way, the government had preferred to look the other way. After Wade Kemp had moved to *The Sun,* Andy Coulson became *News of the World* editor. Coulson was subsequently hired by Prime Minister David Cameron as his press secretary. "The tabloid press in Britain is very powerful, and it's also exceedingly aggressive, and it's not just News Corp.; *The Mail* is very aggressive," said John Whittingdale, a Conservative member of Parliament who is chairman of the Culture, Media and Sport Committee as quoted in *The New York Times.* "They do make or break reputations, so obviously politicians tread warily." [20]

Politicians have always been most afraid of the two News Corp. papers, *The Sun* and its Sunday sister (until it closed), *News of the World.* "'They go on little feeding frenzies against various politicians,' said Roy Greenslade, a professor of journalism at City University London. Until the floodgates opened, when the outrage over the latest phone-hacking revelations had politicians voicing disgust in a cathartic parliamentary session, most members of Parliament were terrified of crossing Mr. Murdoch."[20]

It may be asking too much of the police and the government to serve as a check and balance on the press. Christopher Hitchens, writing for *Slate,* confessed, "Admittedly, it isn't usually the job of these institutions to keep the press honest. (Indeed, I could swear that I read somewhere that the whole concept was the other way about.)"[21]

Many would agree with Hitchens, and might suggest that reputation for ethics could in the long term survive only in an ethical culture. "It's a very personal thing, but throughout my career – from my time as a teacher, to my time as a banker – I have seen just how important culture is to successful organizations," offered Robert Diamond, CEO of Barclays plc. "Culture is difficult to define, I think it's even more difficult to mandate – but for me the evidence of culture is how people behave when no one is watching."[22]

Diamond got it partially right, as the following case study on Barclays shows. Culture comprises values and is evidenced, in part, by how people behave

Reputation, Stock Price, and You

when no one is looking and they have an opportunity for unethical behavior. But this is really a definition of morality. Morality is reflected in the actions of an individual in the face of an unethical opportunity.

On an institutional basis, culture means establishing behavioral norms, monitoring conformance, and mitigating deviations from the norms. These may reaffirm the moral principles of employees; they may rectify them as well. Employees who find the institutional culture incompatible with their own morals will either conform or leave.

At least in principle, boards and management have the potential to reduce "opportunity for deviation" by imposing strong internal controls and compliance mechanisms and to reduce "motive and rationalization for deviation through appropriate incentive-setting, articulation of corporate values, and tone at the top." They also have a legal duty. "'That role has been acknowledged and incorporated into a range of regulatory, commercial, and justice guidance materials, including the Federal Sentencing Guidelines in the U.S., the Ministry of Justice Guidance pertaining to the Anti-Bribery Statute in the UK, and the 2010 OECD Good Practice Guidance on Internal Controls, Ethics, and Compliance,' noted Michael D. Greenberg, director of the RAND Center for Corporate Ethics and Governance (CCEG)."[23]

The Broken Back

The *News of the World* ethical scandal damaged every part of the Murdoch empire, as shown in Table 4-1.

Table 4-1. A Full-Blown Reputational Crisis Is One in Which Every Stakeholder Is Impacted

Quote	Authority	Stakeholder
"Phone-Hacking Scandal Damaged News Corp.'s Image"[24]	Claims filed by News Corp. shareholders led by Amalgamated Bank	Investor
"I think the UK hacking scandal has the potential to damage *The Wall Street Journal*'s reputation."[25]	Jay Ottaway, whose family owned 6.2% of Wall Street Journal publisher Dow Jones & Co before it was sold to News Corp.	Investor
"I think the benefit of the (*Wall Street*) *Journal* is it's above the fray. It's carved out such a strong reputation for so long," he said, but added, "You cannot completely separate it from the muck."[23]	Doug Arthur, a long time newspaper analyst now with Evercore Partners	Analyst

Chapter 4 | Employees

Quote	Authority	Stakeholder
"Rupert Murdoch is torching the reputation of all of his brands."[26]	Arthur Yann, vice president of public relations for the Public Relations Society of America (PRSA)	Media observer
"The reputation of the company we love so much, as well as the press freedoms we value so highly, are all at risk."[27]	Resignation memo from News International chief executive Rebekah Brooks	Employee
"He has too much power over British public life. We've got to look at the situation whereby one person can own more than 20 percent of the newspaper market, the Sky platform and Sky News. I think it's unhealthy."[28]	Opposition Labour Party leader Ed Miliband, calling for a breakup of the media empire	Regulator
"Our committee has jurisdiction to look into these very troubling allegations against News Corp. and find out whether any federal laws were violated such as the Foreign Corrupt Practices Act."[29]	Rep. Bruce Braley (D-Iowa), who sits on the House Oversight and Government Reform Committee	Regulator
"It was totally wrong, and I regret it and I've said it's going to be a blot on my reputation for the rest of my life."[30]	Rupert Murdoch, Chairman of News Corp., testifying before Lord Justice Leveson	Chairman of the Board of Directors
"Tabloids are declining to publish sensational stories about the private lives of celebrities as they fear a backlash from readers disgusted by the revelations of the Leveson Inquiry."[31]	Celebrity publicist Max Clifford speaking to the *London Times*	Customers

Expenses Arising from Employee (In) Action

Costs to settle the growing number of claims for hacking are not insignificant. "News Corp. could end up paying a total of 120 million pounds in damages and legal fees," said Niri Shan, a media lawyer at U.K. law firm Taylor Wessing. Shan based that figure on an average settlement of 30,000 pounds for each of the 4,000 victims identified by police.[32]

Analysts projected costs in the range of $1 billion. As of April 2012, according to *The Independent*, the legal costs associated with phone hacking totaled approximately $37.7 million to date, while $88.2 million went to restructuring after *News of the World* was shut down in July. News Group, the subsidiary that owned the tabloid, also took a $254 million write-off when the paper closed.[33]

Other Costs

On 4 July 2012, *The Huffington Post* summarized[34] the transformations in Murdoch's empire after a 60-year journey that began with a single newspaper in Adelaide, Australia. During the year that followed disclosure of the Milly Dowler affair:

- The *News of the World* newspaper has been closed.
- A parliamentary committee declared Rupert Murdoch "not fit" to lead a major international company.
- A protester assaulted Rupert Murdoch with a shaving-cream pie.
- Rupert Murdoch has apologized repeatedly for the scandal, sent police after his own employees, abandoned his dreams of buying a lucrative satellite company, and made plans to cut off his beloved newspapers from the entertainment properties that keep him enriched.

In addition to Murdoch's personal challenges:

- Murdoch's son James, his heir apparent, has seen his reputation crash and burn due to his role in the scandal.
- Murdoch's trusted deputy Rebekah Brooks has been arrested.
- Murdoch's trusted editor, Andy Coulson, who then became top communications adviser to Prime Minister David Cameron, has been arrested.
- More than 40 other people connected with phone hacking or the bribery of public officials have been arrested.
- Brooks, her husband, and Coulson are facing criminal trials.
- The head of Scotland Yard has resigned.
- Police in the United Kingdom are running three separate investigations into illegal activity by the media.
- The Department of Justice in the United States is probing News Corp.'s operations.

Chapter 4 | Employees

Most painful for Murdoch, according to Robert Monks, founder of Institutional Shareholder Services, the foremost proxy advisor, is that the empire Murdoch had amassed will likely not be passed on to the children. "The family business is simply kaput."[35]

Unethical behavior by a handful of employees, both reporters and their supervisors, who pursued their craft aggressively, co-opted police, and lied to Parliament, operating within a small part of a media empire that generated around 5% of its net income, wiped out 32 times that value. Succinctly, a reputational crisis triggered by the behavior of employees erased 10% of the total News Corp. value in less than two weeks (Table 4-1). The bottom line is $4.4 billion lost.

By ignoring employee deviations from ethical journalistic practices, News Corp. showed that it was suffering from a challenged culture—a *corrupt* culture as headlined in the *Financial Times*.[19]

Barclays

Ironically, Barclays CEO Robert Diamond's failure to distinguish between individual morality and institutional culture cost him personally. His downfall was precipitated by a scandal involving 14 employees at Barclays, along with a handful of employees at other banks, who fiddled with a reference standard called LIBOR (London Interbank Offered Rate) that in 2012 underpinned $360 trillion of global securities.[36] After brewing for months, the alleged improprieties became widespread public knowledge in late June 2012 when Barclays was fined a record 290 million pounds ($453.4 million).

Days later, Diamond and the bank's COO stepped down. In the first week, the reputational crisis also wiped $5 billion in market capitalization from the bank ranked second in the United Kingdom by assets. "Clearly there was behavior that was reprehensible," Diamond acknowledged in testimony to Parliament.[37] As this volume goes to press, Barclays is conducting an internal review into what it called "flawed" business practices while the Serious Fraud Office is investigating the prospect of criminal charges.

And yes, the personal costs mounted. In addition to losing his job, Diamond agreed to forgo up to £20 million in bonuses and shares. And although he walked away with around £2 million in salary and pension payments, the hearings before Parliament cast a shadow. "The comments made at today's hearing have had a terribly unfair impact upon my reputation, which is of paramount concern to me," Diamond said.[38]

Employee Benefits of an Ethical Culture

Employee behavior is one of the most important determinants of an organization's reputation. At an institutional level, both the behavioral norms and the systems designed to foster conformance speak to organizational culture. In an ethical culture, trust and credibility are essential for employee engagement, stabilizing overall culture, and in turn, its reputation.

Although trust can be difficult to define and measure, high levels of trust correlate with high levels of employee engagement. Research has shown that a 10% increase in trust is equivalent to a 36% increase in monetary compensation. If a company is able to increase trust by 10%, it has the equivalent effect on employee life satisfaction as handing out a 36% raise in salary or bonus.[39]

In addition to engaging existing employees, a good ethical reputation can help recruit employees. According to Kelly Services, Inc. the workforce management services firm, "Major public issues such as a company's reputation for strong ethical practices have become critical factors in choosing where to work, even to the point where many employees are prepared to sacrifice pay or promotion in order to work for organizations that are actively engaged in good social responsibility practices. More specifically, concerns about ethical behavior outweigh concerns about the environment by all generations, when making employment choices."[40] Key findings that can impact both recruiting and future salary costs include:

- Almost 90% of respondents say they are more likely to work for an organization that is considered ethically and socially responsible, something that is consistent across all generations.

- Eighty percent are more likely to work for an organization that is considered environmentally responsible, a figure that is considerably higher among people in older age groups.

- In deciding where to work, an organization's reputation for ethical conduct is considered "very important" by 65% of Gen Y, 72% of Gen X, and 77% of baby boomers.

- Forty-six percent of Gen Y would be prepared to forgo higher pay or promotion to work for an organization with a good reputation, rising to 48% for Gen X and 53% for baby boomers.

Chapter 4 | Employees

Consider This

- Organizational culture, the driver of reputation, is a force that can reduce the variances of otherwise unconstrained behaviors—but only to the extent that management and the board care to both monitor and enforce it. Ignorance is tantamount to culpability.

- In any organization, a small group of employees may exercise ethically deviant behavior. Call this group "rogues."

- When the unethical behavior of a group of individuals impacts the institution's overall reputation—that is, when an institution rather than a group of employees is perceived to be culpable—the financial consequences can be catastrophic.

- A strong culture that establishes organizational norms, and a board of directors that will support management even in the face of placing revenue at risk, are essential for driving consistently ethical behavior and mitigating the risk from "rogues."

Innovation

[Innovation is] the design, invention, development and/or implementation of new or altered products, services, processes, systems, organizational structures or business models for the purpose of creating new value for customers and financial returns for the firm. Intellectual Property is part of this. (Table 1-1)

For employees seeking an experience at the cutting edge of their respective fields, a reputation for a culture of innovation is an attraction that facilitates both engagement and alignment. Engagement means lower operating costs as a result of less expensive recruitment and retention incentives, less turnover, less internal friction, and greater effectiveness. Alignment means lower risk-related costs because employees better conform to the company's behavioral guidelines.

Apple Inc.

Profitability on tablet computers that compete with the iPad mini was the topic. "How does Samsung make money in tablets, when Google is partnering with Asus to make a product that makes no money?" asked rhetorically Shaw Wu, an analyst at Sterne Agee & Leach Inc.[41] He had a point. Amazon loses money on every Kindle Fire it sells, with the aim of profiting from sales of books and other digital media. Microsoft, which, with Google, has long worked with Samsung as a hardware partner, was also rolling out a tablet computer under its own brand name.

The challenge as Wu saw it was that Apple had a huge profit advantage. The company had a pricing advantage with consumers and could charge more without sacrificing sales. Moreover, as we explore in Chapter 5, Apple was realizing benefits from its vendors and was able to realize a 37% margin on its larger iPads. Ever since the iPad went on sale in April 2010, Apple has dominated the tablet market—a $66.4 billion market in 2012, of which Apple has a 61% bite.[41]

Apple understands the power of margins. The value of Apple's reputation for innovation, earned by actually being innovative, is that while the most respected company in the world commands only 4% of the telephone handset market, it commands 50% of the profits.[42] That's pricing power in the extreme, a benefit of a superior reputation valued by customers.

For most stakeholders, Apple Inc. has exploited its reputation with innovation, to support tremendous margins. Equally importantly, Apple has exploited that reputation for innovation to engage its employees, create significant enterprise value, and bolster its stock price.

Working for Apple Inc.

Apple Inc., ranked 17th in the 2012 Fortune 500 league table, was launched on April Fool's day 1976 by high school chums Steven Wozniak and Steven Jobs. Pooling the technological expertise of the former, then with Hewlett-Packard, and the marketing vision of the latter, then with Atari, the two college dropouts promoted their garage-built hardware product to the delight of the Silicon Valley hobbyist market.

By 1981, the company employed several thousand, was engaged in international sales, and was expanding with the aid of professional investors. That year, the potential for personal computers that Jobs had recognized mushroomed into massive demand. Waves of competition soon followed, including a market behemoth—IBM.

Two major projects influenced by IBM's presence were evolving in the background. On the technology side, the vision of a graphical user interface initially pioneered by Xerox's Palo Alto Research Center was morphing into the Macintosh—the anti-corporate user-friendly computer. On the business side, the reality of competition set Jobs in search of a CEO who could help Apple punch above its weight. He recruited John Sculley, the then CEO of Pepsi.

Chapter 4 | Employees

In 1984, Apple threw down the gauntlet. During the third quarter of the Super Bowl, Apple aired its famous 60-second commercial introducing the Macintosh. Directed by Ridley Scott, the Orwellian scene depicted the IBM world being shattered by a new machine.[43] Jobs' combative spirit captured the market's attention and gave birth to an Apple culture that today is the underpinning of its success. When Sculley was less enthusiastic about the innovative technology, Jobs was bought out. Sculley won the battle in 1985 but lost the war.

By 1993, Sculley was out, followed by two more CEOs who came and went. In 1997, Jobs returned to the helm, wiser and even more passionate. The company was reinfused with a more focused entrepreneurial culture.

Today, Apple's success rests on a number of intangibles; foremost among them is a built-in fan base that ensures a steady supply of employment applicants and a culture that frames work as a noble mission. It's a proven model. A 10-year study of the world's 50 best businesses, including Apple, shows that founders who centered their businesses on a culture of improving people's lives had a growth rate triple that of competitors in their categories.[44] It also found that "The percentage of engaged employees in world class organizations is double that of average organizations."[45] "This is why Apple can do something unique in the annals of retailing: pay a modest hourly wage and no commission, to individual employees who typically have college degrees and who at the highest performing levels can move as much as $3 million in goods a year (Figure 4-1)."[46] Apple Inc.'s employees move nearly $500 per square foot of retail space per dollar of employee base pay. On an annual basis, the company generates $6,123 per square foot compared to Best Buy's $801 and JC Penny's $135.[47]

It works in reverse, too. "In the U.S. alone, Gallup estimates that the cost of disengaged employees in lost productivity is $370 billion per year."[48]

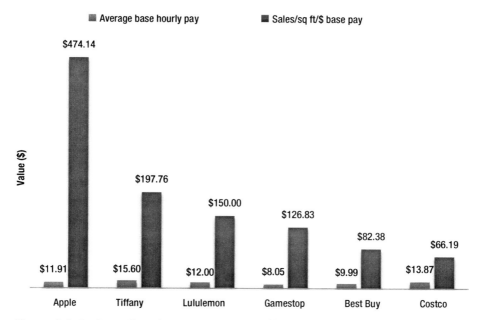

Figure 4-1. Apple retail employees are extremely effective moving nearly $500/sq ft retail space/$1 hourly base pay and dwarfing the performance of other retail operations.

Recruiting Engaged Employees

Denyelle Bruno, then an executive at Macy's West, was one of the first hardcore Apple fans hired for the nascent chain. Charged with building a retail sales force, known internally as specialists, she soon took advantage of Apple's better reputational mousetrap, and people beat a path to the Apple door. Application numbers were so great that statistically it was harder to land a job at an Apple Store than to get into Stanford.

From the outset, Apple recruited candidates who were affable and self-directed rather than tech-savvy. (Technology can be taught, is the theory, while personality is innate.) Those innate advantages are then enhanced with role-playing and pointers on the elaborate etiquette of interacting with customers.

"The phrase that trainees hear time and again, which echoes once they arrive at the stores, is 'enriching people's lives.' The idea is to instill in employees the notion that they are doing something far grander than just selling or fixing products. If there is a secret to Apple's sauce, this is it: the company ennobles employees. It understands that a lot of people will forgo money if they have a sense of higher purpose."[46]

Chapter 4 | Employees

Apple does not incentivize its sales force with commissions. According to Ms. Bruno, the idea was that such incentives would work against the company's primary goals—finding customers the right products, rather than the most expensive ones, and establishing long-term rapport with the brand. It was also thought that commissions would foster employee competition, which would undermine camaraderie.

One two-pronged argument supporting Apple's compensation strategy goes like this: First, "pay-for-performance rules 'crowd out' concern for others' welfare and for ethical rules, making the assumption of selfish opportunism a self-fulfilling prophecy. Second, industries and firms that emphasize incentive pay tend to attract individuals who...are more inclined to selfish behavior than the average."[49]

Empirical evidence supports these arguments. Financial incentives work well for employees who are financially motivated—with the attendant risks. Bradley C. Birkenfeld, the UBS banker who used a variety of ruses to court American clients and help them dodge taxes, told Judge William J. Zloch that the bonus incentives were irresistible. At his sentencing hearing in 2008, he admitted being troubled by the ethics of his actions. "It did concern me, your honor," Mr. Birkenfeld said.[50] He knew he was breaking the law, he told Zloch, but did so because of the "incentives" UBS offered him.

Retaining Engaged Employees

"When you're working for Apple you feel like you're working for this greater good," says a former salesman who asked for anonymity because he didn't want to draw attention to himself.[46] As Apple Inc. explained to the New York Times, "Thousands of incredibly talented professionals...deliver the best customer service in the world." The annual retention rate for Geniuses, the designation for Apple's most advanced salespeople, is almost 90% while the average retention rate in retail sales for the year ending April 2012 was 74%, according to the U.S. Bureau of Labor Statistics.[51]

The company also offers very good benefits for a retailer, including health care, 401(k) contributions, and the chance to buy both company stock and Apple products at a discount. What's more, "Apple" can be a strong credential to have on a résumé.

In a tight job market, this intangible benefit can be invaluable. It is the modern-day analog to doing tours of duty with GE or Procter & Gamble. As P&G's communications department proudly boasts, "More than 130 current and former chief executives at many of the world's top companies began their careers and often spent many years at P&G."[52] David Wiser of Cincinnati-

Reputation, Stock Price, and You 69

based search consultant Wiser Partners added, "P&G is still a golden ticket in terms of leveraging where you've been and where you want to go."

The Other Side of Engagement

And then there is Microsoft. Once, Microsoft was the cool innovator that ran circles around IBM. "They used to point their finger at IBM and laugh," said Bill Hill, a former Microsoft manager. "Now they've become the thing they despised."[53]

It wasn't always so. In 1975, a year before Wozniak and Jobs started selling hardware, Paul Allen and Bill Gates started writing software. The program was called BASIC—Beginner's All-purpose Symbolic Instruction Code—and that year it generated for the duo $16,000. It was a humble start for Microsoft, ranked in 2012 as no. 37 on the Fortune 500 league table.

Microsoft's founders saw evolving before them a computer market divided into hardware and software. They had established a solid reputation with the BASIC language that was on most computers of the day. When they were invited to IBM in New York to discuss developing an operating system for the mainframe behemoth that saw no real future in PCs, "they made what might be one of the most fateful decisions in the history of the computer industry."[54] Rather than developing the operating system and then selling it to IBM, they would license it to them. Every computer that IBM would sell would include that operating system, and in turn they would pay Microsoft a licensing fee. Both IBM and Microsoft were confident that were making the better deal.

IBM marketing muscle pushed the Microsoft operating system into the market. As PC use grew, Microsoft saw that Apple's graphical user interface was the future. Enter Windows and the second fateful decision. Microsoft made it easier for third-party developers to create software that ran on Windows. Applications running on Windows proliferated, to the disadvantage of all other operating systems. The clincher, though, was Microsoft's vision of an office suite—the ability to not only work with the applications simultaneously, but also to copy information from one and seamlessly paste it into another—while maintaining the proper format. That was the heart of the Microsoft monopoly known as Microsoft Office, and it took the company to its peak value of more than $0.55 trillion in 2000.

The principal importance of interoperability and seamless integration remains a key market discriminator. Today, though, the lead provider is Apple, and interoperability is expected to extend across various forms of hardware, all enabling software, and all venues of service including cloud computing. Two Apple products—the iPhone and iPad—alone generate as much revenue as all

Chapter 4 | Employees

of Microsoft's wares combined. Microsoft "since 2000 . . . has fallen flat in every area it entered: e-books, music, search, social networking, etc., etc."[55] What happened?

Change for the worst, Jobs would say. He laid it out in 2004, seven years into the return of Apple Inc. as an innovation powerhouse. After Jobs' return as CEO after an exile engineered by former CEO John Sculley, he told *Businessweek* magazine:

> *People always ask me why did Apple really fail for those years, and it's easy to blame it on certain people or personalities. Certainly, there was some of that. But there's a far more insightful way to think about it. Apple had a monopoly on the graphical user interface for almost 10 years. That's a long time. And how are monopolies lost? Think about it. Some very good product people invent some very good products, and the company achieves a monopoly.*

> *But after that, the product people aren't the ones that drive the company forward anymore. It's the marketing guys or the ones who expand the business into Latin America or whatever. Because what's the point of focusing on making the product even better when the only company you can take business from is yourself?*

> *So a different group of people starts to move up. And who usually ends up running the show? The sales guy. John Akers at IBM is the consummate example. Then one day, the monopoly expires for whatever reason. But by then, the best product people have left, or they're no longer listened to. And so the company goes through this tumultuous time, and it either survives or it doesn't.*

> *Q: Is this common in the industry?*

> *A: Look at Microsoft — who's running Microsoft?*

> *Q: Steve Ballmer.*

> *A: Right, the sales guy. Case closed. And that's what happened at Apple, as well."[56]*

Losing its focus on innovation was bad for Microsoft. Fostering a culture that drove employees to focus on survival made things worse. Losing its reputation for innovation was one of many casualties.

In the August 2012 issue of *Vanity Fair*, Kurt Eichenwald describes how a corrosive management system known as "stack ranking" effectively crippled Microsoft's ability to innovate. The program forced every unit to declare a certain percentage of employees as top performers, good performers, average, and poor.

"Every current and former Microsoft employee I interviewed—*every one*— cited stack ranking as the most destructive process inside of Microsoft, something that drove out untold numbers of employees," Eichenwald writes. "If you were on a team of 10 people, you walked in the first day knowing that, no matter how good everyone was, 2 people were going to get a great review, 7 were going to get mediocre reviews, and 1 was going to get a terrible review," says a former software developer. "It leads to employees focusing on competing with each other rather than competing with other companies."

The differences in employee engagement, driven at Apple by a reputation for innovation and a culture based around the benefits of innovation, have financial consequences. In 2011, Apple Inc. spent 7% of its $108 billion in revenue on sales and general administrative expenses, while Microsoft spent 32.6% of its $69.9 billion on the same types of activities (Figure 4-2). This difference helps explain why equity investors on 6 July 2012 valued Apple 34% more than Microsoft for every dollar of net income, and why Apple Inc. on 20 August became "Wall Street's all-time MVP—that's Most Valuable Property" with the world's highest ever market valuation of $624 billion.[57]

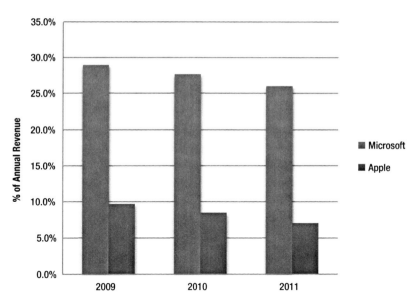

Figure 4-2. Sales, corporate, and other general administrative costs at Apple and Microsoft as a % of revenue. Source: Apple and Microsoft 2011 annual reports. With engaged employees, Apple is able to spend significantly less of its revenue on sales and administrative activities.

Consider This

- Recruiting employees who share an institution's culture tends to create an aligned workforce that is more productive and less costly.

Chapter 4 | Employees

- A consistent, credible reputation, once earned and appreciated, will ensure a steady supply of committed and engaged employees.

Goldman Sachs Group

Standing at London's St. Paul's Cathedral, Goldman Sachs International adviser Brian Griffiths stated: "The injunction of Jesus to love others as ourselves is an endorsement of self-interest.... We have to tolerate the inequality as a way to achieving greater prosperity and opportunity for all."[58] "The lady doth protest too much, methinks," you say? Remember, it was not 20 years ago that the intellectual challenge, power, risk, and reward of investment banking was an alluring siren's song to a generation of some of the most creative, aggressive, and intellectually gifted young adults on the face of this planet.

In financial services today, no institution has a better reputation for attracting the best of the best than Goldman Sachs. In the 1970s, which was a turbulent period when some firms thrived and many others withered on the vine, Goldman was at the center of cutting-edge financial and policy innovation.[59] The firm exuded Gordon Gekko–levels of bravado: "We make the rules, pal. The news, war, peace, famine, upheaval, the price per paper clip. We pick that rabbit out of the hat while everybody sits out there wondering how the hell we did it."[60]

Its innovative bankers were once dubbed "billionaire boy scouts" because of their talent for making fortunes while maintaining a guilt-free, cherubic image.[59] "Becoming a partner at the firm remains the dream of most ambitious financial executives, while joining its ranks remains the goal of most wannabe bankers the world over."[61] In short, over the past 30 years, Goldman has emerged as the iconic innovative bank. Goldman has the "banking equivalent of the celebrity 'it' factor."[62]

The Company

The Goldman Sachs Group, Inc. (NYSE: GS)—the company changed its name from Goldman, Sachs & Co. after it went public in 1999—has been active in the capital markets sector of the financial services industry for more than 100 years. The company operates as a leading global investment banking and securities firm with two main divisions. The first division is Global Capital Markets, which includes investment banking, financial advisory services, trading, and principal investments. The second division is Asset Management and Securities Services, a business unit responsible for investment advisory services. Goldman Sachs's clients include corporations, financial institutions,

Reputation, Stock Price, and You

governments, and wealthy individuals. The company operates more than 40 offices across the globe.

The company was founded by Marcus Goldman, a Bavarian school teacher, who immigrated to the United States in 1848. After supporting himself for some years as a salesman in New Jersey, Goldman moved to Philadelphia, where he operated a small clothing store—he was in the "rags business."

After the Civil War he moved to New York City, where in 1869 he began trading in promissory notes. Goldman would assume the credit risk borne by merchants in lower Manhattan, purchasing at a discount customers' promissory notes from jewelers on Maiden Lane and from leather merchants in an area of the city called "the swamp." Goldman would then sell these jewelry and leather-collateralized loans to commercial banks at a lesser discount.

The Goldman story is the epitome of rags to riches. In the early 1880s, Goldman's son Henry expanded the firm's range of credit exposures and set up operations in Providence, Hartford, Boston, and Philadelphia. In 1887, Goldman, Sachs expanded internationally through a relationship with the British merchant bank Kleinwort Sons. For the next 100 years, the partnership expanded into international commercial finance, foreign-exchange services, and currency arbitrage. As business operations became driven by innovations of increasing complexity, leveraged transactions demanded an ever larger balance sheet.

In early May 1999, the company listed on the New York Stock Exchange, raising $3.6 billion. In 2002, then CEO Henry Paulson, who would go on to be the U.S. Treasury Secretary under President George W. Bush, laid out the company's strategy, declaring, "We want to be the premier global investment bank, securities, and investment management firm. We want to have a disproportionate share of the business of the most important clients in the most important markets." *Businessweek* magazine memorialized those words, adding: "The company must gain a lock on providing financial advice to marquee corporations, government authorities, and superrich individuals in the world's major economies—the U.S., Germany, Britain, Japan, and China."[63] Within four years, Paulson's strategy had propelled the firm "to the top spot in global-equities underwriting and M&A advisory. The trading unit that included fixed income, currency, and commodities generated record net revenues of $5.6 billion, while equities trading added another $1.74 billion. The company generated an annual profit of more than $3 billion, nearly surpassing its earnings at the height of the bull market."[64]

Chapter 4 | Employees

Innovation at Goldman Sachs

When John Havens assumed command of Citigroup's securities and investment business after the 2008 crash, he looked around at his competitors and concluded that Goldman Sachs became a global powerhouse by offering corporate clients smart ideas, innovative products, and flawless execution.[65] Bill Cassano, vice president in the economic derivatives group at Goldman Sachs, concurred: "Financial innovation over the last 25 years has all been about taking the risks that are embedded in assets, isolating them and making them transferable so you can hold the asset, but not hold the risk that isn't part of the reason you're investing."[66] There's money to be made in capturing certain reward while selling uncertain risk.

To strip reward from risk and capture it to the benefit of clients, Goldman Sachs has been introducing financial innovations for more than a century. Initial public offerings are one such model. In the early 20th century, Goldman Sachs established itself as a major player in the initial public offering (IPO) market. Selling shares to the public was innovative; buying them back and structuring retirement options, as Goldman did in the early teens, was even more innovative.[67] Since it was already expert in buying and selling credit, selling and buying equities came naturally—and thus Goldman Sachs found itself in investment banking in the 1930s. In the 1950s, it became a pioneer of certain types of hedging strategies, the precursors to the complex derivative trades that many argue helped to bring about the global financial crisis in 2008.

Innovation is a process driven first and foremost by people. *"Our assets are our people, capital and reputation."*[68] That quote on page 2 of the 2011 Annual Report makes explicit the link between employees and reputation at Goldman.

Innovation is cultural. Goldman Sachs was one of the first financial institutions to recruit MBA graduates from the world's leading business schools, helping it earn a reputation as hiring only the very brightest and most capable. Innovation is enshrined in the firm's credo—the 5th of the 14 Principles:[69]

> 5. We stress creativity and imagination in everything we do. While recognizing that the old way may still be the best way, we constantly strive to find a better solution to a client's problems. We pride ourselves on having pioneered many of the practices and techniques that have become standard in the industry.

Financial Success Metrics

In 2006, Goldman Sachs made more money than any other Wall Street investment bank in history. Its staff shared in a $16 billion bonus pool. The bank was at the top of the global M&A adviser rankings for yet another year,

Reputation, Stock Price, and You

and it was named bank of the year in the International Financing Review (IFR) awards.

The bank won praise for the way it has developed its private equity and hedge fund business—and for the way it combines its roles as adviser and financier with that of co-investor. Goldman was also named equity house of the year and won a new category: Leveraged finance house of the year. That award, introduced to reflect the increasing variety and complexity of financing associated with leveraged buyouts may or may not turn out to be a good win for Goldman.[70] It occurred just as the doom-mongers predicted rising defaults for the next year, a contraction of risk appetite, and an end to the ample global liquidity seen in 2006.

The bank even won an "award" for the way it engineered the exit of one of its corporate directors who had become an embarrassment. Andrew Hill for the *Financial Times* wrote about how Goldman Sachs distanced itself from BP's Lord Browne: "It is rare, for one thing, that Goldman Sachs offers an innovation to the world of business without charging a fee for it. But next time a company chairman wants to hint to a distinguished director that time is up, he need only slide a piece of paper across the boardroom table with two words on it: 'John Browne.'"[71]

Fast forward to 2010, and reputational resilience is still evident. Notwithstanding the terrible bruising suffered by the industry in general and Goldman Sachs in particular, the BBC was still paying tribute to "the world's most revered commercial financial institution." Goldman Sachs topped the industry league tables for financial advice, with 22.8% of the market share and $555 billion in deals[72] (Figure 4-3a). Goldman's average deal size was 15% larger than the average of its peers; and its total deal value was 42% greater than the average of its peers. Goldman Sachs' was also the favorite counterparty of the U.S. Federal Reserve. The company received 22.1% of the Fed's Treasury dealings. The next two major traders, Citigroup and Credit Suisse, received 14.5% and 10.2% respectively.[73] In 2011, notwithstanding a profound slowdown in banking activity, Goldman continued to lead in IPOs (Figure 4-3b).[74] Last, at the end of Q1 of 2012, Goldman Sachs led merger and acquisition advisory services, with 29% of the $1.08 trillion in deals.[75]

For all its faults, challenges, and public missteps, customers still prefer Goldman Sachs and they reward the firm with bigger and better deal opportunities, on which Goldman (generally) effectively delivers. Said William Barker of Brand Finance to the *Financial Times*, "My guess is that their customers are probably very happy with them."[76] As one analyst noted, "Nobody is going to stop doing business with Goldman Sachs. They're just not going to do it—because Goldman is just better than everybody else. And that's the bottom line."[77] To underscore that point, on 29 September 2012,

Chapter 4 | Employees

Barron's magazine cover featured Goldman Sachs in a story titled, "Built to Win."[78]

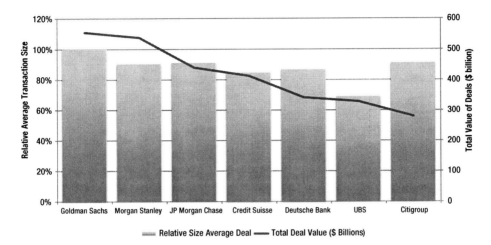

Figure 4-3a. 2010 Financial Advice League table showing Goldman Sachs' advice helped shape more deal value, and that the average value of each deal was greater than that of its closest competitors.

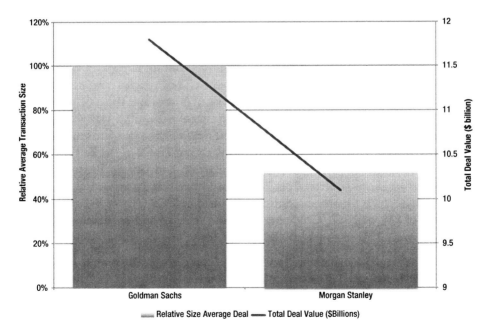

Figure 4-3b. 2011 Financial Advice League table showing Goldman Sachs' services helped raise more capital more deal value, and that the average value of each deal was greater than that of its closest competitors.

Enmity from Non-Stakeholders

Goldman Sachs's reputation for innovation and ubiquity, as well as its superior return among the biggest banks, has made it a target for much of the anger and frustration arising from the global economic chaos. This is best illustrated by the colorful descriptor penned by Matt Taibbi in *Rolling Stone* magazine in July 2009.[79]

In an article titled, "The Great American Bubble Machine," Taibbi charges: "From tech stocks to high gas prices, Goldman Sachs has engineered every major market manipulation since the Great Depression – and they're about to do it again." He then characterizes Goldman Sachs as "a great vampire squid wrapped around the face of humanity, relentlessly jamming its blood funnel into anything that smells like money."

The following month, the *Financial Times* reported that research it commissioned from Brand Asset Consulting comprising a survey of 17,000 Americans found that Goldman's stature—as measured by several gauges of brand strength—had suffered in 2008 and 2009.[75] A similar finding was reported in early 2010 by Harris Interactive in their 2009 Reputation Quotient survey, which placed Goldman Sachs near the bottom of a list of 60 highly visible companies. As an aside, Chapter 9 presents survey data showing that Goldman's peers were more favorably disposed to the company.

Passion and Engagement from Employees

Despite the slide in Goldman Sachs' reputation among the general public, among its employees the company remains an icon. The company seeks to recruit diverse, driven, and innovative team players who have an interest in financial markets, management, and process design. And rather than operate a company of individual stars, it operates a star company.

This is important. Even in investment banking, where many firms coddle top performers, corporate culture is valued by employees. According to *Vault Finance*, a 2010 survey of financial service employees showed the following:

- Percentage of respondents who say firm culture was the single most important factor in deciding to accept their firm's offer over others: **35**

- Percentage who say prestige was the most important factor: **18**

- Percentage who say compensation was the most important: **9**[80]

Chapter 4 | Employees

Goldman's culture helps explain why it is a fixture of *Fortune's* 100 Best Companies to Work For list, a survey-based study involving around 250,000 employees globally. In 2011, Goldman Sachs moved up a slot to no. 23. While that's lower than its 9th place ranking before the financial crisis, Goldman is one of only 13 companies to have earned a spot on the list every year since it debuted in 1998.[81]

The same perceptions go for potential employees. The bonuses and profits that led Goldman Sachs to be labeled a "great vampire squid" are cited by business-school students as proof of the company's strength. And they want to work there. In annual surveys by Universum Group, a Stockholm-based marketing company, as reported by *Fortune*, Goldman Sachs ranked no. 3 or no. 4 among approximately 6,000 MBA candidates at more than 50 business schools worldwide (Figure 4-4).

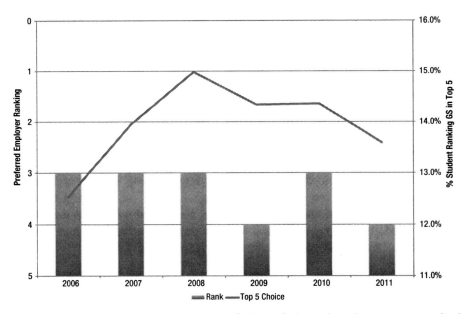

Figure 4-4. MBA students consistently rank Goldman Sachs as their choice investment bank employment opportunity, and as one of the top five employment opportunities consistently. Source: Universum Group annual surveys.

It's not just the fringe benefits nor is it the money. Goldman, for instance, doesn't offer employees free cafeteria chow like Google, ranked the no. 4 choice by existing employees in 2011. It does not provide complimentary recreation and fitness areas like the no. 1 company on the list, SAS. Even Goldman's compensation, though higher than that of many companies, isn't dramatically different from that of other investment banks. (As one former low-level Goldman strategist puts it, "Their compensation system pays you $1 more than whatever is your threshold for leaving Goldman Sachs."[80)]

It's the culture—what many call corporate brand—and what we believe at Goldman Sachs comprises its reputation for innovation. As Stefan Stern who writes on management for the *Financial Times*, summarized: "When it comes to retaining good people or attracting new ones, your image and reputation count."[82]

Last, as every senior executive appreciates, engaged and motivated employees produce more and turn over less. We've seen that Goldman outproduces. What about turnover?

Among financial service companies ranked as one of the top 100 places to work, Goldman turnover was 9.4%; overall industry turnover rates are 10.7%. The 12% lower turnover rate at Goldman translates to lower direct and indirect costs associated. Direct costs that would appear in the Selling, General and Administrative (SG&A) sections of the P&L statement include advertising, headhunter fees, temporary work, overtime pay, signing bonuses, relocation costs for new employees, and training costs. Indirect costs that would appear subtly in the Revenue line of the P&L statement include customer service disruption, emotional costs, loss of morale, burnout/absenteeism among remaining employees, loss of experience, continuity, and "corporate memory."

Goldman Sachs understands explicitly that a good reputation among employees makes for a good corporate reputation and fosters greater productivity and above-average returns.

> Goldman Sachs has one reputation. It can be affected by any number of
> decisions and activities across the firm. Every employee has an equal obligation
> to raise issues or concerns, no matter how small, to protect the firm's
> reputation. We must ensure that our focus on our reputation is as grounded,
> consistent and pervasive as our focus on commercial success.[83]

Goldman Sachs also benefits from this empirically (Figure 4-6). Over the trailing three years, costs in its investment banking division to generate $1 were consistently lower and no less than 4% lower than the average of its peers (Figure 4-5). The exception is the 2011 cost/revenue ratio at JP Morgan Chase which, while better for that year, was offset by an $5.8 billion trading loss in 2012.[84]

Chapter 4 | Employees

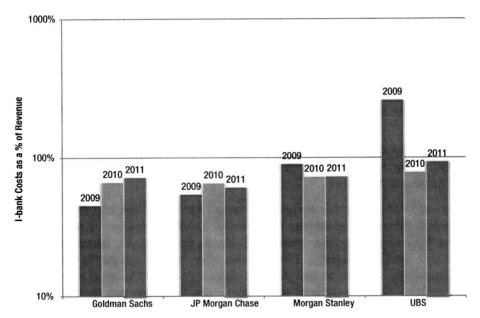

Figure 4-5. Operating costs as a % of revenue generated in the investment banking segments of Goldman Sachs and selected peers illustrating how employee engagement reduces costs. Source: Goldman Sachs, JP Morgan Chase, Morgan Stanley and UBS 2011 Annual reports. JP Morgan Chase, while apparently an exception to the rule in 2011, may have taken risks that manifested only in 2012.[83]

Also, as of mid-July 2012, for every $1 in expected net income, equity investors valued Goldman Sachs more than its six closest competitors: 15% more than JP Morgan Chase, 19% more than Morgan Stanley, 22% more than UBS, 34% more than Citigroup, 64% more than Credit Suisse, and 78% more than Deutsche Bank.[85]

Reputation, Stock Price, and You

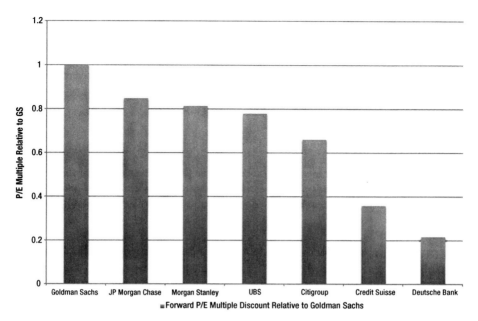

Figure 4-6. Equity investors value Goldman Sachs more. For every $1 of expected future net income, equity investors give Goldman Sachs anywhere from a 15% to a 78% premium over its closest competitors.

Retrospective

Goldman Sachs is an iconic firm respected for its innovation (and the cerebral power behind it). This reputation, and the culture surrounding it, is one that is valued by its employees, and it has enabled the company to sustain its reputation and reap the benefits.

In the capital markets sector, a reputation for innovation is an important differentiator. Goldman Sachs is well aware of the importance of reputation to its value and its ability to compete successfully.

Goldman continues to dominate notwithstanding the great public enmity, increased regulatory scrutiny, and general slowdown, all of which have been adversely impacting the industry as a whole.

Consider This

- Even in industry segments in which compensation is a central motivator, corporate culture is both a competitive differentiator and a primary motivator.

Chapter 4 | Employees

- Engaged and motivated employees outperform their peers, and in most businesses, that is the key to financial success and market domination.

- Stakeholders own a firm's reputation. When customers, clients, and the company are all authentically on the same page, all will benefit from the value generated.

Quality: Domino Pizza Redux

[Quality is] the extent to which a product is free from defects or deficiencies; a service meets or exceeds the expectations of customers or clients, and both products and services conform to measurable and verifiable criteria. (Table 1-1)

The prank impugning the quality of Domino's pizza recorded and uploaded to YouTube on Easter Sunday, 2009, jeopardized Domino's $490 million in domestic revenues and $1.4 billion spent on brand-building during the preceding five years and precipitated a 10% fall in market capitalization in the period immediately following. Trading volume surged.

Yet according to an earnings call transcript by Seeking Alpha, the company lost no more than 2% in domestic same-store sales for the second quarter of 2009. Within one year, Domino's equity value was higher than it had been in years.

Tim McIntyre, vice president of communications at Domino's, who helped shepherd the company through the viral video incident, is on the lecture circuit advising directors that their duties of oversight include social media. Is there a connection? Might it be the $2 million insurance payment the company received following the event? Or perhaps the stock surge is due to the December 2009 launch of new crust, new sauce, and new cheese? After all, quality is a major driver of intangible asset and reputational value in the food sector.

The company did roll out an aggressive campaign to restore its reputation. How effective was it? Simple answer: its returns beat those of two of the three most highly ranked firms in the restaurant sector from that period.

Process: The Secret Sauce

While many might attribute the rebound to excellent marketing, a more satisfying explanation for Domino's reputation resilience was evidence of substantive business processes that engaged its employees to create a quality

Reputation, Stock Price, and You

product, and a communications effort that allowed stakeholders to appreciate its value.

Those quality processes are systems that improve managerial motivation, provide time for managerial oversight, and incorporate technology that enhances quality while reducing opportunities for adverse human intervention, malicious or otherwise.

Domino's greatest reputation risk lurks in and among the employees of the franchisees. Its strategy to mitigate that risk comprises two creative HR-focused processes. First, it requires that every franchise owner be 100% committed to the business—no outside (distracting) revenue opportunities. Domino's wants the fortune of its franchise owners to depend on the success of the franchise. Second, it provides vertically integrated dough manufacturing and supply chain systems that allow the franchise owner to dedicate more time to human resource management rather than engage in the "back-of-store" activity typical of the industry.

Domino's is also constantly innovating to increase quality. It has led the industry with a sturdier corrugated pizza box, a mesh screen that helps cook pizza crust more evenly, and, introduced in 1998, the Domino's HeatWave hot bag that keeps pizzas hot during delivery.

Consider This

- In a business in which quality means meeting customers' expectations for high levels of product or service, processes and controls that drive product quality by engaging employees are proven sources of enterprise value.

- Risk management processes that anticipate and head off crises can reduce volatility. Authentic processes that isolate rogue activities for what they are—rogues—foster reputational resilience.

Guidance

From the perspective of employees, companies' reputations manifest in corporate culture. Culture is what employees experience in their day-to-day operations—the human environment within which instructions are conveyed, goals are set, operations are monitored, and results are rewarded or punished. These experiences establish employee *expectations* that then inform employee actions ranging from ethical decisions to sales execution to, well, making fabulous pizza.

Chapter 4 | Employees

Culture comes from the top. News Corp.'s top leadership came from the rough-and-tumble world of Australian journalism. Within tabloid press, an especially seedy part of the Murdoch empire, an unholy alliance between a capable executive and the head of the enterprise's center of governance lubricated an already slippery slope. Bad behavior was rewarded. There was no internal governor to arrest its proliferation. Consequently, when the ethical problem was exposed, the enterprise had no defense and was found culpable. The full costs are yet to be determined.

Barclays is a similar story. The cost is in the range of half a billion dollars in fines, a few jobs, and the CEO's reputation. The bad behavior—a cultural failure—does not seal the case for more regulation in the financial sector. On the contrary. If a regulator enforces culture, "You get a police state with compliance on the surface and subversion underneath."[86]

As destructive as rogue employees can be to an enterprise's value, engaged employees can create significant value. Apple's culture is a reflection of the values of its founders. Its strong culture attracts employees whose behavior reinforces its reputation for innovation. While that has created significant value by reducing operational costs and boosting revenues, the future will be one in which professional management is at the helm. The world will be watching to see if the culture of innovation will long outlive its original creator.

Microsoft went through the transition to professional management, and the cultural effects on the employees have been well documented. Innovation has been one of many casualties.

Goldman Sachs stands in contrast to Barclays. It has been pilloried in the press, reviled by the general public, parodied by modern-day gonzo journalists, and yet...its customers, employees, and prospective employees hold it in high regard. And this consistently translates to market domination. Say what you wish, but Goldman Sachs' reputation is incredibly resilient.

Domino's shows that employee engagement and a reputation for quality is a consequence of operational controls and properly designed incentives. It shows that authentic controls can protect reputation by enabling a company to distance itself from rogues.

Each of these exemplary companies established reputations that employees understood, valued, and exploited. Awareness of the importance of its reputation—and how it was established—helped Apple and Goldman Sachs dominate their sectors and helped Domino's rebound from a crisis. Conversely, ethical failures poisoned the reputations and accelerated the falls from grace at News Corp. and Barclays.

Reputation, Stock Price, and You

There are practical steps a company can take to prevent employees from exploiting control weaknesses and placing an enterprise's reputation at risk. Supervisors can ask boards to provide evidence of healthy culture, such as functional whistleblowing practices, customer surveys, and employee engagement surveys. The enterprise can invest in systems for challenging "group think" at the board level and technology solutions that provide management and boards with both operational controls and oversight dashboards. Last, a company might consider reputational value insurances where underwriting assesses reputational practices and culture and signals to all stakeholders that the organization is in operational control.

By the Numbers

These case studies illustrate how reputation can affect value-creating and value-destroying actions by employees, and how those economic effects either impact SG&A expenses or create one-time extraordinary charges (Table 4-2).

Table 4-2. Effect of Reputation on Employee-Associated Costs

	P&L Effect	Stock Price Effect
News Corp.	More than $360 million in fees and write-downs	$4.4 billion lost
Barclays	$452 million (£290 million) in one-time extraordinary charges	$5.77 billion (£3.7 billion) lost
Apple	Store sales are 280% more efficient than the average of a reference group. SG&A costs are 65% lower than at Microsoft	Apple 270% 3-year returns Microsoft: 32%; Nasdaq: : 50%; Google: 39%
Goldman Sachs	Average deal size 15% larger than the average of its peers; total deal value 42% greater than the average of its peers. Operating costs per $/revenue no less than 4% lower than average of rivals	Forward P/E multiples 15%–78% greater than all major rivals

Endnotes

1 Russell D. Be ruthless with reputation. *PR Week*. 3 November 2011. Available at: http://www.prweek.com/uk/league_tables/1100806/dean-russell-fleishman-hillard-ruthless-reputation/. Accessed 3 July 2012.

Chapter 4 | Employees

2 Domino's brand takes a hit after YouTube™ "prank" video. *HCD Research*. 17 April 2009. Available at: http://www.mediacurves.com/NationalMediaFocus/J7329-Dominos/. Accessed 3 July 2012

3 Hsieh T. *Wikipedia*. Available at: http://en.wikipedia.org/wiki/Tony_Hsieh. Accessed 2 July 2012.

4 Hsieh T. Available at: http://www.brainyquote.com/quotes/quotes/t/tonyhsieh412218.html. Accessed 2 July 2012.

5 The tipping point. Wikipedia. Available at: http://en.wikipedia.org/wiki/The_Tipping_Point. Accessed 3 July 2012.

6 Chandrasekhar I, Wardrop M, Trotman A. Phone hacking: timeline of the scandal. *The Telegraph*. 13 June 2012. Available at: http://www.telegraph.co.uk/news/uknews/phone-hacking/8634176/Phone-hacking-timeline-of-a-scandal.html. Accessed 3 July 2012.

7 Hughes M. Levi Bellfield found guilty of abducting and murdering Milly Dowler. *The Telegraph*. 23 June 2011. Available at: http://www.telegraph.co.uk/news/uknews/crime/8594367/Levi-Bellfield-found-guilty-of-abducting-and-murdering-Milly-Dowler.html. Accessed 3 July 2012.

8 Davies N, Hill A. Missing Milly Dowler's voicemail was hacked by News of the World. *The Guardian*. 4 July 2011. Available at: http://www.guardian.co.uk/uk/2011/jul/04/milly-dowler-voicemail-hacked-news-of-world. Accessed 3 July 2012.

9 Spitzer E. Prosecute News Corp. *Slate.com*. 12 July 2011. Available at: http://www.slate.com/articles/news_and_politics/the_best_policy/2011/07/prosecute_news_corp.html. Accessed 3 July 2012.

10 Thomson Reuters expands Lipper content through the acquisition of The Globe and Mail's Canadian mutual fund database. Press Release. 1 June 2012. Available at: http://thomsonreuters.com/content/press_room/financial/2012_06_01_thomson_reuters_expands_lipper_through_aquisition. Accessed 4 July 2012.

11 Burman T. Wikipedia. Available at: http://en.wikipedia.org/wiki/Tony_Burman. Accessed 4 July 2012.

12 Hitchens C. Scandal sheets. *Slate*. 11 July 2011. Available at: http://www.slate.com/articles/news_and_politics/fighting_words/2011/07/scandal_sheets.html. Accessed 4 July 2012.

13 Andrews S. Untangling Rebekah Brooks. *Vanity Fair*. February 2012Available at: http://www.vanityfair.com/business/2012/02/rebekah-brooks-201202. Accessed 4 July 2012.

14 Ward RM, DiPaolo DG, Popson HC. College student leaders: meet the alpha female. *Journal of Leadership Education*. 2009; 7(3):100–117.

15 Groth A. How Rebekah Brooks became one of the most powerful women in Britain. *Business Insider*. 9 January 2012. Available at: http://articles.businessinsider.com/2012-01-09/strategy/30606586_1_hacking-scandal-rebekah-brooks-powerful-women. Accessed 11 August 2012.

16 Thakor M. Suits: a woman on Wall Street. *Huffington Post*. 3 March 2011. Available at: http://www.huffingtonpost.com/manisha-thakor/suits-a-woman-on-wall-str_b_830698.html. Accessed 4 July 2012.

Reputation, Stock Price, and You 87

17 Levy G. Rebekah Brooks, the schmoozer hated by Murdoch's wife and daughter. *Daily Mail.* 17 July 2011. Available at: http://www.dailymail.co.uk/femail/article-2015257/Rebekah-Brooks-hated-Rupert-Murdochs-wife-Wendi-daughter-Elisabeth.html#ixzz1zfHoTi8L. Accessed 4 July 2012.

18 Dmitracova O. Hacking was "standard practice" at Murdoch paper: police. *Reuters.* 10 July 2011. Available at: http://www.reuters.com/article/2011/07/10/us-newscorp-police-idUSTRE76902K20110710. Accessed 4 July 2012.

19 Fenton B. Inquiry told of corrupt culture at Murdoch tabloid. *Financial Times.* 27 February 2012. Available at: http://www.ft.com/intl/cms/s/0/c53a70cc-613d-11e1-a738-00144feabdc0.html#axzz1zYqkZk8R. Accessed 4 July 2012/

20 Lyall S. For years, the tabloids' sting kept British politicians in line. *The New York Times.* 9 July 2011 Available at: http://www.nytimes.com/2011/07/10/world/europe/10britain.html?pagewanted=all. Accessed 4 July 2012.

21 Hitchens C. In Britain, the *Guardian* takes on Rupert Murdoch's cynical view of what newspaper readers want to read. *Slate.* 11 July 2011. Available at: http://www.slate.com/articles/news_and_politics/fighting_words/2011/07/scandal_sheets.html. Accessed 11 August 2012.

22 Diamond R. TODAY business lecture 2011. *BBC Radio 4.* 4 November 2011. Available at: http://news.bbc.co.uk/today/hi/today/newsid_9630000/9630673.stm. Accessed 3 July 2012.

23 Kossovsky N. Another British piñata. *Intellectual Asset Management.* 2011; 49:(Sept/Oct) 44–53.

24 Strupp J. Shareholder lawsuit: phone-hacking scandal damaged News Corp.'s image. Media Matters for America. 11 July 2011. Available at: http://mediamatters.org/blog/2011/07/11/shareholder-lawsuit-phone-hacking-scandal-damag/174682. Accessed 3 July 2012.

25 Saba J, Melvin J. Murdoch's newspaper crisis causes jitters in U.S. Reuters. 14 July 2011. Available at: http://us.mobile.reuters.com/article/article/idUSTRE76C7HP20110714?irpc=932. Accessed 3 July 2012.

26 Yann A. PRSA: Rupert Murdoch is torching the reputation of all of his brands. Ragan's PR Daily. 12 July 2011. Available at: http://www.prdaily.com/crisiscommunications/Articles/PRSA_Rupert_Murdoch_is_torching_the_reputation_of_8872.aspx. Accessed 3 July 2012.

27 Phone hacking: Rebekah Brooks resignation statement. The Telegraph. 17 July 2011. Available at: http://www.telegraph.co.uk/news/uknews/phone-hacking/8639598/Phone-hacking-Rebekah-Brooks-resignation-statement.html. Accessed 3 July 2012.

28 . Harrison M. Murdoch makes fresh apology as Brooks is arrested by U.K. Police. Bloomberg Businessweek. 17 July 2011 Available at:http://mobile.businessweek.com/news/2011-07-17/murdoch-makes-fresh-apology-as-brooks-is-arrested-by-u-k-police.html. Accessed 3 July 2012.

29 Yager J. Dem asks Issa to investigate News Corp. The Hill. 14 July 2011. Available at: http://thehill.com/homenews/house/171539-dem-calls-on-issa-to-investigate-news-corp. Accessed 3 July 2012.

30 Sabbagh D. Rupert Murdoch apologises, and says there was a 'cover-up' at the NoW. The Guardian. 26 April 2012. Available at: http://www.guardian.co.uk/media/2012/apr/26/rupert-murdoch-apologises-leveson-inquiry. Accessed 29 August 2012.

Chapter 4 | Employees

31 Leveson inquiry: hearings – day 18. #pressreform. 15 December 2011. Available at: http://pressreform.blogspot.com/2011/12/leveson-inquiry-hearings-day-18.html. Accessed 29 August 2012.

32 Browning J, Morales A. Murdoch makes fresh hacking apology as Miliband urges News Corp. breakup. *Bloomberg.* 17 July 2011. Available at: http://www.bloomberg.com/news/2011-07-17/news-corp-pledges-compensation-co-operation-over-phone-hacking.html. Accessed 4 July 2012.

33 Spanier G. Cost of hacking to Murdoch's empire so far: £239,000,000. *The Independent.* 6 April 2012. Available at: http://www.independent.co.uk/news/uk/crime/cost-of-hacking-to-murdochs-empire-so-far-239000000-7622359.html. Accessed 6 August 2012.

34 Mirkinson J. Phone hacking: a year after Milly Dowler scandal, there is no end in sight to crisis. *Huffington Post.* 4 July 2012. Available at: http://www.huffingtonpost.com/2012/07/04/phone-hacking-milly-dowler-scandal_n_1649200.html. Accessed 4 July 2012.

35 Stern G. Has News Corp's board restored confidence? *B2C.* 9 July 2012. Available at: http://www.business2community.com/finance/has-news-corps-board-restored-confidence-0214626. Accessed 6 August 2012.

36 Armstrong P. Diamond's exit shows Libor only what each bank says it is. *Bloomberg.* 4 July 2012. Available at: http://www.bloomberg.com/news/2012-07-03/diamond-s-exit-shows-libor-only-what-each-bank-says-it-is.html. Accessed 4 July 2012.

37 Westbrook J, Vaughan L. Diamond apologizes for 'reprehensible' Barclays Libor behavior. *Bloomberg.* 4 July 2012. Available at: http://www.sfgate.com/business/bloomberg/article/Diamond-Apologizes-for-Reprehensible-3683997.php. Accessed 4 July 2012.

38 Crowley K, Mustoe H, Moshinksy B. Diamond offers to rebut 'unfair' charges he misled Parliament. *San Francisco Chronicle.* 11 July 2012. Available at: http://www.sfgate.com/business/bloomberg/article/Diamond-Offers-to-Rebut-Unfair-Charges-He-3697627.php. Accessed 11 July 2012.

39 Huang H. Well-being and trust in the workplace. Helliwell JF, NBER Working Paper No. 14589 December 2008.

40 Social responsibility key to attracting top talent. Kelly Services wire story. 28 October 2009. Available at: http://ir.kellyservices.com/releasedetail.cfm?releaseid=419383. Accessed 6 July 2012.

41 Burrows P, Satariano A. Apple said to plan smaller IPad to vie with Google Nexus. *Bloomberg.* 4 July 2012. Available at: http://www.bloomberg.com/news/2012-07-03/here-comes-nexus-7-nightmare-the-ipad-mini.html. Accessed 6 July 2012.

42 Huygens C. Nokia vs. Apple: yearning for a bite. Mission Intangible. 17 February 2011. Available at:http://www.iafinance.org/_blog/MISSION_INTANGIBLE/post/Nokia_vs_Apple_Yearning_for_a_bite/. Accessed 12 July 2012

43 Company history: 1983–1985. Available at: http://www.apple-history.com/h3. Accessed 11 July 2012.

44 Zwilling M. 10 Ways to build a business culture like Apple. *Forbes.* 3 March 2012. Available at: http://www.forbes.com/sites/martinzwilling/2012/03/03/10-ways-to-build-a-business-culture-like-apple/. Accessed 6 July 2012.

Reputation, Stock Price, and You

45 Savitz E. It's time to occupy IT. *Forbes*. 1 June 2012. Available at: http://www.forbes.com/sites/ciocentral/2012/06/01/its-time-to-occupy-it/. Accessed 6 July 2012.

46 Segal D. Apple's retail army, long on loyalty but short on pay. *The New York Times*. 23 June 2012. Available at: http://www.nytimes.com/2012/06/24/business/apple-store-workers-loyal-but-short-on-pay.html?_r=1&ref=business&pagewanted=all. Accessed 6 July 2012.

47 Jopson B. Apple's success a stretch for US retailers. *Financial Times*. 10 August 2012. Available at: http://www.ft.com/intl/cms/s/0/bd72f41a-e1b5-11e1-92f5-00144feab49a.html#axzz23GQOLxlr. Accessed 11 August 2012.

48 Mancini J. It's time to occupy IT. *Forbes*. 1 June 2012. Available at: http://www.forbes.com/sites/ciocentral/2012/06/01/its-time-to-occupy-it/. Accessed 30 September 2012.

49 Klein P. Can say on pay increase social responsibility? *Forbes*. 3 July 2012. Available at: http://www.forbes.com/sites/csr/2012/07/03/can-say-on-pay-increase-social-responsibility/?goback=.gde_2955795_member_130388605. Accessed 7 July 2012.

50 Browning L. Ex-UBS banker pleads guilty in tax evasion. *The New York Times*. 20 June 2008. Available at: http://www.nytimes.com/2008/06/20/business/20tax.html?_r=2&scp=1&sq=Birkenfeld&st=nyt&oref=slogin. Accessed 7 July 2012.

51 Bureau of Labor Statistics. Job openings and labor turnover survey. News Release.. 19 June 2012. Available at: http://www.bls.gov/news.release/jolts.htm/. Accessed 7 July 2012.

52 Monk D. For execs leaving Procter & Gamble, job market remains rosy. *Business Courier*. 13 April 2012. Available at: http://www.bizjournals.com/cincinnati/print-edition/2012/04/13/for-execs-leaving-procter-gamble.html?page=all. Accessed 7 July 2012.

53 Microsoft's downfall: inside the executive e-mails and cannibalistic culture that felled a tech giant. *Vanity Fair*. 3 July 2012. Available at: http://www.vanityfair.com/online/daily/2012/07/microsoft-downfall-emails-steve-ballmer.print. Accessed 7 July 2012.

54 Garvis M. A brief history of how Microsoft (and others) changed the world... Part 1. 7 July 2011. Available at: http://garvis.ca/2011/07/07/a-brief-history-of-how-microsoft-and-others-changed-the-world-part-1/. Accessed 7 July 2012.

55 Allen FE. The terrible management technique that cost Microsoft its creativity. *Forbes*. 3 July 2012. Available at: http://www.forbes.com/sites/frederickallen/2012/07/03/the-terrible-management-technique-that-cost-microsoft-its-creativity/. Accessed 7 July 2012.

56 Carmody T. Why Tim Cook is the best choice to run Apple. *Wired*. 25 November 2011. Available at: http://www.wired.com/business/2011/08/why-tim-cook/. Accessed 7 July 2012.

57 Apple becomes most valuable company ever. *AP Wire Service*. 20 August 2012. Available at: http://www.cbsnews.com/8301-505123_162-57496461/apple-becomes-most-valuable-company-ever/. Accessed 30 September 2012.

58 Chittum R. Bloomberg: Moneychangers in the Temples. *Columbia Journalism Review*, 4 November 2009. Available at: http://www.cjr.org/the_audit/bloomberg_moneychangers_in_the.php. Accessed 7 October 2012.

59 A Brief History of Goldman Sachs, the most hated bank in the world. *Business Insider*. 8 March 2012. Available at: http://articles.businessinsider.com/2012-03-08/wall_street/31134859_1_squid-costumes-goldman-sachs-great-vampire-squid#ixzz20PiCnaRb. Accessed 12 July 2012.

Chapter 4 | Employees

60 "Wall Street's Gekko" film icons and culture. *The Popular History Digest*. Available at: http://www.pophistorydig.com/?tag=wall-street-movie-history. Accessed 12 July 2012.

61 Anderson R. Goldman Sachs' 150-year reputation on the line. *BBC News*. 27 April 2010. Available at: http://news.bbc.co.uk/2/hi/8646264.stm. Accessed 12 July 2012.

62 Tett G. 'BlackRock envy' replaces Goldman allure. *Financial Times*. 14 June 2012. Available at: http://www.ft.com/intl/cms/s/0/c1d6fc24-b63e-11e1-8ad0-00144feabdc0.html#axzz20Po3aOx1. Accessed 12 July 2012.

63 Thornton E. Wall Street's lone ranger. *Businessweek*. 3 March 2002. Available at: http://www.businessweek.com/stories/2002-03-03/wall-streets-lone-ranger. Accessed 14 July 2012.

64 Hank Paulson 1946— biography, *Encyclopedia of Business*, 2nd dd. Available at: http://www.referenceforbusiness.com/biography/M-R/Paulson-Hank-1946.html#ixzz20baZp4QJ. Accessed 14 July 2012.

65 Pimlott D. Havens aims to win hearts, minds and wallets. *Financial Times*. 13 October 2008. http://www.ft.com/intl/cms/s/0/e69f863a-994a-11dd-9d48-000077b07658.html#axzz20Po3aOx1. Accessed 12 July 2012.

66 Hughes J. Customising risk in Chicago. *Financial Times*. 28 October 2005. http://www.ft.com/intl/cms/s/0/2d6aa8d4-474f-11da-b8e5-00000e2511c8.html#axzz20Po3aOx1. 12 July 2012.

67 The Goldman Sachs Group Inc. *History International directory of company histories*, Vol. 51. St. James Press, 2003. Available at: http://www.fundinguniverse.com/company-histories/the-goldman-sachs-group-inc-history/. Accessed 12 July 2012

68 Goldman Sachs 2011 Annual Report, p. 2.

69 Goldman Sachs Business Principles. Corporate Website. Available at: http://www.goldmansachs.com/who-we-are/business-standards/business-principles/index.html. Accessed 30 September 2012.

70 Thomas H. More plaudits for Goldman. *Financial Times*. 18 December 2005. Available at: http://ftalphaville.ft.com/blog/2006/12/18/1469/more-plaudits-for-goldman/. Accessed 12 July 2012.

71 Hill A. The John Browne: dignified new way to separate. *Financial Times*. 11 May 2007. Available at: http://www.ft.com/intl/cms/s/0/eda58376-ff59-11db-aff2-000b5df10621.html#axzz20Po3aOx1. Accessed 12 July 2012.

72 Goldman Tops League table. *New York Times* Dealbook. 3 January 2011. Available at: http://dealbook.nytimes.com/2011/01/03/goldman-tops-league-table/. Accessed 12 July 2012.

73 Harding R. Federal Reserve ♥♥♥ Goldman Sachs. *Financial Times*. 28 September 2012. Available at: http://blogs.ft.com/money-supply/2012/09/28/federal-reserve-%E2%99%A5%E2%99%A5%E2%99%A5-goldman-sachs/#axzz27xj8fQRs. Accessed 30 September 2012.

74 De la Merced MJ. Facebook said to be planning for I.P.O. filing on Wednesday. *New York Times* Dealbook. 31 January 2012. Available at: http://dealbook.nytimes.com/2012/01/31/facebook-plans-to-file-5-billion-i-p-o-on-wednesday/. Accessed 12 July 2012.

75 Robinson G. Goldman Sachs: king of the dealmakers. *Financial Times*. 2 April 2012. Available at: http://ftalphaville.ft.com/blog/tag/goldman-sachs/page/30/. Accessed 12 July 2012.

Reputation, Stock Price, and You

76 Farrell G. Goldman Sachs' reputation tarnished. *Financial Times*. 2 August 2009. Available at: http://www.ft.com/intl/cms/s/0/ae3d459a-7f8e-11de-85dc-00144feabdc0. html#axzz20bj70q2d. Accessed 14 July 2012.

77 PR problems at Goldman Sachs don't keep away clients. *Los Angeles Times*. 6 April 2010. Available at: http://latimesblogs.latimes.com/money_co/2010/04/goldman-sachs-not-being-hit-where-it-hurts.html. Accessed 14 July 2012.

78 Santoli M. Built to win. *Barron's*, 29 September 2012. Available at: http://online.barrons. com/article/SB50001424053111904414004578018594042856164.html?mod=BOL_hpp_highlight_top. Accessed 30 September 2012.

79 Taibbi M. The great American bubble machine. *Rolling Stone*. 9 July 2009. Available at: http://www.rollingstone.com/politics/news/the-great-american-bubble-machine-20100405. Accessed 12 July 2012.

80 Stott P. Goldman Sachs: why reputation matters. 28 April 2010. Available at: http:// vaultcareers.wordpress.com/2010/04/28/goldman-sachs-why-reputation-matters/. Accessed 12 July 2012.

81 Cendrowski S. What's so great about working at Goldman? *CNN Money*. 27 January 2011. Available at: http://money.cnn.com/2011/01/27/news/companies/goldman_sachs_culture. fortune/index.htm. Accessed 12 July 2012.

82 Stern S. Why you should pay attention to your employer brand. *Financial Times*. 1 September 2009. Available at: http://www.ft.com/intl/cms/s/0/5a15b366-9691-11de-84d1-00144feabdc0.html#axzz20Po3aOx1. Accessed 12 July 2012.

83 Goldman Sachs Annual Report 2010, p. 30.

84 Silver-Greenberg J. JPMorgan says trading loss tops $5.8 billion; profit for quarter falls 9%. *The New York Times*. 13 July 2012. Available at: http://dealbook.nytimes.com/2012/07/13/ jpmorgan-reports-second-quarter-profit-of-5-billion-down-9/. Accessed 31 July 2012.

85 Yahoo Finance's summary of Capital IQ and Thomson Reuters Forward P/E data. Available at: http://finance.yahoo.com/q/ks?s=. Accessed 14 July 2012.

86 Hill A. Corporate culture: lofty aspirations. *Financial Times*. 15 July 2012. Available at: http://www.ft.com/intl/cms/s/0/d1b4b71a-ccde-11e1-9960-00144feabdc0. html#axzz20bj70q2d. Accessed 15 July 2012.

CHAPTER

5

Suppliers

*The complexity of supply chains puts your reputation in the hands of the
lowest common denominator.*

—John Hurrell[1]

Just as a steel chain is only as strong as its weakest link, so it is with a supply
chain. A chain with uniformly strong links reduces risk and provides important
benefits to the whole enterprise; but a broken link jeopardizes all.

The strongest chain is one in which each supplier considers his or her
downstream buyer to be his or her preferred customer. As a 2005 survey
made explicit: 75% of the respondent suppliers regularly put their preferred
customers at the top of allocation lists for materials or services in short
supply; 82% said that these customers consistently get first access to new
product or service ideas and technologies; and 87% of the suppliers offer cost
reduction opportunities to their most-preferred customers first.[2] A supplier
to Volvo explained:

> ...*preferred customers are receiving better prices than their other customers.
> They also place their best employees and mechanics with their preferred
> customers primarily, and respond quicker to the needs of their preferred
> customers.*[3]

Such benefits translate to financial gains that vary in size depending on the
dynamics of the buyer/supplier relationship. All things being equal, the benefits
of becoming a "customer of choice" have the potential to deliver value
equivalent to an additional 2%–4% of savings off of the company's total spend
base, according to the Procurement Strategy Council.[4]

Chapter 5 | Suppliers

This chapter explores the role of reputation in establishing "preferred customer" status. It looks at how expectations that suppliers hold about a company help shape that company's reputation; how a company's actions in managing ethics, innovation, quality, safety, sustainability, and security shape suppliers' expectations; what behaviors and benefits result; and how strategies for leveraging reputation to build "customer-of-choice" positions create enterprise-wide benefits that turn into shareholder value.

At one time, companies such as Ford operated under one roof, sourcing raw materials and producing finished goods through an assembly line. Then as assemblies begat subassemblies and supply companies, major manufacturers such as Toyota set them up just outside their gates in what became Toyota City. As logistics and coordination improved, the path from raw material to finished good evolved and extended into a global "supply chain"—the collection and distribution of all the inputs to the production process.[5] Boeing's 777 jet, for example, is assembled from 3 million parts sourced from more than 500 suppliers around the world.[6]

Supply chains have transformed business, reducing labor costs and eliminating warehousing, and they have elevated logistics management to a fine art and information technology to a vital global utility. As supply chains became an increasing source of both value and risk to the penultimate buyer, they also radically transformed the business-to-business relationships between buyers and *their* suppliers. As a source of competitive advantage, maintaining oversight and control of the supply chain to ensure quality at every step has become an overarching concern.

In general, two variables exist in types of relationships between a buyer and a seller in the supply chain: (1) importance of the supply to the buyer's aggregate revenue and (2) scarcity of the supply.[78]

When supplies are important to the business model, but generally easy to obtain, a buyer can push down costs and pit one supplier against another. But when supply is scarce and sources are limited to few suppliers, the buyer will generally prefer a close relationship with a select number of suppliers. For companies that emphasize quality, such as McDonald's, Coca-Cola, Toyota, and Peets, the supply chain relationship tends to follow the closer/fewer model.

When supplies are not especially important points of differentiation in the business, the purchasing strategy may follow one of two paths. When the products are not readily available, a buyer may try to create alternative sources, but when there *are* alternative sources, the buyer's strategy is to reduce administrative (transactional) costs. Known well to students of Coase's theorem, these transactional costs can radically alter the total cost of product acquisition and supply chain operations.

One company's transactional cost, however, may be another company's profit margin. On the other hand, squeezing a supplier too hard can transform a relatively low-value item into a source of extraordinarily high risk.

Reputation Risks in the Supply Chain

The supply chain is a system that creates a complex matrix of "inter-connectedness." And a weak link can create havoc.

Lead paint on children's toys, melamine in a variety of food and consumer products, and tainted pharmaceuticals are examples of remote suppliers creating headline risks for iconic firms. The physical movement of goods from sellers to buyers, the financial information linked to the transactions that relate to the goods purchased, and the business chain process are so rapid and multifarious that today's business processing systems cannot properly integrate the information.

The systems in use, which in the case of many multinationals comprise several generations of computer hardware and software, were not designed to support the current level of global sourcing and distribution. In many ways, this is similar to the failure of systems in the banking sector to identify risk in certain modern complex financial instruments.

With computer system variances and multiple unrelated businesses supporting the global supply chain, inefficiencies are inherent to the system and risks are rampant. The inability of disparate computer systems to extract, transform, and associate data leaves management without full operational control and exposes almost all businesses to an unacceptable range of quality and ethical product perils, credit risks, compliance failures, theft, fraud, and reputational risk.

A report by Mactavish, a consultancy, concluded: "The network of corporate risks is far more systemic than was the case even 5–10 years ago as companies operate in an ever more complicated and interconnected value chain."[1] Among other risks, the Mactavish report identified systemic supply chain disruption caused by company failures and a plethora of efficiency measures throughout the trading system that are reducing resilience and increasing product quality risks.

Iconic firms such as Toyota are invariably the ultimate and most visible bearers of supply chain risk. Regardless of where that risk originated in the chain, it is Toyota's reputation that takes the hit.

Chapter 5 | Suppliers

Mitigating the operational risks in the supply chain and reducing the risk that an operational event will mature into a reputational event is a two-step process. The first consists of basic mainstream managerial strategies—establishing systems that improve visibility and foster control. A 21st-century supply chain, however, requires visibility and control on a scale and scope not yet successfully tackled by any one company. Four challenges stand in the path of success:

Operational Inflexibility. Internal information systems in most companies are optimized for inventory management, transactional processing, and balance sheet–oriented financial reporting. These systems often are composed of entrenched legacy systems that do not easily associate new types of information vital to efficient control of supply chain operations.

Security. Concerns over IT system security make it difficult for most companies to acquire supply chain information that is external to their information systems.

External/Internal Linkage. Associating external data with internal data to provide a coherent view of operations, operational risks, and reputational risks is exceedingly difficult.

Siloed Structures. Enterprise software solutions have broken down the IT barriers separating most operational departments. However, most corporate departments overseeing enterprise-wide issues such as safety, security, ethics, and risk still operate in technology silos.

The challenges in no way reduce the substantial potential benefits, which include overall cost reduction, cost avoidance, revenue enhancement, improved stakeholder service, improved risk management, regulatory risk mitigation, market differentiation, and, ultimately, increased enterprise value (Table 5-1). These potential benefits continue to spur innovative solution frameworks. The Global Trademaster Company, a company in which this book's author has an economic interest, is one of many emerging solutions.

Table 5-1. Operational and Reputation Benefits Arising from Improved Supply Chain Visibility and Control.

Category of Benefit	Type of Benefit
Cost Reduction	Reduced repetitive data entry
	Decreased inventory
	Increased opportunity for sourcing
	Lower insurance rates based on risk distribution resulting from aggregation and analysis of anonymized supply chain data

Category of Benefit	Type of Benefit
	Improved supply chain performance at operating level
Cost Avoidance	Improved planning due to a more stable planning environment
	Improved supply and distribution channel performance
	Potential Green Lane (accelerated border crossing) based on proven transparency and reliability of reporting from the participant's supply and financial chain transactions
Revenue Enhancement	Enhanced transparency of end-to-end supply chain enabling more effective marketing based on predictability of delivery
	Improved market intelligence
	Better system status and performance using third-party metrics
	Improved turnover of inventory
Improved Service	Improved velocity resulting from analysis to resolve choke points and closer integration with manufacturers and carriers
	Greater control for supply chain managers
	Better visibility into the supply chain for operators and customers
	Neutral provision of data on the supply chain
Risk Management	Legal Compliance
	Improved resilience resulting from visibility and ability to re-route shipments to alternative ports not affected by terrorists or natural disasters
	Better security through increasingly better known suppliers
Regulatory Mitigation	Influence over forthcoming regulatory activities and better insight into regulatory objectives and plans
	Enhanced reputation with Customs and Border Protection & Department of Homeland Security
Market Differentiation	Market signaling of a superior (more secure) offering
Enterprise Value Appreciation	Enhanced reputation value arising from operational improvements in processes that ensure safety, security, and quality and potentially capture conformance data on ethics and sustainability

Chapter 5 | Suppliers

The second step in reducing supply chain risks, which reduces the risk that an operational event will mature into a reputational event, is one of engaging supply chain partners. Cases involving McDonald's, Yum! Brands, Coca-Cola, Pepsi, Toyota Motors, and Peet's Coffee illustrate a range of potential strategies.

Quality: McDonald's and YUM!

[Quality is] the extent to which a product is free from defects or deficiencies; a service meets or exceeds the expectations of customers or clients, and both products and services conform to measurable and verifiable criteria. (Table 1-1)

Quality products and services are key success factors for the two largest fast-food franchises: McDonalds Corporation and Yum! Brands. Their reputations for quality are due in no small part to the support they receive from their suppliers. The consequences of their differing supply chain engagement strategies are the centerpiece of this section.

McDonald's Corporation

McDonald's Corporation began humbly in 1955 with three restaurants, several milk-shake mixers, the two McDonald brothers, and a visionary appliance salesman named Ray Kroc. Six years into the venture, brothers Dick and Mac exited with $2.7 million. In 1963, Kroc's growing enterprise had sold a billion burgers, realized net income in excess of $1 million, and was quickly becoming an American icon, Two years later, the company went public. [9]

Today, operating in 119 countries around the world, McDonald's Corporation is the global icon of fast-food franchises and restaurants. McDonald's branded restaurants serve a menu at various price points. As of December 31, 2011, McDonald's had 33,510 restaurants: 27,075 franchised or licensed and 6,435 operated by the company. [10]

McDonald's and its franchisees purchase food, packaging, equipment, and other goods from numerous independent suppliers. From its beginning, the company understood the crucial importance of fresh ingredients and nearly on-time delivery and has focused strongly on the supply chain on which those depend.

By exercising close oversight and operational control of its supply chain, the company has established and strictly enforces product specifications with high quality standards. A quality-leadership board, composed of the company's technical, safety, and supply chain specialists, provides strategic global

Reputation, Stock Price, and You

leadership for all aspects of food quality and safety. The company conducts ongoing product reviews and on-site supplier visits working out of quality centers around the world. In addition, the company works closely with suppliers to encourage innovation, ensure best practices, and drive continuous improvement. By leveraging scale, supply chain infrastructure, and risk management strategies, the company also collaborates with suppliers toward a goal of achieving competitive and predictable food and paper costs over the long term.

Independently owned and operated distribution centers, approved by the company, distribute products and supplies to most McDonald's restaurants. Restaurant personnel are trained in the proper storage, handling, and preparation of products and in the delivery of customer service.

McDonald's oversight extends to the corporate arena. When RHM, the U.K. food group, was divesting itself of its Golden West subsidiary, a provider of burger buns, tomato ketchup, and soft drink syrups, the two firms bidding to acquire RHM first had to be approved by McDonald's.[11]

McDonald's restaurants once offered a menu that was substantially uniform the world over in order to meet customers' *expectations* of a substantially uniform experience—a quality experience—anywhere in the world. Today, McDonald's delivers the same standard quality experience to an international smorgasbord of menus designed to cater to different national tastes. McDonald's calls this value proposition "remaining a trusted brand."[12] It is called here "protecting McDonald's reputation for quality."

Consistency does not mean McDonald's is not open to change. The company works hard to identify, implement, and scale innovative ideas that meet customers' changing needs and preferences. Suppliers play a central role in innovation. It was a McDonald's supplier, after all, that perfected the frozen French fry and the famous secret sauce for the Big Mac. And it was suppliers who saved the day by figuring out how to get chicken into Asia when the other restaurants ran out during the avian flu crisis.[13] McDonald's also engages suppliers in research activities that benefit the company, its franchises, and suppliers.

In recent years, McDonald's has recognized that sustainability has become an important ingredient in its reputation recipe. It works closely with suppliers to more quickly conform to much anticipated climate change–associated regulations and other government-led initiatives.

The company's approach to its relationship with suppliers reflects its ethical culture and the innovations Kroc brought to the business. From the Harvard Business School case study on McDonald's supply chain:

Chapter 5 | Suppliers

> *Unlike most contemporary fast-food franchisers who profited significantly by marking up the goods they required their franchisees to buy, Kroc aligned McDonald's interests with its franchisees' by profiting from excellent restaurant operations. He refused all gifts and special favors offered by suppliers; instead, he focused exclusively on securing the consistent supply, excellent quality, and volume pricing that would facilitate success in the restaurants.*
>
> *Kroc and his staff made other supply chain innovations. Unlike other food retailers at the time, McDonald's established strict standards for the ingredients and appearance of each product; McDonald's staff often visited suppliers without warning to ensure their compliance. Kroc terminated those suppliers that could not consistently provide high quality and dedicated service but he rewarded those that did with loyalty and volume. In effect, he made his suppliers partners in his quest for fast-food greatness.[14]*

Kroc's goal continues into the present: "being a company the public can trust"[15] is borne out, for most of its stakeholders, by fulfilled expectations for quality products as well as ethical behavior and other operational drivers of reputation.

Trust and commitment are the foundation of supply chain management.[16] Both parties are involved; they understand that the relationship and behaviors of each will work to mutual benefit. Trust is conveyed through faith, reliance, belief, or confidence in the supply partner and includes a willingness to forgo opportunistic behavior. Trust is an expectation that one's supply chain partner will act in a consistent manner, will do what he or she says he or she will do, and will maintain the reputation of both partners.

The highest corporate levels of McDonald's are charged with trust assurance. The company brings corporate board–level oversight and operational control to its reputation through the Corporate Responsibility Committee, which advises on all policies and strategies that affect product safety, workplace safety, employee opportunities and training, diversity, and environment and sustainable supply chain initiatives. One step below the corporate board of directors, five corporate-level operational committees monitor and manage reputationally relevant issues on a day-to-day basis.[16] These committees have helped McDonald's implement authentic changes to its supply chain operations, wherever they are regarded "as beneficial for the McDonald's brand" even when they involve additional costs.[17]

Since 2007, consumers and suppliers have been expecting more authentic transparency and accountability from businesses.[18] According to Ben Boyd, Executive Vice President of Edelman, the public relations firm, the most important corporate reputation factors in the 2011 annual survey were:

- Maintains "transparent and honest practices."

- "Offers high-quality products or services."

- "Is a company I can trust."[19]

Collaboration with supply chain partners minimizes risk and maximizes transparency. Rick Blasgen, chief executive of the Illinois-based Council of Supply Chain Management Professionals, says, "You have to trust your partners with information that in the past you might have considered proprietary."[19]

The comfort afforded by reputation holds in check one's fear of self-serving behavior on the part of the others in the supply chain.[20] Commitment is the mutual belief that the trading partners are willing to devote energy to sustaining this relationship[21] and will not act in ways that might adversely affect overall supply chain performance. Trading partners throughout the chain become integrated into their major customers' processes and more tied to their overarching goals.[22] The bottom line is: trust, transparency, and collaboration are essential for the most value to be realized from a supply chain.

A classic fable is illustrative. A pig and a chicken are walking down the road. Chicken says, "Hey Pig, I was thinking we should open a restaurant!" Pig replies, "Hm, maybe, what would we call it?" Chicken responds, "How about 'Ham-n-Eggs'?" Pig thinks for a moment and says, "No thanks. I'd be committed, but you'd only be involved!"[23]

Yum! Brands, Inc.

Yum! Brands may not be instantly recognized by most people as a quick-service restaurant company even though it has approximately 37,000 outlets in more than 120 countries and territories. But the brands it operates sure are: KFC, Pizza Hut, and Taco Bell. It was already a big company in 1977 when it was named Tricon Global Restaurants, Inc., and spun off from PepsiCo.

Under the trademarked aegis of Colonel Sanders, Yum! Brands has been cooking big time ever since. China typifies "the Kentucky Fried Chickenification of the middle classes in the world's emerging economies."[24] A key to their success, explained R. J. Hottovy, an analyst at Morningstar, "is that they built up their supply chain and their distribution system quickly, and that is giving them a real competitive advantage."[25] Yum!'s China operations, for example, increased from 2% of operating profits in 1998 to 33% in 2009.[25]

From the outset, Yum! Brands has operated under a worldwide code of conduct that set behavioral standards for many of the reputationally relevant processes of corporate life. A set of polices governs a spectrum of reputationally related processes and stakeholder relationships.

Chapter 5 | Suppliers

In Yum!'s operations, programs that foster sustainable practices are given major emphasis. Yum! regularly collaborates with its brand leadership teams, franchisees, Unified Foodservice Purchasing Co-op, suppliers, and consultants to help better manage environmental programs and responsibilities. In addition, several markets across the globe are including environmental sustainability as part of Yums! proprietary Supplier Tracking and Recognition (STAR) audit system, recognizing suppliers who have made improvements in this area.

Many premium suppliers of Kids Meal branded products practice environmental principles throughout their organizations and with their factory partners. Such initiatives include the use of environmentally friendly materials whenever possible, including water-based paints, soy-based inks, use of recycled paper for packaging and paper premiums, and the use of nonphthalate plasticizers and lead-free material. Also, key supplier factory partners have implemented initiatives to reduce energy, pollution, and waste.

McDonald's vs. Yum!

There are major strategic differences in how these casual-dining giants approach their businesses. On capital structure, Yum! is more heavily leveraged than McDonald's. On marketing, the company is the brand at McDonald's, whereas at Yum! the corporate enterprise is secondary to the company's several brands.

Yum! benefits from the lower cost structure associated with its China focus. McDonald's appears to be controlling its global supply chain costs better through better overall supplier engagement. McDonald's supply chain is a well-oiled machine that turns over inventory 150 times per year and outpaces Apple Inc., the second most active supply chain, by a factor of 3 (Figure 5-1). In 2011, its second year in the Gartner annual Supply Chain Top 25, McDonald's ranked 8th in a survey of best supply chain operators.[25]

The Gartner survey "identifies the companies that best demonstrate leadership in applying demand-driven principles to drive business results."[26] Apple ranked no. 1, an achievement led by Tim Cook, soon thereafter appointed Apple CEO. The centrality of that operation to overall corporate value has led some to opine that Cook's appointment "may have been one of (Steve) Jobs' most astute moves."[27]

In the 2012 survey, Apple retained its no. 1 spot. McDonald's climbed to no. 3 just behind Amazon. Yum! Brands didn't make it to the top 50.

McDonald's has other badges of distinction valued by its suppliers. McDonald's ranked 49th on *Corporate Responsibility Magazine*'s 2010 Best Corporate

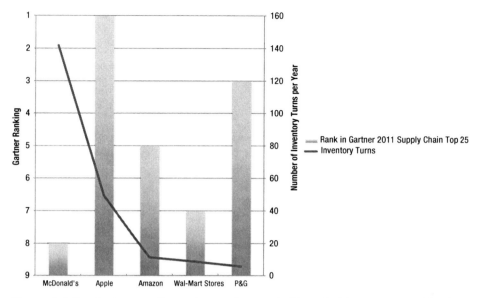

Figure 5-1. Supply chain excellence. Among the most highly ranked firms recognized for their supply chain excellence by Gartner in 2011, McDonald's ranked 8th but had a transactional volume of more than 140 turns per year—outdistancing its closest competitor, Apple Inc., which ranked no. 1.[25,26]

Citizen 100 league table compared to Yum!'s 62nd, and McDonald's trounced Yum! in the 2010 Newsweek Green Rankings 79th to 337th.[28,29] For other customers who value evidence of sustainability practices, McDonald's reputation and credibility lend substantial weight to professional recommendations.[30] They gain some of McDonald's reflected glory.

The value of a multi-stakeholder strategy and better supplier relationships to McDonald's is lower overall supply chain operating costs—and that makes a difference in the bottom line and its stock price. In the contest to win the hearts and minds of analysts and investors, all things being equal, McDonald's consistently appears to pay less in food and paper goods per dollar of labor costs than Yum! (Figure 5-2). In 2009, the cost advantage was about 6%. In 2011, McDonald's cost advantage climbed to more than 10%.

As for the bottom line, in mid-July 2012, McDonald's trailing 12-month profit margin of 20.26% was about 10% higher than Yum!'s 11.69%. This cost advantage helps explain why equity investors priced McDonald's 48% higher than Yum! for every trailing month dollar of sales.

Chapter 5 | Suppliers

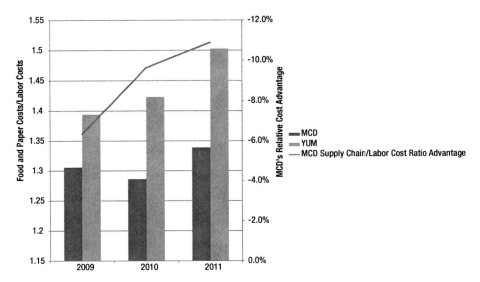

Figure 5-2. Cost of food and paper relative to cost of labor at McDonald's (MCD) and Yum! Brands (YUM) operations. McDonald's pays 10% less for food and paper goods per dollar in wages than its closest fast foods competitor, Yum! Brands.[31]

Retrospective

The secret sauce of McDonald's success is found in the long-term transparent relationships the company has forged with its suppliers. Numbers never tell the whole story, but they provide interesting color. Some of McDonald's deep collaborative relationships with its suppliers have lasted more than 25 years. McDonald's obsession with quality—a reliable, repeatable, trustworthy, and engaging casual dining experience—is transparent, and it is a value that extends to its dealings with its suppliers. Suppliers have long recognized McDonald's obsession with quality as an authentic manifestation of its corporate culture and the underpinning of its reputation. Its suppliers appreciate and value its efforts to deliver consistently that which matters most to its stakeholders. They bestow the coveted status of preferred customer on McDonald's, whose bottom line benefits.

Consider This

- Quality, the consistent delivery of products and services that meet expectations, is a foundation for trust and an authentic reputation.

Reputation, Stock Price, and You | 105

- In supply chains, trust and an authentic reputation help establish long-term relationships, reduce transaction costs, and secure customer-of-choice status.

- Customers-of-choice receive myriad benefits that speak to the bottom line.

Safety: Coke and Pepsi

[Safety is] the state of being certain that a set of conditions will not accidentally cause adverse effects on the well being of employees, the public, or the environment. (Table 1-1)

With combined market capitalizations in excess of $US quarter trillion (Table 5-2), the two beverage companies sell many millions of cans of soda each day. The risks of food safety scares are well appreciated and feared by the two giants in the soft drink producers and bottlers industry: PepsiCo Inc. (NYSE:PEP) and The Coca-Cola Company (NYSE:KO).

Table 5-2. Several key metrics of comparison between PepsiCo Inc. and The Coca-Cola Company

	PepsiCo Inc.	The Coca-Cola Company
Main Exchange	NYSE	NYSE
Market Capitalization March 2012 ($US billion)	98.2	157.5
Profit Margin (ttm)	9.69%	18.42%
Operating Margin (ttm)	15.60%	23.41%
Equity Short % of Float	0.5%	0.6%
Employees	297,000	146,200

Data source: Yahoo Finance and Google Finance.

A study in March 2012 by the Center for Science in the Public Interest showed that high levels of the chemical 4-methylimidazole, part of caramel coloring, were found in both Pepsi and Coke products. Pepsi products, regular Coca-Cola, and Diet Coke had levels high enough to require a warning notice in the state of California. "Coke and Pepsi, with the acquiescence of the FDA, are needlessly exposing millions of Americans to a chemical that causes cancer," said CSPI executive director Michael F. Jacobson. "The coloring is completely

Chapter 5 | Suppliers

cosmetic, adding nothing to the flavor of the product. If companies can make brown food coloring that is carcinogen-free, the industry should use that."[32] Commenting on the allegation, Douglas Karas, FDA spokesman, said that "FDA has no reason to believe there is any immediate risk from the substance. A consumer would have to drink more than a thousand cans of soda in a day to match the doses administered in studies that showed links to cancer in rodents."[33]

Then a new safety sheriff rode into town. The American Cancer Society wrote four months later to U.S. Health Secretary Kathleen Sebelius and drew parallels between the hidden dangers of the world's favorite beverages and the formerly hidden dangers of the world's second-favorite vice product—tobacco. The Society called for a comprehensive safety review along the lines of the U.S. top doctor's landmark report on the dangers of smoking in 1964.[34]

Defining Experience

In June 1999, more than 100 Belgian children were hit by sudden illness, with symptoms of nausea and headaches, after drinking Coca-Cola products. Almost immediately, the Belgian Health Ministry banned the sale of all Coca-Cola beverages and ordered the withdrawal of a range of suspect soft drinks produced by the company in Belgium, France, and Holland, where exports from the Belgian plants are widely sold.

The Coca-Cola Company did not appreciate the magnitude of the storm looming over the safety of its products. The company first declared, "After thorough investigation, no health or safety issues were found" and attributed the problems to others. They blamed a "defective" supply of the carbon dioxide gas used at its Antwerp plant and also claimed that a wood treatment agent used on transportation pallets had caused an "offensive odor on the outside bottom of the can."[35] The manufacturers of the gas, Swede Aga Gas, denied Coca-Cola's claims of "bad" CO_2, saying that the gas was perfectly normal, and that it could provide it with samples of the batch delivered to Belgium.

The company's assertion that it had pinpointed the problem, noting that there was no serious health risk, lacked credibility. Germany refused Coca-Cola imports from Belgium, Saudi Arabia erected barriers, and The Netherlands and Spain raised alerts. Aggravating Coca-Cola's situation, the problems fed into Europe-wide food sensitivity.

Coca-Cola's slow response to a contaminated product lot is an object lesson in the cost of failure to localize a food-safety incident and deal with the consequences of a perceived systemic problem. Recall costs to the company were estimated at $200 million. Costs to the distributor, Coca-Cola Enterprises, were estimated at $130 million. But the real cost—reputational value losses—expressed as the losses to the value of the global brand, at that time estimated at $83.8 billion, was $11 billion.

It is generally understood by today's business leaders that the average cost of an adverse reputational event is about 7% of market capitalization.[36] Coca-Cola's 1999 experience arising from the failure of a quality process was even more expensive at 11%. Coca-Cola learned valuable lessons, and these are apparent in the firm's current risk disclosures.

The Coca-Cola Company

The Coca-Cola Company defines itself narrowly as a beverage company. It originated in 1886 when Atlanta-area pharmacist John Pemberton was experimenting with powerful stimulants, including cola nuts and coca leaves, to add to soda water. The inspiration for his work and that of fellow pharmacists was said to have come from observations of Bolivian Indian workers who chewed coca leaves to ward off fatigue and by West African workers who chewed cola nuts as a stimulant. Pemberton's formula and brand were bought in 1889 for $2300 by Asa Candler, who incorporated The Coca-Cola Company in 1892.

Pemberton's work and Candler's marketing were, by any measure, inspirational, and today the company owns or licenses and markets more than 500 nonalcoholic beverage brands, primarily sparkling beverages but also a variety of still beverages, such as waters, enhanced waters, juice drinks, ready-to-drink teas and coffees, and energy and sports drinks. It owns and markets four of the world's top five nonalcoholic sparkling beverage brands: Coca-Cola, Diet Coke, Fanta, and Sprite.

From a sales and distribution perspective, The Coca-Cola Company is unique in not being directly exposed to retail behemoths. In general, the company and/or subsidiaries only produce syrup concentrate, which is then sold to various bottlers throughout the world who hold a Coca-Cola franchise. Coca-Cola bottlers, who hold territorially exclusive contracts with the company, produce the finished product in cans and bottles from the concentrate in combination with filtered water and sweeteners. The bottlers then sell, distribute, and merchandise the resulting Coca-Cola product to retail stores, vending machines, restaurants, and food service distributors. It is the world's largest beverage distribution system.

As a franchise leader, the financial health and success of its bottling partners are critical to the company's success. The Coca-Cola Company works with its

Chapter 5 | Suppliers

bottling partners to identify system requirements that enable the team to quickly achieve scale and efficiencies, and the company shares best practices with all its bottling partners. The company also designs business models for sparkling and still beverages in specific markets to ensure that it shares the value created by these beverages with its bottling partners.

One notable exception is in the United States, where the company acquired the domestic bottling operation and is responsible for the manufacture and sale of fountain syrups directly to authorized fountain wholesalers and some fountain retailers.

Among Coca-Cola's intangible assets underpinning its reputation is product safety. This has become a driving focus that allows the company to charge a price premium for its sugar water, a focus attributable to the heightened sensitivity sparked by the 1999 Belgian incident. The company now acknowledges, "Our success depends on our ability to maintain consumer confidence in the safety and quality of our products."

The company is also sensitive to global ethics issues with a number of transparent commitments to respect all human rights. These are apparent in its Human Rights Statement and Workplace Rights Policy and Supplier Guiding Principles, its participation in the United Nations Global Compact and its LEAD program, and its participation in the Global Business Initiative on Human Rights.

There is no doubt that reputation risk is top-of-mind. The company is one of the 355 S&P 500 Composite Index constituent members to overtly disclose over the past year the materiality of reputation risk to its operations: "If product safety or quality issues, or negative publicity, even if unwarranted, damage our brand image and corporate reputation, our business may suffer."[37]

Reputation risk disclosures from their most recent annual report highlight the importance of maintaining customer confidence in the safety and quality of its products, and effectively managing its supply chain.

Last, in a disclosure involving operations other than the production of consumable products, the company noted the growing risks of cyber-security breaches. "If we are unable to protect our information systems against service interruption, misappropriation of data or breaches of security, our operations could be disrupted and our reputation may be damaged."[37]

PepsiCo Inc.

In a very competitive business, PepsiCo is one of Coca-Cola's primary competitors in many countries including the United States. Formed in 1965 through the merger of beverage and snack businesses, its origins trace back to the late 1890s when Caleb Bradham, a New Bern, North Carolina, pharmacist, formulated a cocktail to sooth upset stomachs (excess pepsin) without making any overt medical claims. He named the business Pepsi Cola and incorporated in Delaware in 1919.

PepsiCo, Inc. is a global food and snack as well as beverage company. The snack business traces its roots through Frito-Lay, Inc., which was formed by the 1961 merger of two companies first formed in 1932: the Frito Company, founded by Elmer Doolin, and the H. W. Lay Company, founded by Herman W. Lay.

Today, PepsiCo is a leading global food and beverage company with hundreds of brands that are household names throughout the world. Either independently or through contract manufacturers or authorized bottlers, PepsiCo makes, markets, sells, and distributes a variety of foods and beverages in more than 200 countries and territories. Globally recognized brands include Quaker Oats, Tropicana, Gatorade, Lay's, Pepsi, Walkers, Gamesa, and Sabritas.

In addition to Coca-Cola, other significant Pepsi competitors include, but are not limited to, Nestlé, Dr. Pepper Snapple Group, Inc., Groupe Danone, Kraft Foods Inc., and Unilever. In certain markets, competition includes beer companies. The company also competes against numerous regional and local companies and, in some markets, against retailers that have developed their own store or private label beverage brands.

While competing on two fronts with both beverages and foods might appear to be inefficient, as analysts have suggested, Pepsi reaffirmed as recently as February 2012 its commitment to remaining an integrated food and beverage company. Indra Nooyi, the PepsiCo CEO, declared the group "financially and operationally benefits" from its "Power of One" strategy, which was devised last year to bring its food and drink operations in the United States closer together. She told analysts that the idea of splitting the company in two has been "taken off the table."[38]

For Pepsi, two operational issues stand out. From a sales and distribution perspective, PepsiCo is heavily exposed to Walton family stores. In 2011, sales to Wal-Mart Stores, Inc. (Wal-Mart), including Sam's Club (Sam's), represented approximately 11% of PepsiCo's total net revenue. Its top five retail customers represented approximately 30% of its 2011 North American net revenue, with Wal-Mart (including Sam's) representing approximately 18%. These percentages include concentrate sales to independent bottlers that were used in finished goods sold by them to these retailers.

Its largest competitor is The Coca-Cola Company, but its beverage, snack, and food brands compete against global, regional, local, and private label

Chapter 5 | Suppliers

manufacturers and other discount-price competitors. Pepsi charges a price premium for its sugar water—a capability enabled by the value-add of the company's intangibles. Of the six major intangible assets comprising business processes underpinning reputation, Pepsi emphasizes sustainability (Table 5-2). In 2011, PepsiCo earned a place on the prestigious Dow Jones Sustainability World Index for the fifth consecutive year, the North America Index for the sixth consecutive year, and in the Food and Beverage Supersector was ranked number one.

Reputation risk is top-of-mind for Pepsi. "Any damage to our reputation could have a material adverse effect on our business, financial condition and results of operations."[39]

The disclosure details how failures in ethical controls, quality, safety, innovation, security, and sustainability could each damage PepsiCo's reputation.

Most of the disclosures focus on business processes that would be of concern to consumers of the company's products and they conclude with the acknowledgment that damage to PepsiCo's reputation or loss of consumer confidence in products for any reason could result in decreased demand for products and could have a material adverse effect on the business, financial condition, and results of operations, as well as require additional resources to rebuild the company's reputation.

Implications for Reputation Management

The Pepsi-Coke rivalry is legendary. Although some suggest the feud really heated up with the Pepsi Challenge in 1975, the brands have been fighting each other for more than a century. For many, this battle for the hearts, minds, and palates of the global consumer has been all about brand.

Today, it is about more. A brand is a promise that creates expectations. Those expectations create an impression among stakeholders we encapsulate in the term *reputation*.

Unlike the marketing-driven communications of the brand wars, reputation-shaping communications travel through a range of nontraditional channels. In our social media–dominated environment, informal, incidental, and nontraditional channels of communication are more likely to be used to report to stakeholders on a firm's ethics, quality, innovation, safety, security, and sustainability practices. As outlined in Table 5-1 and as implied in the list of reputation risks disclosed by each of the firms, many operational decisions produce outcomes that communicate something about the firm to its stakeholders.

In 2010, both Pepsi and Coca-Cola took full ownership of their North American supply chain partners, explaining that they needed more flexibility and direct control of production, distribution, and new product innovation cycles. PepsiCo was first to do so, acquiring both Pepsi Bottling Group Inc. and PepsiAmericas Inc. for $7.8 billion. Coca-Cola followed later with its acquisition of the North American operations of Coca-Cola Enterprises for $15 billion.

Creating Reputation Value

It cannot be overstated that many improvements in the process underpinning reputation create visible improvements on the profit and loss (P&L) statement that translate to additional enterprise value. Hence today's cola wars, whose battles for the hearts and minds of stakeholders are being waged by the operational teams that manage the supply chain; ensure ethical conformance; drive innovation; ensure quality; and drive safety, security, and sustainability. They are also being waged at the level of the board of directors through superior oversight, risk management, and the perpetuation of a corporate culture that is obsessed with delighting the firm's stakeholders.

Retrospective

McDonald's understood the value of a committed and integrated supply chain from the outset. The Coca-Cola Company learned the lesson through trial by fire. But once learned, as with the food icons, the economic effects of the different relationships the beverage companies have with their supply chains appear on the P&L statement. Mirroring the benefits realized from closer operational integration and trust, Coke's costs for producing and distributing products at The Coca-Cola Company are lower than Pepsi's (Figure 5-3).

Chapter 5 | Suppliers

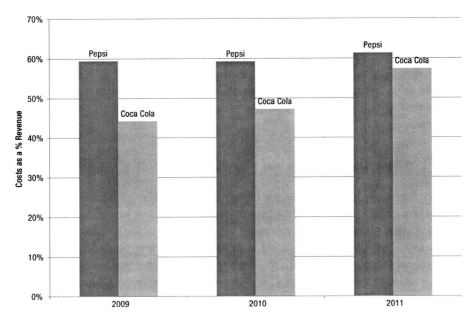

Figure 5-3. Combined costs for production and distribution represented as a fraction of revenues. Notwithstanding PepsiCo's Power of One strategy, The Coca-Cola Company consistently spends less on making and distributing its products than it arch rival.[40]

Consider This

- Management of complex supply chains is a source of competitive advantage.
- Authentic integration and commitment to supply chain oversight and management, sources of real value, are benefits of a reputation for ethical collaboration.
- Once burned, never again.

Toyota Motor Corporation

Echoing observations in the food and beverage industries, a recent study of the automobile supply chain showed that supplier trust in the buyer creates value. In a sample of 344 supplier–automaker exchange relationships in the United States, Japan, and Korea, perceived trustworthiness substantially reduced transaction costs. The most trusted automakers spent significantly less in face-to-face supplier interaction time on contracting and haggling when compared to the least trusted automaker. This translated into procurement (transaction) costs that were five times lower for the most trusted automaker.[41]

In January 2010, Toyota learned how those costs multiply when that trust is broken.

In the automotive industry, Toyota Motor Corporation is an iconic firm. Commencing operations in 1933 as the automobile division of Toyota Industries Corporation (formerly, Toyoda Automatic Loom Works, Ltd.), Toyota became a separate company on August 28, 1937. In 1982, the Toyota Motor Company and Toyota Motor Sales merged into one company, the Toyota Motor Corporation of today.

Toyota's automotive operations include the design, manufacture, assembly, and sale of passenger cars, minivans, and commercial vehicles, such as trucks, as well as related parts and accessories. Toyota also provides financing services to dealers and their customers for the purchase or lease of Toyota vehicles, and provides retail leasing through the purchase of lease contracts originated by Toyota dealers.

As of March 31, 2009, Toyota operated through 529 consolidated subsidiaries and 229 affiliated companies through 53 overseas manufacturing companies in 27 countries and regions. The company also has an extensive supply chain through which raw materials are transformed into parts and subassemblies by unaffiliated companies.

In fiscal 2009, Toyota sold 7.56 million vehicles in more than 170 countries and regions, and the company had net revenues of ¥20,529.5 billion ($208.9 billion) and a net loss of ¥436.9 billion ($4.4 billion) (see Table 5-3).

Table 5-3. Key Financial Performance Indicators for Toyota as of End of February, 2010[42]

Performance Indicator	Value
Market Cap (intraday)	$114.66 billion
Profit Margin (ttm)	−3.89%
Revenue (ttm) $US	$190.76 billion
Qtrly Revenue Growth (yoy)	10.20%
Gross Profit (ttm)	$21.11 billion
EBITDA (ttm)	$8.89 billion

The Toyota Supply Chain

Toyota purchases parts, components, raw materials, equipment, and other supplies from several competing suppliers located around the world. Toyota

Chapter 5 | Suppliers

collaborates with its suppliers to encourage technological innovation, cost reduction, and other competitive measures. During fiscal 2009, no single supplier accounted for more than 5% of Toyota's consolidated purchases of raw materials, parts, and equipment, with the single exception of an affiliate of Toyota, Denso Corporation, which supplied approximately 10% of Toyota's purchases.

Toyota procures parts and components locally in the country of the production site as well as in third-world countries. In order to realize timely and efficient distribution through an increasingly complex system at the same time keeping total costs at a minimum, Toyota developed a standardized system of global distribution and supports the operation of the system at each production base. This system is at the heart of Toyota's famous manufacturing process (Table 5-4).

Table 5-4. An Overview of the Automobile Industry Supply Chain

Process Step	Value Added	Example
Design	High	Demand-driven process of satisfying consumer wants and needs. Yield prototypes or "concept" cars.
Raw Materials	Low	These include rubber, glass, steel, plastic, and aluminum.
Parts	Medium	Tires, windshields, and air bags are examples of parts.
Assembly	Medium	An unenviable gray zone with subassembly and major assembly steps subject to the greatest pressures to cut costs.
Marketing	High	Marketing is a major basis for consumers' perceived values.
Distribution and Sales	High	First step of the customer experience.

As Toyota acknowledged in its 2009 annual report, its "ability to continue to obtain supplies in an efficient manner is subject to a number of factors, some of which are not in Toyota's control. These include the ability of its suppliers to provide a continued source of supplies and the effect on Toyota of competition by other users in obtaining the supplies."

Parts and assembly are among the lowest sources of added value and the greatest potential sources of cost savings. Appropriately, Toyota is working to improve profitability and enhance operating efficiencies by continuing to pursue aggressive cost reduction programs.

Design changes to achieve the reduction in the number of platforms used in vehicle production are one approach. Because platforms are the essential structures that form the base of different vehicle models, by using a common platform for the production of a greater number of models, Toyota decreases the substantial expenditures required to design and develop vehicles.

Toyota also continues to focus on other methods of increasing the commonality of parts and components used in different models. Steps include reducing model variations and the number of parts used in each model. A common global database to enable plants in different areas of the world to purchase parts and materials from the most competitive sources is utilized in order to increase the efficiency of procurement from outside suppliers.

Toyota's Business Philosophy

Harmony, honor, and a near fanatical devotion to quality have characterized the company's business philosophy for nearly half a century. The values of harmony and honor were memorialized in 1962 in a pact between management and labor that created a unique cooperative work environment present nowhere else in the industry. The four-point "Labor and Management Resolutions for the 21st Century" were summarized as follows in the unedited translation:[43]

- "As a global company, we will endeavor for the progress of the world economy, and at the same time contribute to international society.

- The relationship between labor and management shall be based upon mutual trust and respect.

- In order to create a company environment in which workers can fully utilize their potential and additional value can be obtained, we, labor and management will endeavor to faithfully perform the roles entrusted to us, while standing on common ground.

- We will contribute to the realization of a truly affluent society and life for working people, taking into consideration the future of Japan as a whole."

This unique team approach, in turn, enabled a cooperative company-wide effort to reduce the costs of defects and waste in accordance with the quality principles of Edward Deming. In 1965, Toyota won the Deming Application Prize for quality control. In 1992, Toyota issued a seven-point credo. Key intangible values addressed include honor, respect, safety, quality, and

Chapter 5 | Suppliers

innovation. The last three are among the six major business processes that drive reputation value.

The Perfect Storm

The largest automobile assembler in the world operated for 50 years with business processes that ensure harmony, honor, and quality for all under its direct corporate control. But it faced increasing cost pressures as the U.S. and European markets became saturated and price-sensitive Asian markets came on line. Then more cost pressures came as the global financial markets melted down. Toyota management created further cost pressures in pursuit of market share and its obsession with outgrowing General Motors. Rather than sow discord in its own labor force, Toyota pursued two cost reduction strategies: (1) standardize parts across a greater range of vehicles and (2) squeeze parts suppliers aggressively.

> *Lean supply chain strategies are coming back to haunt manufacturers. Manufacturers simply don't have the tools to manage the suppliers they depend on.*
>
> —Jim Lawton, General Manager,
> Dun & Bradsteet Supply Management Solutions

Toyota's aggressive tactics following 2008, its first year of loss in 59 years, drove suppliers' profits down to negligible levels. Toyota slashed production and even hired private detectives to identify suppliers at risk for bankruptcies who would need to be quickly replaced. Bloomberg quoted Kazushi Kawabata, president of Toyota supplier Comco Holdings, as saying: "The suppliers are totally in Toyota's grip."[44]

On the software front, information systems began to exert a greater influence on vehicle safety than the underlying mechanical systems. Experts voiced fears that old-style quality controls over manufacturing were outdated and inadequate for cyber risks.

Things started failing. Lacking adequate oversight and visibility in post-production follow-up, problems associated with common components began to crop up globally and go unobserved. The "dots were not connected" until third parties began to bring pressure to bear. The results: headline risks were realized, and failed components forced the recall of more than 8 million vehicles. Toyota's reputation sank, and the financial consequences of the recall began manifesting.

Adding to the woes were concerns of ethical lapses, consequences that potentially included civil and possibly criminal penalties. Internal Toyota

Reputation, Stock Price, and You 117

memos tell how the automaker saved more than $100 million by negotiating with U.S. federal regulators to stop an investigation into accelerator complaints in exchange for a product recall in September 2007.[45]

Ethics, safety, and quality—a headline risk-trifecta. The thing about headline risks and reputation perils, of course, is that they can snowball. Toyota was facing both headline-generating criminal probes and Congressional investigations into its safety problems. Both were overshadowed by the myriad class-action lawsuits filed. Moreover, automobile insurers were preparing to subrogate past auto accident claims involving Toyota vehicles. This is the "pile-on of the trial lawyers and regulators and the mommy-bloggers," said Chris Gidez, Director of Risk Management and Crisis Communications at the marketing firm Hill and Knowlton.[46]

In late January 2010, Toyota's stock price tanked, taking with it approximately $25 billion in market capitalization. On the credit side, five-year credit default swaps (CDSs) on Toyota Motor Corp. debt were quoted at 95–115 basis points (bps) early February, up 38 bps from the month before. The equivalent CDS on Honda Motor Corp. was quoted at about 82 bps according to Markit. In addition, in early February Toyota Motor's five-year CDSs briefly dropped below AA-rated Japan's sovereign five-year CDSs for the first time on data going back to 2007.

Although the recall notice didn't come until late January, Toyota sales for the month fell 16%, to their lowest level in more than a decade, while sales of other cars were rising by 6%. And Toyota's market share fell to 14%, dropping from 17% for 2009. According to Kelley Blue Book, which tracks tens of thousands of new and used-car transactions each week based on data from manufacturers, dealers, and wholesalers, prices for new Toyotas moved lower and were closer to dealer invoices.

Reputation loss was also affecting Toyota's pricing power for vehicles not affected by the recall—used cars. Data from Kelley Blue Book showed prices for used Toyotas fell by 1.5% in the first week after the recall, and by the third week, another 1.5% drop.[47]

Retrospective

This case study on risk and reputation management looks at what happened when executives at an iconic firm in the automobile industry, Toyota, subverted their culture, and in doing so, lost visibility and control of the human behaviors impacting critical elements of their supply chain. It traces how Toyota's famed standard for supply chain management excellence was compromised by senior management's focus on other metrics—growing market share, aka profit without purpose. The quality and safety failures arising were then compounded

Chapter 5 | Suppliers

by potential ethical lapses in internal assessment and reporting. The impact is quantified in metrics memorializing the costs of damaging three major pillars of reputation value: quality, safety, and ethics.

Risk lurks at the periphery of vision. That which is not seen or is ignored, and thus not controlled or managed, can wreak havoc when it impacts a critical source of intangible asset and reputation value. Supply chains sweep in worldwide risk from suppliers, licensees, franchisees, and other partners and it all lands at the doorstep of the large iconic global assemblers, retailers, and distributors. When risk manifests and is headline-grade, the financial impact can be substantial or even catastrophic. All companies that depend on a supply chain are exposed.

Toyota faced headline risk highlighting ethics, safety, and quality issues. Equity costs as of February 2010 were in the $25 billion range. Pricing power dropped around 3%. Market share fell another 3% for 2010, and sales in January 2010 fell 16% to their lowest level in a decade.[47]

Operating costs are difficult to estimate—it was in Toyota's effort to control them that risk arose. Adding to future expected operating costs will be regulatory costs, possible fines and penalties, litigation costs, insurance subrogation costs, and inferior vendor terms. Credit default swap pricing is up almost 30% foreshadowing higher credit costs. All told, the estimated early reputational impact was an immediate $2 billion cost to earnings and a $25 billion cost to market capitalization (Table 5-5).

Table 5-5. Toyota's Reputation Losses: Income Statement Impact.[47]

P&L Entry	Description	$US Billions
Revenue		
	Lost sales	26.75
	Lost pricing power	4.21
	New lost gross profit	0.90
Operating Expenses		
	Nonrecurring	0.50
Other Expenses		
	Additional interest expense	0.07
	Additional depreciation expense	0.54
Net Cost		
	Cost to earnings	2.01

Supply chain–based headline risks will continue to haunt iconic global firms. Outsourcing has created dependencies that currently exceed management's capacity to oversee and control, and these risks will persist until the global supply chain evolves a complementary information management system. Increasingly, suppliers are analyzing the cost to serve their key accounts. In some cases, they are de-prioritizing, or even de-selecting, high–cost-to-serve customers. Removing burdens on suppliers from unnecessary cost-to-serve situations improves end-to-end supply chain economics for all concerned and helps to secure customer of choice status.

Consider This

- The network of corporate risks is far more systemic than ever as companies operate in an ever more complicated and interconnected supply chain.

- Reputational risk exacerbates operational risk. It can threaten the future of companies wounded by operational failures.

- Controls mitigate risk. An integrated view of operational, financial, and reputational risk can give management and corporate boards the level of visibility they, and their stakeholders, now demand.

Sustainability: Peet's Coffee & Tea Inc.

[Sustainability is] the making, using, offering for sale or selling products and services that meet the needs of the present without compromising the ability of future generations to meet their own needs. (Table 1-1)

Peet's Coffee & Tea is a small specialty coffee roaster and marketer of fresh-roasted coffee and tea. It was named for Alfred Peet, who founded the company in Berkeley, California, in 1966 and who later mentored Starbucks' co-founder Gerald Baldwin, who subsequently sold the Starbucks chain and bought Peet's. Baldwin served as Peet's chief executive officer for about 23 years and remains a board member after more than four decades.

In late July 2012, investors were wagering that rival bidders would attempt to top a near $1 billion takeover offer that already ranks as the most expensive U.S. beverage deal. Including net cash, the $941 million offer valued the owner of specialty cafes and grocery products at 21 times earnings before interest, taxes, depreciation, and amortization, the richest multiple for an American maker of nonalcoholic drinks in deals larger than $500 million, according to

Chapter 5 | Suppliers

data compiled by Bloomberg.[48] The expected winning bidder was Starbucks, with its market value of $36 billion (Table 5-5). Peet's "is perceived actually as a more premium offering than Starbucks on the grocery shelf, and they have consistently been able to charge $1 more per 12-ounce bag on the grocery shelf... That is something that Starbucks covets," said Nick Setyan, a Los Angeles-based analyst at Wedbush.[49] Sales of beans through grocery stores generated net revenues of 22.5%; Peet's coffee sold through one of its 196 retail stores generated margins of only 4.5%. The pricing power has been something that Starbucks coveted and may be willing to pay 32 times expected forward earnings. Starbucks traded late July 2012 at 20.36 times forward earnings.[50]

Table 5-5. Several Key Metrics of Comparison Between Peet's Coffee & Tea Inc. and Starbucks Corporation

	Peet's Coffee & Tea Inc.	Starbucks Corporation
Main Exchange	NDAQ	NDAQ
Market Capitalization August 2012 ($B)	0.99	33.2
Profit Margin (ttm)	4.14%	10.67%
Operating Margin (ttm)	7.34%	13.25%
Equity Short % of Float	35.5%	1.1%
Employees	811	149,000

Data source: Yahoo Finance and Google Finance.

The secret to Peet's value is its supply chain management strategy, all focused on relationships on the delivery-to-customer end of the chain. Peet's distributes through a network of grocery stores, mass merchandisers, and club stores through a direct store delivery (DSD) selling and merchandising system in which DSD route sales representatives deliver directly to their stores anywhere between one and four times per week, properly shelve the product, rotate the stock to ensure freshness, and forge store-level selling relationships. Peet's also ships directly to certain customers, offering them fresh-roasted coffee shipped directly from its roastery to their doors and a wider selection of coffees than is available in their retail stores or at grocery store partners.

Through its customer service representatives and coffee experts, the customer service team provides in-depth coffee information to guide

Reputation, Stock Price, and You

customers through their coffee explorations. Data compiled by Bloomberg indicate that sales from Peet's grocery-store business increased more than 92% in three years to $98.9 million in 2011.

On the supplier side, Peet's competes with procurement giants. In addition to Starbucks, JM Smucker Co.—the $8.4 billion maker of Folgers coffee—and the $70-billion–market-valued Kraft Foods Inc.—which sells Maxwell House and Yuban brand coffee products—have significant buying power and could leverage that power to become preferred customers. But Peet's relationships top all.

In coffee-producing countries, the coffee crop undergoes weather-related changes in quality. Furthermore, as a trade commodity, coffee prices can fluctuate depending on weather conditions in various coffee-producing countries, economic and political conditions affecting those countries, foreign currency fluctuations, the ability of coffee-producing countries to agree on export quotas, and world economic conditions that make commodities more or less attractive investment options.

Peet's procures coffee from 23 countries, with a large percentage of coffee coming from Central and South America from more than 30 different exporters, brokers, and growers. They purchase only high-quality Arabica coffee beans, which are considered superior to beans traded in the commodity market. Arabica beans tend to trade on a negotiated basis at a substantial premium above commodity coffee prices, depending on the supply and demand at the time of purchase.

Peet's access to high-quality Arabica beans depends on its relationships with coffee brokers, exporters, and growers, with long-term relationships helping ensure a steady supply of coffee beans. Peet's believes that its reputation built over 45 years gives them access to some of the highest-quality coffee beans from the finest estates and growing regions around the world. They are also occasionally offered opportunities to purchase unique and special coffees.

Given their common heritage, it's not surprising that both Peet's and Starbucks emphasize sustainable practices that inure to the benefit of their suppliers. Peet's website provides details on the company's "commitment to sustainable business practices." Starbucks, to help ensure sustainability and future supply of high-quality green coffees and reinforce its leadership role in the coffee industry, operates Farmer Support Centers in Costa Rica and Rwanda, among other locations. These Farmer Support Centers are staffed with agronomists and sustainability experts who work with coffee farming communities to promote best practices in coffee production designed to improve both coffee quality and yields.

Chapter 5 | Suppliers

Starbuck's reputation is closely associated with its Corporate Social Responsibility programs, balancing profitability with a social conscience. This umbrella program provides social benefits to many stakeholders and encompasses the sustainability programs.

By the Numbers

The case studies in this chapter illustrate how reputation can affect value-creating and value-destroying actions by vendors and suppliers (Table 5-6).

Table 5-6. Effects of Reputation on Supplier and Vendor-Associated Costs

	P&L Effect	**Stock Price Effect**
Automotive sector: customer of choice status	2%–4% lower cost of goods sold	Increase
McDonald's: supply chain engagement strategy	10% *lower* adjusted costs for food and paper goods than Yum! Brands 10% higher profit margin	48% premium over Yum! Brands for every trailing month of dollar sales
Coca-Cola: supply chain engagement strategy	4% *lower* cost of sales, bottling, and distribution than Pepsi	2009: crisis erased 11% of market cap 2011: 13% greater equity value per expected $1 of net income than Pepsi
Toyota: supply chain operational event evolving into a reputational event	Credit default swap prices up 0.6%–0.7% 16% fall in monthly sales 14% fall in annual market share 3% fall in secondary market pricing power (inventory value) Total P&L impact of $2 billion	$25 billion lost
Peet's	Higher pricing power for store-bought coffee beans	Shares at pending acquisition currently priced at a 50% premium to expected earnings relative to Starbucks

Endnotes

1 Davies PJ. John Hurrell (Chief Executive, Association of Insurance and Risk Managers) quotation from "Not out of the woods yet." *Financial Times*. 12 February 2010. Available at: http://www.ft.com/intl/cms/s/0/146fea72-17ef-11df-a74d-00144feab49a. html#axzz20ybGaDCE. Accessed 18 July 2012.

Reputation, Stock Price, and You

2 Lindwall C, Ellmo A, Rehme J, Kowalkowski C. *Increasing customer attractiveness through upstream brand equity.* The International IPSERA workshop on Customer attractiveness, supplier satisfaction and customer value. 25–26 November 2010. Available at: http://urn.kb.se/resolve?urn=urn:nbn:se:liu:diva-63092. Accessed 17 July 2012.

3 Skogman L, Tiselius K. *Developing strategic supplier relationships at Volvo Powertrain.* Master of Science thesis in the Master Degree Program Supply Chain Management 2012. Department of Technology Management and Economics, Division of Industrial Marketing. Chalmers University of Technology. Report No. E2012:029.

4 Bew R. The new customer of choice imperative: ensuring supply availability, productivity gains, and supplier innovation. *92d Annual International Supply Management Conference*, Las Vegas, May 2007.

5 Supply-chain management. *Economist.* 6 April 2009. Available at: http://www.economist.com/node/13432670. Accessed 20 July 2012.

6 Boeing 777 Facts, 777 Family. Available at: http://www.boeing.com/commercial/777family/pf/pf_facts.html. Accessed 20 July 2012.

7 Van de Rijt J, Sanema SC. A conceptual model for interactions between suppliers and buyers: from uni-faced to multi-faced B2B sales organizations. Paper presented at the *International IPSERA Workshop on Customer Attractiveness, Supplier Satisfaction and Customer Value*, November 2010, University of Twente.

8 Kraljic P. Purchasing must become supply management, *Harvard Business Review* 1983; September–October: 109–117.

9 A brief history of McDonald's. Available at: http://www.mcspotlight.org/company/company_history.html. Accessed 18 July 2012.

10 McDonald's Corporation. *Google Finance.* Available at: http://www.google.com/finance?cid=22568. Accessed 18 July 2012.

11 Urry M. RHM receives two Golden West bids. *Financial Times.* 26 March 2005. Available at: http://www.ft.com/intl/cms/s/0/eb54ac20-9d9d-11d9-a227-00000e2511c8.html#axzz20ybGaDCE. Accessed 18 July 2012.

12 McDonald's Corporation *2011 Annual Report* (Form 10K), p. 8.

13 Vitasek K, Manrodt V. What five great economists can tell us about Outsourcing. *Supply Chain Management Review.* July/August 2012 pp 18-25.

14 Goldberg RA, Yagan JD. McDonald's Corporation: managing a sustainable supply chain. *Harvard Business School.* 16 April 2007. Case 9-907-414.

15 McDonald's *2009 Worldwide Corporate Responsibility Report.* p. 14. Available at: http://www.scribd.com/doc/93473994/1/Corporate-Governance-Ethics. Accessed 18 July 2012.

16 Lee HL, Billington C. Managing supply chain inventories: pitfalls and opportunities. *Sloan Management Review.* 1992; Spring: 65–73.

17 Fletcher C. McDonald's pledges sustainable Filet-O-Fish in Europe. *Bloomberg.* 8 June 2011. Available at: http://www.bloomberg.com/news/2011-06-07/mcdonald-s-pledges-sustainably-sourced-filet-o-fish-in-europe.html. Accessed 18 July 2012.

18 Jackson A-L, Feld A. Domino's 'brutally honest' ads attract sales as consumer spending falters. *Bloomberg.* 17 October 2011. Available at: http://www.bloomberg.com/news/2011-10-

Chapter 5 | Suppliers

17/domino-s-brutally-honest-ads-offset-slowing-consumer-spending.html. Accessed 19 July 2012.

19 Taylor P. Supply chain is a strategic discipline. *Financial Times*. 25 January 2011. Available at: http://www.ft.com/intl/cms/s/0/eb1cf8ca-2749-11e0-80d7-00144feab49a. html#axzz20ybGaDCE. Accessed 18 July 2012.

20 Nooteboom B, Berger H, Noorderhaven N. Effects of trust and governance on relational risk. *Academy of Management Journal*. 1997; 40(2):8–38.

21 Dion P, Banting P, Picard S, Blenkhorn D. JIT implementation: a growth opportunity for purchasing. *International Journal of Purchasing and Materials Management*. 1992; 28 (4):33.

22 Spekman RE, Kamauff JW, Myhr N. An empirical investigation into supply chain management: a perspective on partnerships. *International Journal of Physical Distribution & Logistics Management*. 1998; 28(8):630–650.

23 The Chicken and the Pig. Wikipedia. Available at: http://en.wikipedia.org/wiki/The_Chicken_and_the_Pig. Accessed 18 July 2012.

24 Foley S. How Yum! Brands is conquering the world. *Bloomberg Businessweek*. 14 July 2010. Available at: http://www.businessweek.com/globalbiz/content/jul2010/gb20100714_088544. htm. Accessed 19 July 2012.

25 Taylor P. Supply chain leaders identified. *Financial Times*. 25 July 2011. Available at: http://www.ft.com/intl/cms/s/0/509f9722-b6db-11e0-a8b8-00144feabdc0.html#axzz20ybGaDCE. Accessed 18 July 2012.

26 Gartner supply chain top 25. *Gartner Research*. Available at: http://www.gartner.com/technology/supply-chain/top25.jsp. Accessed 20 July 2012.

27 Plimmer G. Supply-chain experts arrive at the top. *Financial Times*. 26 October 2011. Available at: http://www.ft.com/intl/cms/s/0/718ad57c-ef76-11e0-941e-00144feab49a. html#axzz20ybGaDCE. Accessed 18 July 2012.

28 100 best corporate citizens. *Corporate Responsibility Magazine*. Available at: http://www.thecro.com/content/100-best-corporate-citizens. Accessed 20 July 2012.

29 Green Rankings 2010: U.S. Companies. *Daily Beast*. Available at: http://www.thedailybeast.com/newsweek/2010/10/18/green-rankings-us-companies.html. Accessed 20 July 2012.

30 Salminen RT, Arpalo J, Pekkarinen, O, Jalkala A, Mirola T. Characteristics of a good customer reference for a process equipment supplier. 2008. Presentation of the RELI project – Developing Reference-based Business. Available at: http://www.tbrc.fi/eng/projects/?PCID=32&PID=58. Accessed 20 July 2012.

31 Data source: Compiled from the respective 2009, 2010, and 2011 annual reports for McDonalds Corporation and YUM! Brands.

32 Lab tests find carcinogen in regular and Diet Coke and Pepsi. Center for Science in the Public Interest. 5 March 2012. Available at: http://www.cspinet.org/new/201203051.html. Accessed 20 July 2012.

33 Consumer group claims soda-cancer link. *Bloomberg* 5 March 2012. Available at: http://www.chron.com/news/article/Consumer-group-claims-soda-cancer-link-3383014.php. Accessed 20 July 2012.

Reputation, Stock Price, and You 125

34 Cancer group asks U.S. to study sugary drinks, obesity. *Reuters*. 4 July 2012. Available at: http://in.reuters.com/article/2012/07/03/usa-obesity-soda-cancer-idINL2E8I3AO120120703. Accessed 20 July 2012.

35 Hays CL. Coke Products Are Ordered Off the Shelves in Four Countries. *New York Times*. 16 June 1999. http://www.nytimes.com/1999/06/16/business/coke-products-are-ordered-off-the-shelves-in-four-countries.html?pagewanted=all&src=pm. Accessed 10 October 2012.

36 Greenberg MD. On breaking the log jam: the how and why of corporate reputation leadership. *Corporate Finance Review*. 2012; 17(1):11–17.

37 The Coca-Cola Company Annual Report, 2011.

38 Russell M. In the spotlight – PepsiCo's plans beg more questions. *Just Food*. 10 February 2012. Available at: http://www.just-food.com/analysis/in-the-spotlight-pepsicos-plans-beg-more-questions_id118218.aspx. Accessed 31 August 2012.

39 PepsiCo. Annual Report, 2011.

40 Data source: Compiled from the respective 2009, 2010, and 2011 annual reports for The Coca-Cola Company and PepsiCo.

41 Dyer JH, Chu W. The role of trustworthiness in reducing transaction costs and improving performance: empirical evidence from the United States, Japan and Korea. *Organization Science*. 2003;14 (1): 57–68.

42 Compiled from Yahoo Finance company statistics. http://finance.yahoo.com/q/ks?s=TM+Key+Statistics. Accessed February 2010.

43 Labor–management relations. Toyota. Available at: http://www.toyota.co.jp/en/environmental_rep/03/jyugyoin.html. Accessed 1 September 2012.

44 Kitamura M, Horie M. Toyota partmakers in Japan hire detectives to hunt bankruptcies. *Bloomberg*. 1 May 2009. Available at: http://www.bloomberg.com/apps/news?pid=newsarchive&sid=aGcEKX2DBZ4M&refer=japan. Accessed 10 August 2010.

45 Memos show regulators cut short Toyota probe in 2007. *Reuters*. 22 February 2010. Available at: http://www.reuters.com/article/2010/02/22/retire-us-toyota-nhtsa-idUSTRE61L4TC20100222. Accessed 10 August 2010.

46 McDonald C. Toyota, Tylenol recalls 'Worlds Apart,' crisis mgt. expert says. *Property Casualty 360*. 5 February 2010. Available at: http://www.propertycasualty360.com/2010/02/05/toyota-tylenol-recalls-worlds-apart-crisis-mgt-expert-says. Accessed 10 August 2012.

47 Kossovsky N. Foggy supply chain claims another victim (case study). *Intellectual Asset Management*. 2010; 41(May/June): 19–27.

48 Barinka A. Peet's seen tempting Starbucks to top richest Java bid: real M&A. *Bloomberg*. 31 July 2012. Available at: http://www.sfgate.com/business/bloomberg/article/Peet-s-Seen-Tempting-Starbucks-to-Top-Richest-3752232.php. Accessed 1 August 2012.

49 Franklin M. Could Starbucks Acquire Peet's Coffee? The Daily Meal, 30 July 2012. Available at: http://www.thedailymeal.com/could-starbucks-acquire-peets-coffee. Accessed 10 October 2012.

50 Yahoo Finance, SBUX, Key Statistics. Available at: http://finance.yahoo.com/q/ks?s=SBUX+Key+Statistics. Accessed 2 October 2012.

CHAPTER 6

Creditors

A man I do not trust could not get money from me on all the bonds in Christendom.

—J. P. Morgan[1]

John Pierpont Morgan, patriarch of the banking dynasty, famously asserted that credit was based on trust. Knowing whom he was lending to was more important than either cash or property collateral, he explained to Congress in 1912. In today's commercial relationships, trust still denotes an expectation of behavior that is the foundation for commercial credit.

One hundred years after Morgan's statement, superior reputations that foster trust are still associated with better credit terms. Today, when it is no longer clear exactly who "owns" any given security, when buyer and seller usually never meet, and where there is never any apparent opportunity for trust to develop, reputations matter even more to borrowers and creditors.[2] Risk is the issue. High trust, or reputation, translates into lower credit risk. Lesser reputation means higher credit risk.

Yet today most of the finance literature focuses on the "hard" aspects of credit risk, including such quantifiable elements as repayment history and credit ratings, which tend to constrict the meaning of reputation. Neglect of the intangibles may explain why the literature has not been very successful on the subject of pricing credit risk. Prior studies have been able to explain only a small fraction of the variation in credit spreads.[3,4,5,6] Reliance on hard information, such as balance sheet and market data, ignores such intangible factors as firm reputation—that which J. P. Morgan considered essential. Alan Greenspan spoke of this issue when he lamented, "I am ... distressed at how far we have let concerns for reputation slip in recent years."[7]

Chapter 6 | Creditors

Volkswagen AG

The Volkswagen Group's August 2012 acquisition of Porsche illustrates how reputation can trump oversimplified quantitative world views. The largest carmaker in Europe, the VW Group aspires to surpass both General Motors and Toyota and become the largest carmaker in the world. In 2011, it delivered 8.3 million vehicles, up by 1 million from the year before. Sales revenue increased by 25.6% to €159.3 billion ($212 billion), and operating profits rose to €11.3 billion ($15 billion)—a new record.

The Group, better known to generations of aging hippies as the manufacturer of the Beetle and the Microbus, consisted of ten brands from seven European countries: Volkswagen Passenger Cars, Audi, S☐KODA, SEAT, Bentley, Volkswagen Commercial Vehicles, Scania, MAN, Bugatti, and Lamborghini. Each brand has its own character and operates as an independent entity to meet the specific needs of different market segments and countries.

On 3 August 2012, Volkswagen added to its stable of brands Porsche Zwischenholding GmbH as the 11th in the VW Group. In the lead up to the deal's closing, credit markets held differing opinions about the economic benefits of adding Porsche's reputation to the Group. On 9 July 2012, *Bloomberg* reported that VW had committed to spending €4.46 billion ($5.5 billion) of cash to add to its 49.9% stake and complete its acquisition of Porsche SE, and that it also took on €2.5 billion ($3.2 billion) of debt along with the 50.1% of the iconic sports carmaker that it didn't already own. Moody's was dubious, commenting that the cash payment created a deterioration in VW's leverage ratio, with adjusted net debt–to-earnings ratio rising to 0.7 times from 0.4 times before the transaction. Fitch was more optimistic, affirming its existing ratings and revising Volkswagen's outlook to Positive from Stable.[8]

But investors, more attuned to reputation, were unabashedly enthusiastic. They concluded that the acquisition of a premium brand made Volkswagen more creditworthy and they pushed VW's bonds to record highs. VW's €1.25 billion bonds with a face value of 2.75% rose in price, cutting the yield to 1.3%. Credit default swaps (CDSs) protecting the company's debt were the most traded of any corporate contracts globally in the week through June 29 and fell the most compared with other European auto firms in July, according to Credit Market Analysis (CMA), a part of S&P Capital IQ.[9]

Reputation Matters

There are a few academic studies that quantify the relationship between credit costs and the six business pillars that underpin reputation. These pillars are

Reputation, Stock Price, and You

among the categories of corporate investments that have no visibility on traditional balance sheets yet represent essential "economic competencies"—a term used by Charles Hulten, professor of economics at the University of Maryland.[10] Bauer and Hann showed that credit costs correlate with reputation-associated operational risks in *safety* and *sustainability*.[11] Using information on the environmental profile of 582 U.S. public corporations between 1995 and 2006, and controlling for numerous credit risk determinants, they showed that firms with questions about their environmental performance pay a premium on the cost of debt financing and have lower credit ratings. The corporate activities underlying this *sustainability* connection were related mainly to regulatory and climate change issues. In contrast, firms with a reputation for proactive environmental engagement are charged a lower cost of debt.

Commitments to *innovate* and execute practices with environmental benefits are also associated with lower bond spreads, as observed for firms in industries both that are traditionally low and high in environmental risk. Also, the relevance of corporate environmental management has increased over recent years as a result of the growing climate change concerns and investors' awareness of associated regulatory risks.

Scott Mitchell, Chairman of Open Compliance and Ethics Group (OCEG), a not-for-profit performance management think tank, argues that the Enron and WorldCom scandals forced investors to consider extra-financial factors. "Creditors are looking for high financial performance, but with a degree of both responsibility and integrity." Companies that are seriously committed to driving principled performance through integrated governance, risk, and compliance activities based on publicly vetted tools and resources invariably end up with better reputations.[12]

Reputational risk should not be conflated with moral risk. All other things being equal, there is no evidence that companies operating in the alcohol, gaming, or adult entertainment industries—so-called sin industries—face a higher cost of debt or a lower bond rating. However, the tobacco industry does because of additional regulatory risks.[13] In October of 2011, S&P reminded corporate boards and managers that its analysts take corporate safety measures into account when rating creditworthiness.[14] While they may not have the tools to estimate improved cash flows from enhanced reputations, the credit ratings agencies are not unaware of the risks to cash flows from the failure of any of the six business processes underpinning reputation enumerated in Table 1-1.

A few academic studies do quantify the relationship between credit costs and reputation directly. Each year, *Fortune* magazine surveys industry experts along dimensions such as the *quality*, integrity, and character of a firm's managers;

Chapter 6 | Creditors

the *innovativeness* of the firm; the quality of its products; and the firm's ability to attract, retain, and train talented workers. They use these as important factors for gauging reputation. Their ranking of "Most Admired Companies," described further in Chapter 9, is used by academics in a number of disciplines as a measure corporate reputation.[15,16]

Another survey-based ranking of the world's "Most Respected Companies" is published by *Barron's*. Unlike the *Fortune* survey, *Barron's* limits its survey respondents to professional money managers. In May and June 2012, 116 investors nationally scored each of the world's 100 largest companies on a scale of 1 to 5. One key question asks the degree they respect, or don't, the world's largest companies.

Research based on these reputation scorings consistently shows that a favorable reputation correlates with lower expectations for adverse credit events—a benefit factored into credit pricing. In a 2011 study, using the Most Admired Company rankings as a proxy for reputation, Anginer et al. found a robust inverse relationship between a firm's reputation as measured by the *Fortune* survey and the credit spread on its bonds: [17] A higher reputation score was associated with lower monthly credit spreads. A half-point (0.5) improvement in the reputation score, or moving up one quintile in the Fortune reputation rankings, reduced the cost of debt capital by 10–20 basis points (bps), even taking into account all other firm-level and macro-level variables affecting credit risk.

In the pricing of CDSs also, firms with superior reputations benefit. Marc Lucier, a director of Deutsche Bank, reported in 2009 that companies with higher reputation rankings tend to have lower credit costs, reflected in lower spreads of CDSs. The converse is also true: 49% of the variance in the average relative CDS cost was explained by the average reputation rankings.[18]

A 2012 study for this book using the *Barron's* survey data as the proxy for reputation showed that lower CDS prices correlated with higher levels of "respect." In an analysis of 30 of the world's largest companies, two variables, the Barron's respect scores and the Total Debt/earnings before interest, taxes, depreciation, and amortization (EBITDA) ratio, explained 15% of the variance in pricing of CDSs. Controlling for the Debt/EBITDA ratio, the *Barron's* Respect score explained 12% of the CDS pricing variance, and a move one full notch up the Respect scale moved the 3 August 2012 CDS price down 15.6 bps (Figure 6-1).

In addition to better pricing, superior reputations are associated both with larger credit tranches and better terms. A study of 181 deals with a median value of $408 million showed that the General Partner's reputation is significantly related to leverage and deal structure.[19] The study found that

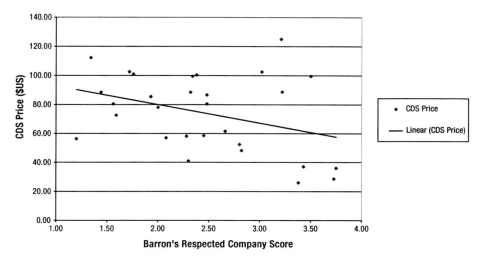

Figure 6-1. Correlation of CDS prices 3 August 2012 with the *Barron's* Respect Score. The debt of companies with better reputations can be insured at a lower cost.

reputable private equity groups pay narrower bank and institutional loan spreads, have longer loan maturities, and rely more on institutional loans.[20]

Conversely, reputational damage can lower credit ratings and increase credit costs. After its reputational crisis, BP was briefly unable to borrow money at any price. Two days after Carnival Corp's. *Costa Concordia* cruise ship capsized, Standard & Poor's issued a bulletin saying that costs associated with the disaster would negatively affect Carnival's 2012 operating performance, including "any investment associated with restoring the reputation of the Costa brand, which is one of Carnival's largest and most well-known."[21] And the failure of MF Global, the financial derivatives broker, and the ensuing legal, regulatory, and reputational damage, led Standard & Poor's to reduce the ratings of the parent, CME Group Inc.[22]

Security: The Johnson & Johnson Case

> [Security is] the degree of protection a company offers against events undertaken by actors intentionally, criminally or maliciously, for purposes that adversely affect the firm. Because fear is the great disruptor of life and commerce, it is useful to think of security, the most ethereal of the intangible assets, as "absence of fear." (Table 1-1)

There was nothing Johnson & Johnson could have done to signal more convincingly its ethical culture than its enterprise-wide behavior during the 1982 Tylenol poisonings. At that time, Tylenol was the undisputed leader in

Chapter 6 | Creditors

the painkiller field, accounting for a 37% market share. Had Tylenol been a public corporation, profits would have placed it in the top half of the Fortune 500.

The recounting of the security crisis the company endured forged a powerful linkage between the words "corporate ethics" and Johnson & Johnson. During the fall of 1982, a malevolent person or persons replaced Tylenol Extra-Strength capsules with cyanide-laced capsules, resealed the packages, and deposited them on the shelves of at least a half-dozen pharmacies and food stores in the Chicago area. By the end of the crisis, seven people had purchased the tainted capsules, ingested them, and died.

Having learned about the developing crisis from a phone query by a Chicago reporter, Johnson & Johnson Chairman James Burke charged a seven-member strategy team with two goals: protecting people and saving the product.[23] The company's first actions were to alert consumers nationwide immediately through the media not to consume any Tylenol product. After two more contaminated bottles of Tylenol were found, Mr. Burke ordered a national withdrawal of every capsule.

The crisis generated unprecedented news coverage. More than 100,000 separate news stories ran in U.S. newspapers and garnered hundreds of hours of national and local television coverage. The company's post-crisis study revealed that more than 90% of the U.S. population had heard of the Chicago deaths within the first week of the crisis. Two news clipping services found more than 125,000 clips on the Tylenol story, and one of them claimed that the story had received the widest U.S. news coverage since President John F. Kennedy's assassination.[24]

Extensive coverage enabled the company to communicate to its stakeholders what it was doing to mitigate the disaster and restore its reputation—actions proving that ethical behavior was a cultural standard at Johnson & Johnson.

When the dust had settled, the central message stakeholders received was that the company was moral, revered its customers, and was itself a victim of a wanton act of terrorism. Its reputation was secured for the next quarter-century. Surveys consistently ranked the firm at or near the top of almost every reputational ranking, and press coverage tended to be favorable (Figure 6-2). The company's low CDS costs reflected the benefits of its long-term superior reputation and perceived superior creditworthiness (Figure 6-3).

Reputation, Stock Price, and You

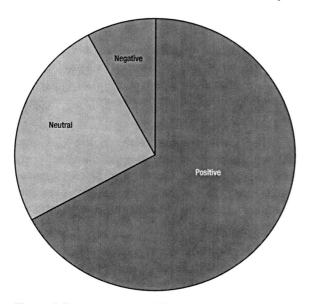

Figure 6-2. Analysis of the 167 articles appearing in the business media during the 12 months preceding 15 May 2009 concerning Johnson & Johnson and reputation show an overwhelming positive sentiment, with a positive to negative ratio of 8.38. Source: Newssift.com, a *Financial Times* service.

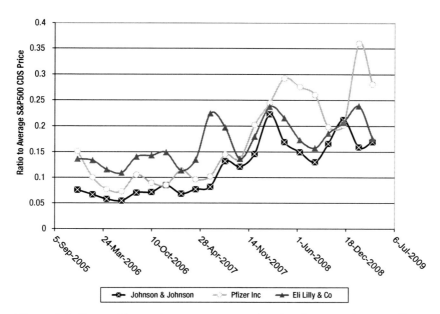

Figure 6-3. Firms with superior reputations tend to face lower credit costs. Shown are the company and two peers, and their respective costs of credit as measured by the ratio of their CDS price relative to the average CDS price of the S&P 500. Source: Kossovsky N. J&J, a credo and a reputation (case study). *Intellectual Asset Management*. 2010; 39: (January/February): 30–34.

Chapter 6 | Creditors

Guidance

Creditors are obviously at an informational disadvantage, since there is no way they can fully comprehend the motives or anticipate the potential behaviors of a borrower. They are forced to depend upon the body of information beyond direct knowledge that is encapsulated in the word "reputation."

Hypothesizing in 1982 what J. P. Morgan knew empirically in 1912, Milgrom and Roberts suggested that reputations would play a role in credit relationships."[25] Along this same line of thought, Berger and Udell suggested that older firms accessed credit more easily than younger firms because enough time had passed to establish the firm's public reputation, thereby mitigating asymmetric information problems.[26]

Looking at consistency of repayment alone is inadequate for distinguishing healthy firms with similar repayment records. Firms may adopt a wide range of other actions that influence how their creditworthiness is perceived. A firm may, for example, hire quality managers or take a conservative approach to risk management, leading it to be perceived as a high-quality firm in terms of its credit risk. These and other qualitative features are factored into the bond rating agencies rankings.

While we prefer the term "reputation," qualitative features not present on standard corporate financial statements are also known in financial circles as "non-financial" or "extra-financial" information. In its 1996 Measures that Matter study, Cap Gemini Ernst & Young, a global accountancy, established that non-financial performance plays a critical role in how public companies are valued, accounting for as much as 35% of institutional investors' valuation.[27] In 2005, PwC, another global accountancy, reported controlled experiments showing that extra-financial data and intangible asset value calculations swayed 40% of analysts to change their target valuations of public companies. That same year, Thomson Extel, the publishing group, reported that 6% of buy-side brokerages devoted material resources to extra-financial data to determine intangible asset value. A year later, that figure was updated to 32% of buy-side brokerages.[28]

More investment managers also seem to be collecting extra-financial information. In 2007, Vigeo, a provider of extra-financial data, reported that they had been retained by ABP Fund, which had €200 billion ($280 billion) in assets under management. Also, in 2007, the Enhanced Analytics Initiative, international extra-financial investment information cooperative, reported that its membership had a total of US$2.4 trillion of assets under management. Today, that increased attention to extra-financial information has grown to encompass, among others, groups with investment strategies informed by

Reputation, Stock Price, and You 135

corporate environmental, social, and governance practices under the rubric of socially responsible investing.

In 2000, Cap Gemini Ernst & Young declared "the market at once demands and relies on non-financial information in company evaluations and valuation decisions."[29] As seen with the VW case, 12 years later some investors are still comfortable factoring extra-financial information into the pricing of equities or debt. Anecdotally, select members of the professional credit community—regional bankers—may be similarly inclined.

The credit experience of Pittsburgh-based Littlearth Productions, a women's accessories manufacturer, is illustrative. A licensee of the National Football League, Littlearth's products, sold under the Pro-Fan-ity brand, are made for the female sports enthusiast. The company's globally distributed operations and supply chain call for levels of working capital augmented through lines of credit. Robert J. Brandegee, CEO, attributes the strength of his banking relationships to the intangible value of his license. "The bank is willing to work with us when we are not quite in 'formula' because they know how much we will sell this upcoming NFL season," he says. His bank manager, like many citizens of Pittsburgh—a "drinking town with a football problem"[29]—is an enthusiast of the local professional team, the Steelers. Rob adds, "His understanding of the emotional power of our brand is a benefit that makes all of the difference for us in terms of our ability to grow through conventional financing!"

But other members of the stakeholder community of creditors, even if they are sports fans, are often not moved this way. The fact that such different comfort levels exist for something as fundamental as credit risk explains, in part, why the Nobel Committee has awarded two separate prizes in 1996 and 2001 for work in the field of markets with asymmetric information.

Economists as far back as Adam Smith[30] observed that, as interest rates rise, the best borrowers drop out of the market. However, it was the work of Michael Spence, who along with George Akerlof and Joseph Stiglitz was awarded the Nobel Prize in Economics, that explained how credit rating agencies and insurers helped translate extra-financial information—reputation—into information that can be appreciated and valued by all stakeholders.[31]

Because reputation is difficult to value, commercial insurances can be unusually valuable in signaling information about credit risk related to reputation risk arising from operational risk. The art is in the detail. The strongest signals on creditworthiness come from insurances that indemnify policyholders against reputational value loss and that incentivize better reputation risk management.

Chapter 6 | Creditors

In 2011, both AIG and Zurich Financial Services, in cooperation with Aon, introduced reputation insurances that primarily provide indemnifications for crisis communications expenses. In 2012, Kiln Group in cooperation with Steel City Re introduced a different type of product—Reputational Value Insurance. Reputational Value Insurance protects against first-party loss to a company's reputation arising from a failed business process and consequential adverse media attention. Evidence of reputation risk control is a condition of underwriting the insurance, and loss limits are indexed to reputational value metrics.[32] Insurances are discussed further in Chapter 8.

Consider This

- Reputation is an umbrella term for the extra-financial information on intangible assets that lenders can factor into their assessment of the creditworthiness of a borrower.

- Among the largest companies, a better reputation can enhance the creditworthiness of a borrower and the benefits can persist for years.

- Insurances are among the most cost-effective instruments for signaling reputation-driven enhanced creditworthiness. Properly designed reputation insurances can help stakeholders appreciate and value a company's state of reputation risk control.

By the Numbers

Table 6-1. Effects of Reputation on Credit Costs

	P&L Effect	**Stock Price Effect**
VW Group	Corporate bond yield dropped to record low of 1.3%. Funding advantage of at least 400 bps over its main European rivals.[33]	85% 3 yr ROE compared to 33% for world markets, 20% for DAX
Johnson & Johnson	Post-crisis CDS prices lower by 5–10 basis points than peers and as low as 5% of the average for all S&P 500 companies.	Equity price resilience

Multiple studies	Credit spreads for the World's Most Admired Companies are ~0.75% lower than the prices for those with the worst reputations. CDS prices for the World's Most Respected (Largest) Companies are ~0.60% lower than the prices for those with the worst reputations.	Increase

Endnotes

1 Surowiecki J. The trust crunch. *The New Yorker*. 20 October 2008. Available at: http://www.newyorker.com/talk/financial/2008/10/20/081020ta_talk_surowiecki. Accessed 2 August 2012.

2 Authers J. A return to vision of J. P. Morgan. *Financial Times*. 29 July 2012. Available at: http://www.ft.com/intl/cms/s/0/e6e6a57c-d7d2-11e1-80a8-00144feabdc0.html#axzz22O9ypWml. Accessed 2 August 2012.

3 Collin-Dufresne P, Goldstein RS, Martin JS. The determinants of credit spread changes, *Journal of Finance*. 2001; 56:2177–2207.

4 Duffee GR. Estimating the price of default risk. *Review of Financial Studies*. 1999; 12:197–266.

5 Amato J, Remolona E. The credit spread puzzle, *BIS Quarterly Review*. 2003; 51–63.

6 Elton EJ, Gruber MJ, Agrawal D, Mann C. Explaining the rate spread on corporate bonds. *Journal of Finance*. 2001; 56:247–277.

7 Goodman PS. Taking hard new look at a Greenspan legacy. *The New York Times*. 8 October 2008. http://www.nytimes.com/2008/10/09/business/economy/09greenspan.html?pagewanted=all. Accessed 2 August 2012.

8 Fitch affirms Volkswagen at 'A–' on Porsche acquisition. Press Release. *Reuters*. 5 July 2012. Available at: http://in.reuters.com/article/2012/07/05/idINWNA042820120705. Accessed 3 August 2012.

9 Benjamin H. Porsche joins Bugatti to spur VW bonds record: corporate finance. *Bloomberg*. 9 July 2012. Available at: http://www.businessweek.com/news/2012-07-08/porsche-joins-bugatti-to-spur-vw-bonds-record-corporate-finance. Accessed 3 August 2012.

10 Hulten C. Agnostic blessings: how to count intangibles. Mission Intangible Monthly Briefing. 3 December 2010. Audio recordings available from the Intangible Asset Finance Society: http://iafinance.org/monthly-briefings. Accessed 15 September 2012.

11 Bauer R, Hann D. Corporate environmental management and credit risk. Working paper, European Centre for Corporate Engagement, June 30, 2010. Available at: http://ssrn.com/abstract=1660470 or http://dx.doi.org/10.2139/ssrn.1660470. Accessed 3 August 2012

12 Mitchell SL. How reputation drives principled performance. Mission Intangible Monthly Briefing, 1 April 2011. Audio recordings available from the Intangible Asset Finance Society: http://iafinance.org/monthly-briefings.

Chapter 6 | Creditors

13 Dassen S. Sin companies and credit risk. Master's Thesis. Maastricht University, Faculty of Economics and Business Administration, Maastricht, 24 May 2011.

14 Chapelle T. S&P emphasizes safety as factor in credit scores. *Agenda*. 24 October 2011.

15 Davies G. *Corporate reputation and competitiveness*. New York: Psychology Press, 2003.

16 Fombrun, CJ, Gardberg NA, Sever JM. The reputation quotient: a multi-stakeholder measure of corporate reputation. *Journal of Brand Management*. 1999; 7: 241–255.

17 Anginer D, Warburton AJ, Yildizhan C. Corporate reputation and cost of debt. Available at: SSRN: http://ssrn.com/abstract=1873803 or http://dx.doi.org/10.2139/ssrn.1873803. Accessed 3 August 2012

18 Lucier M. Quantifying the financial impact of reputation. In *Building and enforcing intellectual property value 2010*. IP Media Group, 2010; 15–20.

19 James C. Buyout financing: the changing role of banks in deal financing. Available at: www.frbsf.org/csip/research/200710_Chris_James.pdf. Accessed 3 August 2012.

20 Demiroglu C, James CM. The role of private equity group reputation in LBO financing. *Journal of Financial Economics*. 2010; 96(2):306–330

21 Reputation risk in focus at credit rating agencies. *Business Insurance*. 26 February 2012. Available at: http://www.businessinsurance.com/article/20120226/NEWS06/302269975. Accessed 2 August 2012.

22 Polansek T. S&P cuts CME Group rating due to MF Global risk. *Reuters*. 10 February 2012. Available at: http://www.porknetwork.com/pork-news/SP-cuts-CME-Group-rating-due-to-MF-Global-risk-139044309.html?view=all. Accessed 2 August 2012.

23 Crisis communications case study: Tylenol. *BCMpedia*. Available at: http://www.bcmpedia.org/wiki/Crisis_Communications_Case_Study_Tylenol. Accessed 12 August 2012.

24 Case study: the Johnson & Johnson Tylenol crisis. Crisis Communication Strategies. DoD Joint Course in Communication. Available at: http://www.ou.edu/deptcomm/dodjcc/groups/02C2/Johnson%20&%20Johnson.htm. Accessed 12 August 2012.

25 Milgrom P, Roberts J. Predation, reputation, and entry deterrence. *Journal of Economic Theory*. 1982; 27:280–312.

26 Berger AN, Udell GF. Relationship lending and lines of credit in small firm finance. *Journal of Business*. 1995; 68:351–382. Available at: http://dx.doi.org/10.1086/296668. Accessed 3 August 2012

27 Measuring the future: the value creation index. Cap Gemini Ernst & Young Center for Business Innovation, 2000; 3.

28 Kossovsky N. Accounting for intangibles: from IP to CEO. *Patent Strategy & Management*. 2007; 8(7):3–4.

29 Pittsburgh. *Urban dictionary*. Available at: http://www.urbandictionary.com/define.php?term=pittsburgh&page=2. Accessed 1 September 2012.

30 Smith A. *An inquiry into the nature and causes of the wealth of nations*. London: Strahan & Cadell, 1776.

31 Spence AM. Consumer misperceptions, product failure and producer liability. *Review of Economic Studies*. 1977; 44:561–572.

Reputation, Stock Price, and You

32 Steel City Re. Protecting reputation value. Available at: http://www.steelcityre.com/protecting_value.shtml. Accessed 1 September 2012.

33 Tait N, Kirk S. Lex in depth: Volkswagen. *Financial Times*. 5 September 2012. http://www.ft.com/intl/cms/s/0/8723e25e-f761-11e1-8c9d-00144feabdc0.html#axzz25h3VSeTG. Accessed 6 September 2012.

Controls

CHAPTER

7

Equity Investors

Given the recent reputational, legal and regulatory risks ... we believe the board is in need of independent leadership.

—Class A Equity Investors of News Corporation[1]

Equity investors express their expectations mostly by buying or selling shares. Through these direct behaviors, they establish stock prices and earnings multiples. Firms with superior reputations benefit from higher multiples on earnings. Poor reputations tend to result in higher stock price volatility and greater vulnerability to headline risks. In a reputational crisis, any firm may experience a collapse in stock price.

Recently, investors have begun voicing their expectations with increasing frequency through their proxies. Some of their expectations may reflect social values; many others are reactions to financial performance alone. In very recent years, investors have become far more active in their expression of disappointment, through voting against board members and against management plans, with increasing attention to "Nay on pay."[2] Also, increased numbers of these shareholders are taking their displeasure to the courts. Individual corporate executives and board members may also suffer personal reputation damage when their companies endure an adverse reputational event.

Investors are not yet storming the Bastille, but their concerns about the reputations of their companies are being taken very seriously. The following studies illustrate some of the widely varied examples of growing shareholder influence on corporate behaviors and their reputations.

Facebook Inc.

Most equity investors buy stocks that they expect to be able to sell at a higher price within a reasonable period. Before Facebook's initial public offering (IPO), Reuters reported that it was already oversubscribed with one week left. For the "IPO of the Decade," analysts expected that the upper end of the projected price range of $28 to $35 would be raised. In turn, Facebook would raise more than the expected $10.6 billion, and shares could be expected to rise once the IPO was complete.[3] Expectations were high. Just ten weeks later, the shorts were high.

This historic 18 May 2012 Facebook Inc. IPO did not go as many had expected. Facebook shares, which opened up 11%, closed just above their $38 IPO price. More than 576 million shares changed hands, setting a trading volume record for U.S. market debuts.[4] Most investors had expected a first-day pop, but five days later, Facebook equity was hemorrhaging value (Figure 7-1).

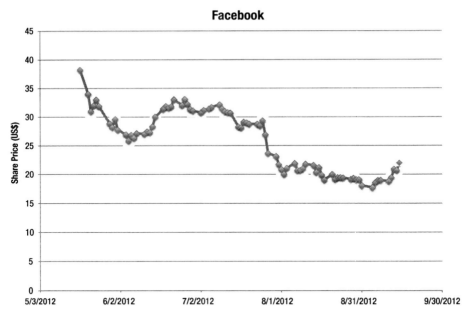

Figure 7-1. Time series chart showing Facebook's stock price from its May launch through early August. Within 10 weeks, Facebook equity had shed 47% of its IPO value. Source: Yahoo Finance.[5]

The company had priced its IPO at the top end of its target range and increased the size of the offering, becoming the first U.S. company to go public with a valuation greater than $100 billion. On 2 August, after less than three months, that valuation dipped briefly to $42.8 billion. At a valuation of

Reputation, Stock Price, and You

122 times historic earnings, those expectations arguably still could be irrationally exuberant.

When the stock was still above $30, long before the magnitude of the mismatch between equity investor expectations and broad market behavior became apparent, *Vanity Fair* published a tongue-in-cheek indictment of all potentially culpable parties, namely, everyone[6]:

> **The Underwriters…**
> *…for lowering their expectations of earnings just before the IPO, and informing only a select number of larger clients.*
>
> **Your Stupid Cell Phone…**
> *…for enabling mobile advertising that is less lucrative to Facebook and worrying the underwriters.*
>
> **The Media…**
> *…for propping up Facebook and confusing a terrific social-media service with a hot stock. The journalists should have been savvy enough to see through Wall Street's foolish promises.*
>
> **General Motors…**
> *…for yanking its advertising from the site just before the IPO.*
>
> **Barack Hussein Obama…**
> *…Why not?*
>
> **NASDAQ…**
> *…when on IPO, day, a glitch "delayed Facebook's market debut by roughly half an hour, and later delayed order confirmations."*
>
> **Facebook.com…**
> *…for alleged "registration and prospectus (that) were materially false."*

Not everyone was disappointed in Facebook Inc.'s huge drop. Some European investors bought structured products benefiting from the stock's decline.[7] A put warrant that predicted Facebook would be at $22 by March 2013 cost 6 euro cents ($0.07) to buy in the week after Facebook went public. On 6 August, the warrant was worth 36 euro cents, a return of more than 500%.

Reputation and Information Processing

Equity investors have the luxury of assessing the expected benefits of the drivers of value on customers, employees, vendors, and creditors and then

Chapter 7 | Equity Investors

determining if the current stock price is reasonable, too high, or too low. Major macroeconomic events, regional microeconomic events, and specific corporate events can all reset current expectations.

The Facebook IPO illustrates a confusion between reputation and brand that can impact stakeholder behavior. Reputation, which is an expectation of behavior held by stakeholders, should not be conflated with brand, which is an emotional construct. Corporate reputation creates a powerful aggregation of information that draws from an enormous and diverse array of sources. In general, the process of its formation is cognitive and provides a framework through which investors process current events. Brands, on the other hand, can create an emotional attachment that obscures reality and undermines rational choice.

Consider how investors processed news about Facebook just before its IPO. James Gorman, CEO of Morgan Stanley, the lead underwriter, disclosed that he "had unprecedented retail demand" and "people calling in from every part of the country." Gorman confirmed that 26% of the shares were placed in the hands of individual investors.[8] Individual investors who were users of the product were often passionate supporters. Retail investors had always been key to Facebook's IPO strategy, in part because it had more than 900 million users globally. "We want to dump a lot of money into Facebook," said one aspiring investor, citing peers' activity on the site as evidence of its longevity. "You're on Facebook half your day, if not more. It's a necessity. It's water, it's death, and now it's Facebook."[9] Such passion drove extraordinary expectations and created a company brand that acted as a powerful news filter. "The demand is insane," said one retail broker to the *Financial Times*. "You could write that Facebook was the worst company in the world, and retail would still want the stock."[10]

Writing about the rush for shares at the IPO of Arsenal, an English football club, the *Financial Times* observed in 2010 that investors' willingness to pay an "ego premium" can add roughly 25% to a company's sale price.[11] That would put the fair value of Facebook at $32 per share, all other things being equal.

While only a few were overtly disparaging the firm, there was ample information to properly determine more factually grounded, business-oriented expectations about Facebook's advertising-linked revenue model. Two weeks before the IPO, Marin Software, a digital marketing platform that processed more than $100 million worth of spending on Facebook, found the cost per click for Facebook's standard ads, which made up an estimated three-quarters of the social network's advertising revenues, had fallen 26% over the prior year.[12] A full month before the IPO, Facebook published quarterly numbers that showed the rate of revenue growth was slowing, seasonality factors were kicking in, and costs were soaring. The net effect for the first quarter of 2012

Reputation, Stock Price, and You

was a 36% slump in the company's operating profit margin, down from 53% the year before.[13]

Ignoring reality is never a good strategy for investors. But when adverse events obscure reality, a good reputation can provide visibility to investors and dispel fear, uncertainty, and doubt.

Recall that Johnson & Johnson emerged in 1982 from its crisis with an unimpeachable reputation for ethics. Not often appreciated is that a second Johnson & Johnson Tylenol poisoning had also occurred. While the first attack in 1982 caused significant financial damage, the second in 1986 didn't. The primary differences between the two events were that by 1986, Johnson & Johnson had strengthened its control over the security processes that ensured safety in its products, and it had established a stellar reputation for ethical behavior.

With its ethical reputation, Johnson & Johnson's contentions were credible: that it was in control of its supply chain, that the poisoning was a rogue criminal act, and that all other products were safe. Equity investors took the cue.

After the initial event in 1982, the company's market value fell by $1 billion, or 30% of its equity value, and took 2.5 years to equilibrate; during the course of the 1986 event, the company recovered its lost reputational value as equity investors boosted its stock price by 30% (Figure 7-2).

The company's diligence in ensuring the safety and security of all its business processes was communicated so effectively that it bolstered J&J's reputation among consumers, and the company recovered 70% of its market share within five months of the crisis. Investors' concerns receded in less than two months, and the company outperformed the S&P 500 index over the course of the year. Subsequent research revealed that many consumers were so reassured by the steps that J&J had taken that, instead of deserting Tylenol, they actually switched to it from other painkillers.

Conversely, a bad reputation can exacerbate bad news. So it was for Knight Capital Group. In the summer of 2012, the entire financial services sector was at a reputational low point with customers and regulators, as well as other stakeholders. For a financial services company, it was a bad time to have a reputational crisis arising from an operational failure.

On 1 August 2012, Knight, a major market maker in global equities, watched briefly as its electronic systems began trading for themselves. According to *The New York Times*, technical problems "led the firm's computers to rapidly buy and sell millions of shares in over a hundred stocks for about 45 minutes after the markets opened. Those trades pushed the value of many stocks up,

Chapter 7 | Equity Investors

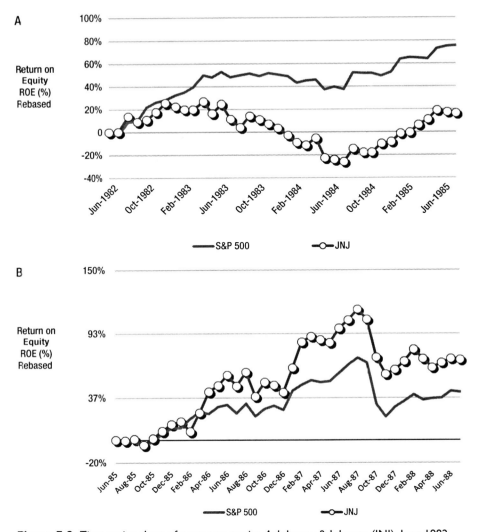

Figure 7-2. Time series chart of return on equity. A: Johnson & Johnson (JNJ), June 1982 through June 1985. The stock took 2.5 years to recover value from the fall 1982 Tylenol crisis. Following the incident, J&J invested time and effort into strengthening its reputation resilience by improving the underlying business processes that previously had allowed the product tampering to occur. B: Johnson & Johnson June 1985 through June 1988. There was no meaningful adverse impact of a second Tylenol crisis in 1986. In fact, the stock price actually rose and outperformed the S&P 500 by 30%. Source: Kossovsky N. *Mission Intangible: Managing risk and reputation to create enterprise value*. Intangible Asset Finance Society/Trafford, 2010. Reproduced with permission.

and the company's losses appear to have occurred when it had to sell the overvalued shares back into the market at a lower price."[14] Knight Capital's tab for the bad trades: $440 million.

Reputation, Stock Price, and You 149

Knight's safety system, like BP's blowout protector on the Deepwater Horizon, failed. Two days later, with its stock price down from $10.50 to below $3 at the start of trading, Knight's reputation as a safe platform for U.S. equity trades was in tatters. Customers, employees, and regulators all wondered why it took the firm so long to stop trades that were losing $10 million per minute. "Even just a minute or two would have been surprising to me. On these time scales, that is an eternity," said David Lauer, a one-time trader at a high-speed firm. "To have something going on for 30 minutes is shocking."[15] The losses threatened the stability of the firm, and Knight Capital acknowledged that its capital base, the money it used to conduct its business, had been "severely impacted" by the event and that it was "actively pursuing its strategic and financing alternatives."[14]

Meanwhile, the regulators—soon to be followed by the litigators—were joining the bloggers in outrage. "Existing rules make it clear that when broker-dealers with access to our markets use computers to trade, trade fast, or trade frequently, they must check those systems to ensure they are operating properly," SEC Chairman Mary Schapiro said two days after the event. "And, naturally, we will consider whether such compliance measures were followed in this case."[16]

Five days after the business process failure at Knight, and with adverse publicity mushrooming, Wall Street bailed out one of its own. A group of investors led by Jefferies, the investment bank that structured the deal; Blackstone; Getco; Stephens; Stifel Financial; and TD Ameritrade acquired control and about 70% of Knight for around $1.50 a share.[17]

Operational failures from computer system malfunctions are risks that companies like Knight Capital Group routinely disclose in their annual reports.

> Capacity constraints, systems failures and delays may occur in the future and could cause, among other things, unanticipated problems with our trading or operating systems...decreased levels of client service and client satisfaction, and harm to our reputation. If any of these events were to occur, we could suffer substantial financial losses, a loss of clients...litigation or other client claims, and regulatory sanctions or additional regulatory burdens.[18]

It is not clear what, if any, systems Knight Capital had in place to mitigate those risks. Nor is it clear that the company contemplated a precipitous failure. But the data show that controls that mitigate reputational risks arising from operational values do more than protect against losses. When companies make operational improvements in reputational risk management in a way that can be appreciated and valued by equity investors, value is added.

Chapter 7 | Equity Investors

Constituent members of the S&P 500 index were scanned in the winter of each year for firms that appeared to have latent reputation value as suggested by their Steel City Re Corporate Reputation Rankings. The algorithm underpinning the RepuStars Variety Corporate Reputation Index, calculated by Dow Jones indexes, was used to accomplish this. Portfolios of up to 57 companies were structured each year and the one-year returns were compared with the baseline S&P 500 index returns (Figure 7-3). On average, those companies filtered for latent reputation value outperformed the broader market by 6.5% annually over the 10-year study period.[19]

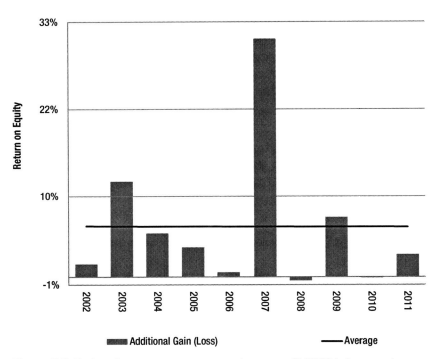

Figure 7-3. Re-based one-year returns on equity among S&P 500 index constituent members identified by the RepuStars Variety algorithm (RepuSPX) as having as-yet unrealized reputation value. The average value is 6.5%. The baseline levels of return are the S&P 500 index. Source: Mission: Intangible blog of the Intangible Asset Finance Society. Reproduced with permission.[20]

Consider This

From the perspective of equity investors:

Reputation, a cognitive expectation of behavior held by stakeholders, should not be conflated with brand, an emotional construct.

- Superior reputations can mitigate the reputational consequences of adverse events.

- When a corporation operates in an industry sector held in low esteem, it is even more vulnerable to a reputational stumble.

- Unexpected gains (or losses) in reputational value among major companies can be expected on average to add (or subtract) 6%–7% to (from) the market capitalization.

WPP plc

In May 2011, WPP plc, the world's largest marketing services group, teamed up with both Aon, one of the world's largest insurance brokers, and Zurich Financial Services, a leading insurer, to create a supersized reputation restoration insurance product: $100 million for advertising, lobbying, and public relations.[21] WPP's role in the product is to act as a kind of loss adjuster for the policy, advising on and directing spending for a crisis-hit company. In a vividly ironic twist, one year later, the CEO of WPP, Sir Martin Sorrell, was facing his own reputational crisis.

A proposed 56% pay boost for Sorrel on top of a prior year's substantial turn toward global retrenchment was inconsistent with shareholders' evolving expectations of meeting certain economic responsibilities. One evolving notion is that a CEO cannot lose a lot of money for shareholders and expect to be rewarded. WPP was not unaware of this expectation. Adding insult to injury, in January 2012, a consortium of the conglomerate's communications companies announced at Davos that "major global brands have more work to close the gap between their performance in the marketplace and their citizenship."[22]

As is almost always the case, a failure of a business process was at the bottom of the WPP reputational crisis. Board governance failed thrice. The first was not processing shareholder concerns effectively. A second was failing to understand that the politics of pay in the United Kingdom had changed. Last, according to The Telegraph, they were relying too heavily on compensation consultants.[23]

All of this may be true, but the simple answer is that the reputation of the firm had been deteriorating. "If you look at the long-term performance in general in the media industry, it has been dismal," said Sanford C. Bernstein

Chapter 7 | Equity Investors

analyst Claudio Aspesi. When investors are disappointed with the performance of their companies, they look to the CEO. "So scrutiny over what management teams have done to justify their pay packages is entirely appropriate," added Aspesi.[23]

The reputations of companies and CEOs are often conflated. Serial studies over 10 years by Weber Shandwick's Chief Reputation Strategist, Dr. Leslie Gaines-Ross, suggest that executives believe that 50% of a company's reputation is attributable to the CEO. In a May 2012 update, 66% of the general public said that their perceptions of top leadership also affected their opinions of company reputations from a great deal to a moderate degree. Only 7% said that there is no link between the two.[24]

On 13 June 2012, 60% of WPP investors voted against the remuneration packages of directors, including Sorrell. The nay vote came on the heels of a protest vote from 40% of investors in 2011. "We're disappointed by the result of the vote," Sorrell said in an e-mail. "But the shareowners have spoken."[25]

Jeffrey Rosen, head of WPP's remuneration committee, said: "If we take anything away from this, it is that we should have a more continuous program of dialogue with shareholders." Twenty-two percent of shareholders thought the time for dialogue had passed and voted against Rosen's reappointment. Two other directors had even higher votes against.[25] Only 2% voted against Sorrell's reappointment—it was his pay level that they rejected.

Given the linkage between CEO and the company reputation, scrutiny does not reveal a pretty picture of the reputations of CEOs. Gaines-Ross reported in 2009 that in the wake of the global financial meltdown of 2008, only 14% of American executives held a positive view of chief executives,[26] and among the general public, probably an even lower percentage. Added Gaines-Ross: "Companies and leaders fall, often trip a second time as they institute change but, on the third try, you definitely lose investor and customer patience. After a third attempt or three sequential mishaps, your reputation gets a scarlet R."[27]

The investor rebellion at WPP was one of the biggest since 2009, when 90% of Royal Bank of Scotland Group plc shareholders turned down the pension plan for the lender's former chief, Fred Goodwin. Goodwin, who had built the Royal Bank of Scotland into one of the world's largest banks, also led the bank to ruin within four years, posting the biggest loss in U.K. corporate history—£24 billion ($38 billion). The British government had to spend £45 billion ($71 billion) bailing out and nationalizing RBS for an 82% stake.

Leading the bank to near-collapse and then walking away with a fat pension so infuriated the British public that Goodwin was stripped of his knighthood in January 2012. Having "brought the honors system into disrepute," in the

Reputation, Stock Price, and You

words of the *Huffington Post*, "he found himself in the company of British spy Anthony Blunt, Zimbabwean President Robert Mugabe, and Romanian dictator Nicolae Ceausescu."[28]

Say-on-Pay and Other Vocalizations

Evolving legislation in the United States and United Kingdom has given shareholders a greater voice in corporate governance, but like many politically initiated shifts in power, the instigators are voters. Shareholders who have regularly rubber-stamped management-inspired proposals on governance and pay are increasingly becoming voters and taking issue with executive pay programs.

Sir Francis Bacon, a liberal-minded reformer of his day, famously wrote that knowledge is power.[29] Because of social media, shareholder/voters today are more aware than ever, and they are exercising their newly found powers to some effect. Even at historically docile Japanese companies, shareholder meetings the summer of 2012 were marked by a flurry of proposals from investors challenging management by opposing board appointments, for example, or simply expressing anger at executives.[30]

WPP's dissenting shareholders had ample company. In 2012, more than 30% of investors in "the Pru," the UK's largest insurer, opted to vote against the company's pay plan. Sixteen percent of shareholders voted against the CEO pay package at Aberdeen Asset Management. At Aviva, chief executive Andrew Moss resigned from the company after shareholders rejected the insurance group's pay policies. Nearly 50% of shareholders of William Hill, the United Kingdom's biggest bookmaker, voted against the firm's remuneration report. Shareholders at Trinity Mirror, the newspaper company, prompted the resignation of CEO Sly Bailey after a quarter of the firm's shareholders pressured the board to reduce her pay.

Angry over domestic energy prices, nearly 12% of shareholders voted against remuneration packages at Centrica, the owner of British Gas. Cookson, the U.K. materials technology company, took a beating at the annual general meeting after 32% of its shareholders voted against the re-election of the entire board following its decision to award £20 million ($32 million) in shares to directors. According to the *Daily Telegraph*, dissenters included Lord Myners, the Labour peer and chairman of Cevian, a 14% investor in the firm. Nearly 32% of votes cast at the annual general meeting opposed the directors' remuneration report.

Financial institutions are favored targets of shareholder rage. After dismal returns, around 15% of shareholders rejected the remuneration report of

Chapter 7 | Equity Investors

Man Group, the U.K. hedge fund firm, piling more pressure on chief executive Peter Clarke to resign. At Barclays, even before the LIBOR (London Interbank Offered Rate) scandal became public, anger at Bob Diamond's pay package spilled out into open mutiny at the bank's annual general meeting when 27% of investors voted against it. UBS was hit with a 36.84% rejection of its compensation report and Credit Suisse with a 31.6% rejection. Across the pond, in an almost unprecedented revolt, 55% of the Citibank's shareholders rejected a $49 million pay package for its chief executive, Vikram Pandit.[31] "The only surprise about this vote was that so many shareholders still voted in favor. Citigroup's stock has declined more than 90 percent in the last five years, and the company has been a prime example of mismanagement in the years leading up to the financial crisis."[32]

Rage and anger here are being driven by a perception that the bankers have skewed values. "The majority of people feel it's just a culture of greed," explained one executive coach.[33] Or perhaps not sharing the benefits of that greed. Proxy advisory groups such as Institutional Shareholder Services and Glass Lewis have been credited with influencing many of the successful nay campaigns of 2012. But they have not been successful when a bank's reputation among shareholders, economic returns, and executive pay has been generally aligned.

Shareholders in the United States who are not themselves activists actually have little in common with Occupy Wall Street protesters. Except in fairly extraordinary circumstances, it appears they don't much care about how much people get paid, as long as earnings and share prices keep rising.[34] The banks have deservedly received outsized attention because of persistent headline risk brought on by pockets of truly bad behavior in the financial sector, but compensation has otherwise not been a major battleground.

Correlating Respect and Pay

Using the *Barron's* Respect data introduced earlier as a proxy for a firm's reputation among its shareholding professional investors, the data show that greater respect goes hand in hand with greater CEO salary in the financial sector. *Barron's* Respect scores explained 27% of the variance in salary levels among CEO's of the world's largest financial institutions, and each additional full notch of additional *Barron's* Respect translated to an additional $800,000 in salary (Figure 7-4).

Three companies stood apart from the model. Berkshire Hathaway had the second highest mean *Barron's* Respect score among the largest financial institutions, just behind Visa. Visa's CEO's nominal salary was $4.23 million and was low relative to the respect earned from investors. Berkshire's CEO, one of the five wealthiest men in the world, took home only $490,000 in salary, an exceptionally low salary nominal salary that is heavily supplemented with contingent compensation. At the other end of the spectrum, Citigroup had the second lowest mean *Barron's* Respect score, just above AIG. While AIG's CEO's salary was $3.02 million, and his compensation package was approved by 99.19% of the votes cast, Citigroup's CEO's nominal salary was significantly above the trend line at $7.02 million; his compensation package was approved by only 45% of the votes cast.

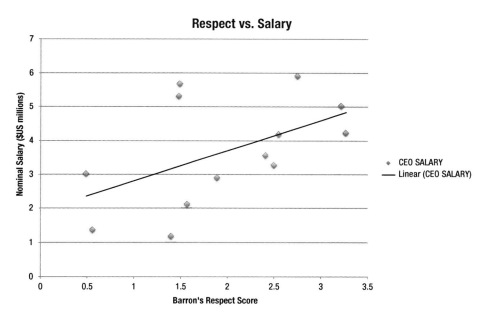

Figure 7-4. Correlation between CEO base pay level ($ millions) and Barron's Respect score. In financial services, being respected by investors translates into better pay, and when within reason, into harmonious annual general meetings. Source: Salary data drawn from most recent annual reports as published by Yahoo Finance. Available at: http://finance.yahoo.com/.

Again using the *Barron's* Respect data as a proxy for a firm's reputation, the data show that greater respect does not explain CEO salary in the Consumer Non-Durables sector (Figure 7-5). Exemplary companies are Altria Group, Procter & Gamble, PepsiCo, Diageo, L'Oreal, SAB Miller, LVMH Moët Hennessy, Kraft Foods, and Coca-Cola. *Barron's* Respect scores explained none of the variance in salary levels among CEOs of the world's largest food, beverage, and related products companies.

It is the goal of this volume to present the data rather than speculate on the lack of any correlation. However, this is not to say that investors are completely

Chapter 7 | Equity Investors

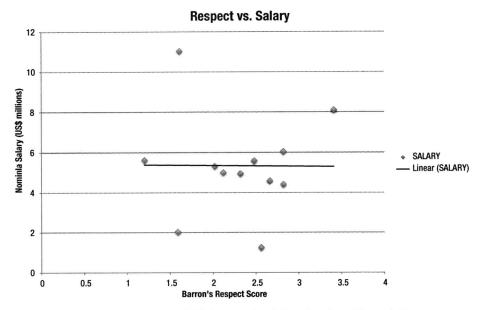

Figure 7-5. Correlation between CEO base pay level ($ millions) and Barron's Respect score. In the consumer non-durables section, being respected by investors does not translate into better pay. Source: Salary data drawn from most recent annual reports as published by Yahoo Finance. Available at: http://finance.yahoo.com/.

indifferent to the pay of executives at non-financial companies. Shareholders have disapproved executive compensation systems at some U.S. companies such as Big Lots (31% approval), Cooper Industries (30%), Simon Property Group (27%), Pitney Bowes (35%), and Chiquita Brands (20%). Outsized pay for performance is the dominating issue. According to Towers Watson, the compensation consultancy, companies whose shareholder returns were consistently in the bottom quartile over five years were about nine times more likely to fail their say-on-pay votes than neutral performers.[35]

Companies that outperform can pretty much do what they want, even when the CEO is barely known. Benefitting from Apple's stellar reputation, CEO Tim Cook's $378 million 10-year package was approved with 83% of the votes cast. "If a company is doing well," said Doug Friske, a Towers Watson's consultant, "shareholders have no problem with pay that recognizes that."[35] But not always. Proxy advisor ISS recommended against the compensation package at the Walt Disney Company, a firm with a good reputation among all stakeholders. The company protested that it "had (reported a) record financial performance in Fiscal Year 2011...(with) total shareholder return more than four times greater than that of the S&P 500 during Mr. Iger's more than six years of leadership."

Reputation, Stock Price, and You | 157

But with Disney, a company widely respected, the issue for the powerful proxy advisor wasn't pay or performance—it was governance. ISS recommended against voting for the members of Disney's Governance and Nominating Committee as a result of appointing its CEO as Chairman of the Board as part of a reasoned CEO succession strategy. ISS is generally opposed to CEOs serving jointly as their own boss as chairpersons. ISS has also recommended against Disney's position on say-on-pay.[36] The package squeezed by with 57% of the votes cast.

ISS had recommended a vote against pay packages at 14% of the companies it assessed in 2012, up from 12% last year. Shareholder support was 30% lower at companies with a negative say-on-pay assessment from ISS.[37]

"Even if we haven't seen widespread shareholder revolt," Friske said, "there's definitely been a change in boardroom attitudes. Maybe it's not a shareholder spring, but perhaps we can call it a shareholder thaw."[35]

Nevertheless, executive compensation systems put to a say-on-pay vote continue to be approved by shareholders of most companies, often by large majorities. Semler Brossy, a compensation advisor, reported in June 2012 that at midyear say-on-pay votes in the Russell 3000 found only 40 of 1,594 corporations, or 2.5%, had failed. Ninety percent of the large companies won at least 70% approval from shareholders in such votes, according to another consultancy, Davis Polk.[37] Though the press talked up a "shareholder spring," the failure rate of approximately 2% for the first half of 2012 was comparable to the rates for 2011.[38]

Then there is litigation. Shareholders who express their feelings through their proxies and are ignored by their companies can sell their equity, of course, but they have recourse to that more explicit communication channel as well.

When, over shareholder protests, the board at Cincinnati Bell Inc. bumped up the compensation of the top executives by up to 80% despite a 68% drop in 2010 net earnings, they were sued, becoming the first company to garner a "no" vote for executive compensation under Dodd-Frank—a distinction of sorts.[39] The lawsuit was brought by Illinois-based NECA-IBEW Pension Fund, a Bell shareholder, and accused Cincinnati Bell Inc.'s outside directors of breaching their duty to investors and the company's top executives of "unjust enrichment" over pay raises. The suit sought return or impoundment of the pay increases and implementation of internal controls preventing excessive compensation to the company's top executives.

"Companies may not have to abide by shareholder advisory say-on-pay votes mandated under the Dodd-Frank Act," the *Wall Street Journal* noted in June 2011, "but lawyers specialized in securities class action suits have already brought a half dozen suits against directors and executives for ignoring their

Chapter 7 | Equity Investors

results."[40] A number of firms have tried to settle the claims quickly. Among those that have settled are KeyCorp and Occidental Petroleum. Others that have faced suits were Beazer Homes, Hercules Offshore, and Umpqua Holdings, and law firms had pending investigations at Dex One, Masco Corp., and Stanley Black & Decker, among others. "In addition to legal fees," the *Journal* stated, "the suits could impact companies more widely in areas like the cost of director and officers' liability insurance, and how much compensation consultants charge."

Guidance

Many Facebook investors, enthralled with the company and its brand, took the plunge and bought high, only to sell low. Professional investors with less emotional engagement, and wary of the market's reputation for disappointing investors caught up in the new, new thing, were more prudent. Innovation may make for good companies; it may not necessarily make for good investments.

Investors in Johnson & Johnson in the late 1980s invested in a good company. The company's culture had been tested by fire in 1983. Its security systems were tested in 1986 and proven to be better than anyone had imagined. Shareholders found a company in which risks previously felt to be inherent in the sector had been eliminated through superior processes. Appreciation of that reduction in risk helped shareholders better value the firm and discover an additional 30% in enterprise value.

Paul Liebman, a compliance attorney who notably has worked for both the largest public and private companies in the United States, ExxonMobil Corporation and Koch Industries, recounted a story of Charles Koch's investment philosophy. "Koch," he said, "only wanted to own businesses that operated legally, ethically, safely, and profitably." Liebman, who was at the time Chief Compliance Counsel at Dell, a technology company, added, "If anyone of those four were missing, then he didn't want to be involved."[41] Most equity investors, at the end of the day, are similarly inclined.

Despite their enhanced influence with management and board composition, investors' message to management remains stable: create value and shareholders will reward management. Lose value and shareholders will support management as long as management's reputation for *eventually* rewarding shareholders remains intact.

Frederick D. Lipman, head of the Association of Audit Committee Members, Inc., points out that Warren Buffet takes the contrarian position that stock

Reputation, Stock Price, and You

price is not really controlled by the executives of his companies, so he sees no reason to either reward or punish them for its volatility.[42]

The investors' message also comes with a warning. Lose value, signal disregard for shareholders, and cause shareholders to expect little from management, and they will fight on pay or seek the removal of management and/or the board. For lost reputation, even Buffet will be ruthless.[43]

Consider This

- Because the reputations of CEOs and the companies they lead are often conflated, investor behaviors toward one are shaped by the other.

- Empowered by recent legislation, shareholders are using conversations on CEO pay as one behavior to express their beliefs.

- When either a company or a CEO has a good reputation, shareholders will support most strategies.

By the Numbers

These discussions illustrate how reputation can affect shareholder behavior, and how those behaviors affect the executive team's freedom to operate, set compensation, and execute their business strategies (Table 7-1).

Table 7-1. Effect of Reputation on Investor-Associated Behaviors

	Operations Effect	Stock Price Effect
Facebook Inc.	Irrational exuberance conflating brand with reputation	50% loss on equity 500% gain on equity derivatives
Johnson & Johnson	Market share growth from unexpected reputational boost even in the face of an adverse event	30% boost in projected market cap
S&P500	Unexpected reputational boost	Average annual market cap boost of 6.5% over 10-year study period
Financial institutions	Correlation of investor respect metric with CEO salary: $800,000 per full notch up	N/A

	Operations Effect	**Stock Price Effect**
All companies	Consistent bottom quartile ROE are nine times more likely to fail "say-on-pay"	N/A

Endnotes

1 Rushton K. Rupert Murdoch faces shareholder revolt at News Corporation AGM. *The Telegraph.* 18 July 2012. Available at: http://www.telegraph.co.uk/finance/newsbysector/mediatechnologyandtelecoms/media/9410035/Rupert-Murdoch-faces-shareholder-revolt-at-News-Corporation-AGM.html. Accessed 6 August 2012.

2 Myles D. Stronger say-on-pay means shareholder spring to stay. *IFLR.* 26 July 2012. Available at: http://www.iflr.com/Article/3066760/Corporate/Stronger-say-on-pay-means-Shareholder-Spring-to-stay.html. Accessed 4 August 2012.

3 Facebook IPO demand above expectations. *24/7 Wall Street.* 11 May 2012. Available at: http://247wallst.com/2012/05/11/facebook-ipo-demand-above-expectations/. Accessed 7 August 2012.

4 Oreskovic A. Historic Facebook debut falls short of expectations. Reuters. 18 May 2012. Available at: http://news.yahoo.com/facebook-prices-top-range-landmark-ipo-005337198--sector.html. Accessed 7 August 2012.

5 http://finance.yahoo.com/q/hp?s=FB+Historical+Prices

6 Weiner J. Who's to blame for the Facebook I.P.O. disaster? Blame must be assigned! *Vanity Fair.* 23 May 2012. Available at: http://www.vanityfair.com/online/daily/2012/05/Whos-to-Blame-for-the-Facebook-IPO-Disaster-Blame-Must-Be-Assigned. Accessed 7 August 2012.

7 Marsh A. Facebook bears garner 500% profit from structured product bets. *Bloomberg.* 6 August 2012. Available at: http://www.bloomberg.com/news/2012-08-06/facebook-bears-garner-500-profit-from-structured-product-bets.html. Accessed 7 August 2012.

8 Demos T. Gorman calls Facebook investors 'naive.' *Financial Times.* 31 May 2012. Available at: http://www.ft.com/intl/cms/s/0/d84a2ab0-ab64-11e1-b675-00144feabdc0.html#axzz22rXUquye. Accessed 7 August 2012.

9 Demos T. Retail demand for Facebook risks inflating IPO. *Financial Times.* 16 May 2012. Available at: http://www.ft.com/intl/cms/s/0/1f8d58f0-9ed8-11e1-a767-00144feabdc0.html#axzz22rXUquye. Accessed 7 August 2012.

10 Darila M, Santa M. Retail brokers stop accepting orders on Facebook shares. *World Business Press.* 17 May 2012. Available at: http://wbponline.com/Articles/View/5026. Accessed 7 August 2012.

11 Lex. Psychic income. *Financial Times.* 20 August 2010.

12 Bradshaw T, Dembosky A. Facebook's premium ad prices still rising. *Financial Times.* 6 May 2012. Available at: http://www.ft.com/intl/cms/s/0/77a89c04-9774-11e1-83f3-00144feabdc0.html#axzz22rXUquye. Accessed 7 August 2012.

Reputation, Stock Price, and You

13 Waters R. Facebook gives the bulls pause for thought. *Financial Times*. 24 April 2012. Available at: http://blogs.ft.com/tech-blog/2012/04/facebook-gives-the-bulls-pause-for-thought/#axzz22sWPhcYk. Accessed 7 August 2012.

14 Popper N. Knight Capital says trading glitch cost it $440 million. *The New York Times*. 2 August 2012. Available at: http://dealbook.nytimes.com/2012/08/02/knight-capital-says-trading-mishap-cost-it-440-million/. Accessed 7 August 2012.

15 Silver-Greenberg J, Popper N, de la Merced MJ. Trading program ran amok, with no 'off' switch. *The New York Times*. 3 August 2012. Available at: http://dealbook.nytimes.com/2012/08/03/trading-program-ran-amok-with-no-off-switch/. Accessed 7 August 2012.

16 Chairman Schapiro statement on Knight Capital Group trading issue. Press Release. US Securities and Exchange Commission, 3 August 2012. Available at: http://www.sec.gov/news/press/2012/2012-151.htm. Accessed 4 October 2012.

17 Mackenzie M, Alloway T. Outside investors take control of Knight. *Financial Times*. 6 August 2012. Available at: http://www.ft.com/intl/cms/s/0/616e6ea6-dff8-11e1-a96a-00144feab49a.html#axzz22rXUquye. Accessed 7 August 2012.

18 Knight Capital Group Annual Report, 2011, pp. 19–20.

19 Greenberg MD. On breaking the log jam: the how and why of corporate reputation leadership. *Corporate Finance Review*. 2012; 17(1):11–17.

20 Huygens, C. Reputational value symmetry. *Mission: Intangible*, 4 February 2012. Available at: http://www.iafinance.org/_blog/MISSION_INTANGIBLE/post/Reputational_Value_Symmetry/. Accessed 13 October 2012.

21 Davies PJ. Insurance for groups to restore reputations. *Financial Times*. 8 May 2011. Available at: http://www.ft.com/intl/cms/s/0/8a61e98a-79a3-11e0-86bd-00144feabdc0.html#axzz22rXUquye. Accessed 8 August 2012.

22 Global corporate reputation index finds major brands lag citizenship qualities. Press Release. WPP. 27 January 2012.

23 Reece D. Sir Martin Sorrell's pay in dock but it's WPP board who should take the blame. *The Telegraph*. 13 June 2012. Available at: http://www.telegraph.co.uk/finance/comment/damianreece/9330589/Sir-Martin-Sorrells-pay-in-dock-but-its-WPP-board-who-should-take-the-blame.html. Accessed 8 August 2012.

24 Gaines-Ross L. CEO reputation still going strong. *CEO.com*. 3 May 2012. Available at: www.ceo.com/flink/?lnk=http%3A%2F%2Freputationxchange.com%2F2012%2F05%2F03%2Fceo-reputation-still-going-strong%2F. Accessed 8 August 2012.

25 WPP investors vote against pay package of CEO Martin Sorrell. *Bloomberg*. 13 June 2012. Available at: http://www.bloomberg.com/news/2012-06-13/wpp-investors-vote-against-pay-package-of-chief-martin-sorrell.html\. Accessed 8 August 2012.

26 Gaines-Ross L. Resetting CEO reputation. *Huffington Post*. 11 November 2009. Available at: www.huffingtonpost.com/dr-leslie-gainesross/resetting-ceo-reputation_b_354147.html. Accessed 8 August 2012.

27 Gaines-Ross L. Timing is everything in reputation. reputationXchange. 8 August 2012. Available at: reputationxchange.com. Accessed 8 August 2012.

Chapter 7 | Equity Investors

28 Lawless J. Ex-RBS CEO Fred Goodwin stripped of knighthood. *Huffington Post.* 31 January 2012. Available at: http://www.huffingtonpost.com/huff-wires/20120131/eu-britain-rbs/. Accessed 8 August 2012.

29 Knowledge is power. Sir Francis Bacon, *Religious Meditations, Of Heresies*, 1597. Cited in The Quotations Page. Available at: http://www.quotationspage.com/quote/2060.html. Accessed 10 August 2012.

30 Tabuchi H. Japanese shareholders starting to show their teeth. *The New York Times.*27 June 2012. Available at: http://www.nytimes.com/2012/06/28/business/global/japanese-shareholders-starting-to-show-their-teeth.html?pagewanted=all. Accessed 10 August 2012.

31 The shareholder spring: investor revolts in 2012. *Financial News.* 8 August 2012. Available at: http://www.efinancialnews.com/gallery/in-pictures-shareholder-revolts/3. Accessed 8 August 2012.

32 Davidoff SM. Furor over executive pay is not the revolt it appears to be. *New York Times.* 1 May 2012. Available at: http://dealbook.nytimes.com/2012/05/01/furor-over-executive-pay-is-not-the-revolt-it-appears-to-be/. Accessed 3 September 2012.

33 Schuffham M, Bart K. Credit Suisse and Barclays investors revolt over pay. *Reuters.* 27 April 2012. Available at: http://www.reuters.com/article/2012/04/27/us-barclays-creditsuisse-agm-idUSBRE83Q0VP20120427. Accessed 10 August 2012.

34 Gongloff M. Bank shareholders' executive pay revolt no match for big returns. *Huffington Post.* 7 May 2012. Available at: http://www.huffingtonpost.com/2012/05/07/say-on-banker-pay_n_1496133.html. Accessed 10 August 2012.

35 Brady D. Say on pay: boards listen when shareholders speak. *Bloomberg Businessweek.* 7 June 2012. Available at: http://www.businessweek.com/articles/2012-06-07/say-on-pay-boards-listen-when-shareholders-speak. Accessed 10 August 2012.

36 Quinlivan S. Disney at odds with ISS again: Making sense of Dodd-Frank. 1 March 2012. Available at: http://dodd-frank.com/disney-at-odds-with-iss-again/. Accessed 10 August 2012.

37 Frankel A. Shareholder spring? Not so much, new study says. *Reuters.* 8 June 2012. Available at: http://blogs.reuters.com/alison-frankel/2012/06/08/shareholder-spring-not-so-much-new-study-says/. Accessed 10 August 2012.

38 Sandler RJ. Mid-season update on the 2012 proxy season. *Harvard Law School Forum on Corporate Governance and Financial Regulation.* 7 June 2012. Available at: http://blogs.law.harvard.edu/corpgov/2012/06/07/mid-season-update-on-the-2012-proxy-season/. Accessed 10 August 2012.

39 Cincinnati Bell settles 'say on pay' shareholder suit. *Business Courier.* 21 December 2011. Available at: http://www.bizjournals.com/cincinnati/news/2011/12/21/cincinnati-bell-settles-say-on-pay.html. Accessed 10 August 2012.

40 Chasan E. Say-on-pay turns into sue-on-pay. *Wall Street Journal.* 30 June 2011. Available at: http://blogs.wsj.com/cfo/2011/06/30/say-on-pay-turns-into-sue-on-pay/. Accessed 10 August 2012.

41 Liebman P. How reputation drives principled performance. Mission Intangible Monthly Briefing, 1 April 2011. Audio recordings available from the Intangible Asset Finance Society. Available at: http://iafinance.org/monthly-briefings. Accessed 5 October 2012.

Reputation, Stock Price, and You

42 Lipman FD. Intangible incentives: compensation and corporate performance. Mission Intangible Monthly Briefing. 13 January 2012. Audio recordings available from the Intangible Asset Finance Society, http://iafinance.org/monthly-briefings. Accessed 5 October 2012.

43 Russell D. Be ruthless with reputation. *PR Week*. 3 November 2011. Available at: http://www.prweek.com/uk/league_tables/1100806/dean-russell-fleishman-hillard-ruthless-reputation/. Accessed 3 July 2012.

CHAPTER

8

Boards of Directors

This has now turned into a reputation matter, a financial squeeze for BP, and a political matter, and that is why you will now see more of me. As this is now turning to a different type of crisis, that is where I come in.

—Carl-Henric Svanberg, Chairman BP[1]

Elected by shareholders, the board of directors in a stock corporation is the highest management authority. Its most critical duties are to select and compensate senior management, protect the assets of the corporation, and approve strategy—the company's approach to marshaling and deploying resources to meet corporate objectives. Each of these duties leads to corporate actions that establish a company's reputation among its various stakeholders.

Governance is the umbrella term for processes that boards use to execute their duties. *Culture*, an expression of corporate values, gives tone to governance—often called the *tone at the top*—and is ultimately reflected in reputation.[2] Bob Diamond, Barclays' former chief executive, directly referred to "culture" 50 times as he testified for three hours before a House of Commons committee about the U.K. bank's role in the industry-wide rigging of benchmark interest rates.

Writing tongue-in-cheek for the *Financial Times*, Andrew Hill observed:

> There is a lot of it about. Culture was the "secret sauce" at Goldman Sachs, of which there is now "virtually no trace", according to Greg Smith, a disgruntled former employee of the US investment bank. The "ingrained conventions of Japanese culture" were behind the crisis at the tsunami-hit Fukushima nuclear

Chapter 8 | Boards of Directors

plant, says the man chairing the probe into the disaster. British pharmaceutical group GlaxoSmithKline has made "a culture of putting patients first" a priority, having clamped down on aggressive selling and marketing of blockbuster drugs that this month resulted in a $3 billion settlement with the US government.[3]

Today, governance needs to demand a culture sensitive to corporate reputation. As shown earlier, the ability of a company to bring products and services to market and generate greater revenues and lower costs is directly linked to a company's reputation. "An executive team's understanding of this aspect of business is central to their stewardship of the company's assets," observed Aron Cramer, President and CEO of BSR, a corporate social responsibility consultancy.[4]

Ultimately, the board is where the buck stops with regard to corporate culture. Eternal vigilance must be a watchword, since even the top performers can fall from grace. In fact, they are often the most at risk, since their behaviors tend to become unconscious and automatic and may reduce the ability of the organization to adapt to changes in the business environment.

Oversight is a board-level responsibility, but it is undeniably a managerial process. This chapter shows how sensitivity to what's at stake in reputation risk can inform board-level actions. To both remain informed and enable stakeholders to appreciate and value their efforts, boards will find the tools introduced in this chapter particularly helpful as they select and compensate senior management, protect the assets of the corporation, and approve strategy in the context of corporate reputation.

Say-on-Pay: Compensation Committee

Heading the list of the top 10 compensation committee agenda items for 2012 published by Pearl Meyer & Partners, the executive compensation firm, is the charge to "understand your company's pay-for-performance linkage."[5] "The starting point is to really understand company strategy and the key metrics that drive it," advises Simon Patterson, Managing Director.[6] "Use industry-relevant performance metrics that support the short- and long-term business objectives of the company and creation of shareholder value," adds John L. Anderson, lead senior executive compensation consultant at Meridian Compensation Partners.[6] Ann Murray, partner at McKenna Long & Aldridge LLP, a law firm, warns that boards need to act defensively and anticipate shareholder reaction. "Failed" say-on-pay votes triggered derivative litigation against directors in about 20% of the cases in 2011.[7]

The case studies that follow show how sensitivity to reputation evolved to become a central pillar of corporate strategy; it represents 11% of the CEO's bonus compensation at UBS and is factored into compensation at both JP Morgan Chase and Goldman Sachs. Metrics that report on reputation—especially reputational value metrics—have a clear role in supporting the board's execution of its duties of compensating key executives and driving shareholder value.

There are also compelling personal reasons. "Personal reputation risk, being sued, being challenged by regulators, being challenged by shareholders" are just a few of the risks faced by compensation committee members, said Dennis Whalen, executive director of KPMG's audit committee institute.[8] Reputational value metrics can help boards explain their compensation packages to stakeholders, and they can help protect the directors' personal reputations and wealth.

UBS

Formed in 1998 from the merger of two Swiss giants, SBC and Union Bank of Switzerland, UBS in 2012 celebrated 150 years of banking services. It is today a world-class wealth manager, the biggest universal bank in Switzerland, and the second largest institutional asset manager globally.

2011 was a challenging year for the industry as a whole. Markets had ongoing concerns surrounding eurozone sovereign debt, the European banking system, the U.S. federal budget deficit, and economic growth issues—all of which affected client confidence. Activity levels were subdued as investors sought out safe-haven investments and remained on the sidelines of markets for most of the second half of the year.[9]

At UBS, although profits were depressed, they were present until a surprise $2.3 billion loss was acknowledged in September 2011. That's when UBS revealed that a rogue trader had lost a quantity of money so large that it potentially wiped out profits for the entire quarter.[10] The trader, Kweku M. Adoboli, made speculative bets with the company's own money on various benchmarks. "Concealed" through "fictitious trades," those positions violated the firm's risk limits. The firm was surprised once more by a loss it had not anticipated, and throughout the financial community, there was an exasperated cry, as Douglas Adams, the science fiction humorist, might have written, "Oh no, not again."

In 1998, UBS had an inauspicious start as Europe's biggest bank, losing in the year of its formation CHF750 million ($520 million) and heading the league table for the largest single loser in the collapse of Long-Term Capital Management, the infamous U.S. hedge fund.[11] Among the casualties was

Chapter 8 | Boards of Directors

Chairman Mathis Cabiallavetta, who, after a tenure of only 4 months, "fell on his sword" and resigned.[12]

The 21st century brought more drama. While the go-go years of the early aughts were good for UBS, it was UBS's announcement disclosing that it was the first Wall Street firm to suffer heavy losses that marked the end of that period of irrational exuberance and the beginning of the 2007 subprime mortgage crisis. By December, UBS reported writedowns for the year of CHF21.6 billion ($18 billion).[13] UBS turned to the Government of Singapore Investment Corporation (GIC) and an unnamed investor from the Middle East for SFr19.4 billion ($17.2 billion) to shore up its balance sheet.[14] By March 2008, the writedown had grown to $37 billion, the biggest single-year loss of any company in Swiss history, and Chairman Marcel Ospel reluctantly stepped down.[15]

Before a full year had passed, UBS was expensing $780 million more in disgorgement of profits, interest, penalties, and restitution of unpaid taxes to the U.S. government.[16] The payments were part of a deferred prosecution agreement on charges of conspiring to defraud the United States by impeding the Internal Revenue Service and for failing to register with the Securities and Exchange Commission (SEC) as a broker/dealer and investment adviser for U.S. citizens. The UBS case became a centerpiece in a U.S. crackdown on offshore tax evasion.[17] With less than 1 year on the job, Chairman Peter Kurer agreed to step down.[18]

On 26 February 2009, UBS lured Oscar Grubel, a Board member at Winterthur Group, out of retirement to take over as CEO. Having spent his entire career in the banking sector, he understood the ramifications of the reputational crisis at UBS. Speaking to the company's 65,000 staff 30 months later, "From my first day on the job, I placed the reputation of the bank above all else."[19] A few months later, at the 2009 Annual General Meeting of UBS, Kaspar Villiger was elected to the Board of Directors and was soon after appointed Chairman of the Board. He served as Finance Minister and Head of the Swiss Federal Department of Finance for 8 years, until he stepped down at the end of 2003. After leaving government, he was elected to the boards of Nestlé, Swiss Re, and the Neue Zürcher Zeitung, from which he resigned in 2009 when he took on the UBS chairmanship.[20] Gruber and Villiger embarked on a major effort to transform UBS's culture into one that recognized and mitigated reputational risk.

At the same time, leaders of the G20 were holding their second summit for the year in Pittsburgh, where they endorsed the Financial Stability Board's (FSB) Principles for Sound Compensation Practices and their Implementation Standards.[21] The FSB, established in London after the 2008 global banking crisis and successor to the Financial Stability Forum formed after the 1998 global banking crisis, includes members of most key groups of finance ministries, central bankers, and international financial bodies.

FSB concluded that the banking behaviors triggering the two major crises were promoted by incentives that centralized reward but socialized risk. Convinced that a short-term bonus culture had triggered excessive risk taking before the financial crisis, they have pushed banks to align their payment structures better with risks and institutional performance.[22] The FSB proposed that compensation structures be adjusted to account for all types of risk, "including difficult to measure risks such as liquidity risk and reputation risk."[21] Another suggestion, being implemented in the United States, is to link banks' pay plans to payments made into governments' deposit insurance schemes.[23]

Grubel and Villiger recognized they had to strengthen UBS's risk culture. They used the FSB standards for making the cultural changes stick by linking reputation risk to compensation. The language and emphasis on reputational factors in the company's annual reports reflects these changes. One indicator is that the number of citations of the word *reputation* doubled to 42 mentions between the 2008 and 2009 annual reports (Figure 8-1).

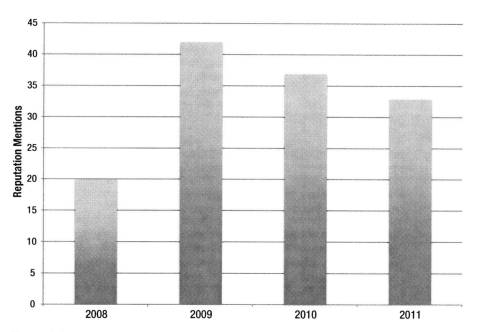

Figure 8-1. Number of mentions of the word *reputation* in UBS annual reports, 2008–2011.

Chapter 8 | Boards of Directors

More substantive are the changes in the language of the risk disclosures, risk management principles, and compensation-linked incentives. With each passing year after the crisis of 2007–2008, the prominence of reputation risk grew as the drivers of the risk became better defined. At the same time, reputation risk increasingly became a driver for the compensation of most senior executives.

The clearest insight into board values and thinking is the corporate annual report. The following table details the subtle but definite shift in language over recent years toward a reputational focus (Table 8-1).

Table 8-1a. Evolving Prominence of Reputation as a Disclosed Strategic Risk Factor in UBS's Annual Reports

	Order in List of Risk Factors	Nature of Risk
2008	Last of 11	"UBS's reputation is critical in maintaining its relationships with clients, investors, regulators and the general public."
2011	Second of 17	"Damage to our reputation can have fundamental negative effects on our business and prospects. Our reputation is critical to the success of our strategic plans. We recognize(d) that restoring our reputation …(is) essential to maintaining our relationships with clients, investors, regulators and the general public, as well as with our employees."

Table 8-1b. Evolving Prominence of Reputation Protection in Discussions of Risk Management and Control Principles in the Company's Annual Reports

	"Five pillars/key principles support our efforts to achieve an appropriate balance between risk and return"
2008	"#5- Protection of UBS's reputation depends, among other things, on the effective management and control of the risks incurred in the course of its business. All employees should make the protection of UBS's reputation an overriding concern."
2011	"#2-Reputation protection through a sound risk culture characterized by a holistic and integrated view of risk, performance and reward, and by full compliance with our standards and principles, particularly our Code of Business Conduct and Ethics."

Reputation, Stock Price, and You 171

Table 8-1c. Evolving Prominence of Reputation in the Letter from the Chair of the Human Resources and Compensation Committee in the Company's Annual ReportsFactor

	Reputation Factor	Highlights
2008	No	The final amount awarded to executives depends on their achievement of performance targets linked to long-term, risk-adjusted value creation. Three year claw-back structure for all cash bonus awards to "alter the UBS corporate culture."
2011	Yes	"While a number of improvements were made to strengthen how we identify key risk-takers and measure their performance, no specific changes were made to the overall framework in 2011. It thus offers stability and continuity, as well as the necessary features. Group Executive Board compensation factors: Group and divisional performance information, including risk-adjusted profitability and other financial and non-financial factors such as leadership effectiveness, strategy execution, and <u>reputational impact</u>. Risk Committee's involvement in compensation matters: …to ensure that compensation plans are aligned with our business strategy, and that policies are designed to enhance risk awareness and…the possibility of <u>reputational risk</u>."

Within 4 months of disclosing the September 2011 losses, Chairman Kaspar Villiger announced his decision to step down a year early, leaving UBS to face its fifth chairman in 14 years.[24] His work, however, was not done. Over the next few months, he would take two more opportunities to impact UBS's evolving culture of reputation risk awareness and management that would propel UBS ahead of the 2009 FSB standards. And he would do so with the new head of UBS's Human Resources and Compensation Committee, Ann Godbehere.

A financial sector veteran, Godbehere had been on the board with Villiger since 2009, and was known to him before then when she was CFO at Swiss Re. She had done significant repair work as interim chief financial officer and executive director of Northern Rock post-nationalization prior to joining the board at UBS. She has been a non-executive director of British American Tobacco plc since 2011, non-executive director of Atrium Underwriting Group Limited and Ariel Group Limited since 2007, non-executive director of Prudential plc since 2007, and chairman of its audit committee since 2009.[25]

On 15 November 2011, UBS appointed a new CEO who affirmed the importance of reputation management. Chatting with the media on his first official day on the job, Sergio Ermotti, the former UniCredit Deputy Chief

Chapter 8 | Boards of Directors

Executive Officer who just joined UBS in April, said, "No profit is worth more than our reputation as a bank."[26] With only 1 week before his end of tenure, on 23 April 2012, UBS Chairman Kaspar Villiger pushed both the benefits and costs of reputation right to the top. "The idea behind this is that you try to evaluate the CEO according to what's necessary for executing the company's strategy in the long term. There are nine criteria in total, of which some shall be qualitative. Reputation is one of them. It will count more than one ninth."[27]

The existing framework allows UBS "on one hand, to motivate our employees by rewarding strong performance, and on the other hand, to withdraw or reduce incentives where performance has been weak or where employees act against the interests of the firm…We will keep our framework under review to ensure that it continues to meet our key goal of aligning employee and shareholder interests," Ann Godbehere said in the lender's annual compensation report for 2011.[27] "The CEO is very much in agreement with this," Villiger said. "I would find it important that this would be done by more people."

At Barclays Bank, the new chairman, David Walker, said in August 2012 that he was undertaking a top-to-bottom review of the embattled business, telling a British newspaper that he wasn't wedded to any of his predecessor's policies.[28] Charged with rebuilding Barclays' reputation in the wake of the LIBOR (London Interbank Offered Rate) scandal, Walker said finding a new chief executive was his number one priority, though a rewrite of the bank's pay policy was also in the cards. Walker, who led a review of banking culture for the Labour government in the aftermath of the 2008 banking crisis, framed the governance priorities: "The board absolutely does not need a clearout, but it does need to be supplemented. Three significant roles have gone – the chairman, the chief executive, and the chairman of the remuneration committee."[29]

Linking Compensation to Reputation

Linking CEO compensation to corporate reputation is a natural extension of the FSB recommendations. While it is not clear all CEOs are taking as kindly to it as UBS's Ermotti, most are resigned to it. When questioned by Representative Barney Frank at a House hearing on the JP Morgan Chase losses of 2012, CEO Jamie Dimon said he did not know if he would be the subject of potential clawbacks by the board of directors that determines his compensation. "I can't tell my board what to do," Dimon told Frank.[30]

Although the CEO's compensation at JP Morgan Chase is not tied to reputation explicitly, reputation is a factor in the company's compensation plan. It's worth considering, since in the opinion of many, JP Morgan Chase is

Reputation, Stock Price, and You

still having a reputational crisis as this volume goes to press. The onslaught of regulators, litigators, and bloggers triggered by a $2 billion hedging loss in the spring of 2012 suggests that something went wrong.

Consider the conflicting interests of regulators, shareholders, management, corporate directors, and employees on the matter of incentive pay clawbacks. Similar to the UBS model and others conforming to the FSB recommendations, according to Bloomberg, JP Morgan Chase "can cancel stock awards or demand they be repaid if an employee 'engages in conduct that causes material financial or reputational harm,'" JPMorgan said in its annual proxy statement.

The same goes for Goldman Sachs. "Equity awards should be subject to vesting and other restrictions over an extended period of time. A clawback should also exist for cause, including any individual misconduct that results in legal or reputational harm."[31] JP Morgan Chase adds the teaser, "The company will claw back pay if it's appropriate. . ."[32]

"Appropriate" is a squishy word. The market wants to know what formula will be used to convert the magnitude of the alleged damage into the magnitude of clawbacks, and when, after the alleged damage was precipitated, the magnitude of the damage will be assessed. Remember that millions of dollars of compensation and bonus pay are at risk. Bloomberg reported that "New York City Comptroller John Liu said that JP Morgan should tell shareholders it will 'aggressively claw back every single dollar possible from the executives responsible for the $2 billion loss.'" Employees subject to the clawback will probably have other opinions.

JP Morgan Chase's corporate directors will find little comfort in subjective measures of reputation, caught as they are between regulators on one hand and litigators on the other—employees and investors tend to speak through litigators. This means that the company's directors' and officers' insurance carriers are no doubt wishing that the directors would turn to objective measures and establish standards before they effect a clawback. More generally, every corporate board of directors that has identified reputation to be material to their company's business should be seeking a solution to their need for objective reputation metrics, if only to preempt future issues.

Fund managers and financial advisers, given the prevalence of concern about reputation risk, would also like objective measures. Auditors would no doubt appreciate objective measures as well, not only in the context of controls, but also because reputation has now been identified as a driver of liquidity. Even communications professionals would likely find better ways to shape the stories surrounding JP Morgan Chase—and every other publicly traded client company—if they had objective measures of reputation.

Chapter 8 | Boards of Directors

Reputational value metrics today are essential managerial and oversight tools. They objectify what would otherwise be subjective decisions at risk for being second-guessed. Moreover, they apprise the market of the status of an asset increasingly felt to be a vital part of a company's value.

Many different stakeholders today need quantitative reputational value metrics for a wide range of core business activities. Since companies have already disclosed the materiality of reputation risks, they have opened the door to reputational management. In our culture, we tend to manage that which we can measure. As the JP Morgan Chase clawback issue shows, the need to adopt quantitative measures of reputation is a time-sensitive matter for many stakeholders.

Consider This

- Linking reputation and compensation at the highest levels of a corporation is at the top of today's best practices for driving a reputation-focused risk culture throughout the organization.

- Linking compensation and clawbacks to a company's reputation requires reputational value metric systems to monitor, measure, and report reputation.

Asset Protection

Accountants may struggle with the valuation of reputation, but most corporate directors have long accepted that it is a vital corporate asset. Leslie Gaines Ross, chief reputation strategist for Weber Shandwick, a public relations agency, explained to *Forbes*: "In certain industries, it's 90% trust and reputation, like in the financial services industry...It's like health care companies, or pharmaceutical companies, airlines. If you don't trust an airline, you're not going to fly it."[33] In other words, in certain industries, a lost reputation is tantamount to a fatal enterprise-level wound.

Unlike other corporate assets, however, reputation is damaged through the interplay of a failed business process, adverse publicity, and stakeholder expectations. Above and beyond implementing business process controls, protecting corporate reputation value may include waging an active battle with activists for the hearts and minds of stakeholders.

In the *Harvard Business Review* article, "Reputation Warfare," Gaines Ross wrote: "Companies trying to protect their good names are increasingly coming under assault from small-scale antagonists: dissatisfied customers, disgruntled employees—virtually anyone with a personal computer and an ax to grind."[34] It is a battle well known to the Walt Disney Company, whose "brand asset" is valued at $29 billion.[35]

Modern communication strategies—empower your team, respond promptly, and embrace social media—are all fine and good, but as shown in the study below, asymmetric warfare demands additional strategies. They are, according to Gaines-Ross, stockpiling credentials for future use, avoiding disproportionate show-of-force, and finding sympathetic third parties to serve as "force multipliers."

To stockpile credentials, companies need to establish an authentic reputation—a goal whose value has been demonstrated throughout this volume. To show force—marketing and legal muscle—proportionately, companies need a scorecard to measure the reputational impact of an attack. Reputational value metrics, discussed at length in Chapters 9 and 12 and earlier in this chapter, can inform show-of-force strategies.

There's much to be said about the value of sympathetic third parties, but in the court of public opinion, the opinions of such third parties are discounted because they are known to be, well, sympathetic. There's more to be said about the value of dispassionate third parties. In the next section, the value of insurances, a staple of markets with asymmetric information, is explored in the context of a dispassionate communications strategy. After all, as an editorial in *Corporate Board Member* helpfully reminded its readers, "The most important insurance is sleep insurance–knowing that your personal and corporate assets are covered in the event of a crisis."[36]

The Walt Disney Company

Robert A. Iger was celebrating his 14th month as CEO of The Walt Disney Company when he received a fax from Hong Kong just in time for Christmas 2006. The cover memo concluded ominously, "We look forward to discussing with you the improvement of labor conditions in Disney supplier factories in China and elsewhere on or before December 22."[37] Attached to the five-page memo was a 31-page report entitled, *A Second Attempt at Looking for Mickey Mouse's Conscience: A Survey of the Working Conditions of Disney's Supplier Factories in China.*

Iger had risen through Disney's ranks on the Capital Cities/ABC Television side of the company and previously had served as President and COO. Since January 2000, he had been deeply aware of the ethical labor challenge in China, and, in December of that year, CBC Marketplace received reports from human rights activists documenting the unethical practices in Disney factories in China. CBC's broadcast that month described a report called *The*

Chapter 8 | Boards of Directors

Secret Life of Toys alleging sweatshop conditions. Although the major toy distributors employed inspectors to monitor labor conditions, the monitoring was felt to be flawed. According to Jenny Chan, "In a recent report on child labour, UNICEF revealed that young factory workers in developing countries are often hidden in closets or stuffed into boxes when monitors arrive to inspect the premises."[38]

The letter's author had launched the Hong Kong–based labor watchdog group, Students & Scholars Against Corporate Misbehavior (SACOM), in 2005. SACOM's inaugural report, the 32-page *Looking for Mickey Mouse's Conscience: A Survey of the Working Conditions of Disney's Supplier Factories in China*, called attention to 10 international labor standards violations:

- High occurrence of occupational injuries and accidents
- Violations of women workers' rights
- Wages well below the local legal minimum
- Nontransparent and problematic wage calculations
- Long working hours
- Terrible work environment on the shop floor
- Poor living environment
- Horrible food
- False trails of factory inspection
- Restrictions on resignation with 45 days of wages held in security

During the first year of Iger's tenure as CEO, SACOM went on a media offensive. It made an 11-minute documentary film, *Those with Justice—A Disney Factory in China*, jointly produced with Sweatshop Watch, "to visualize the collective struggles of the workers based in Shenzhen," released through press conferences in Hong Kong and New York in coordination with the National Labor Committee, currently known as the Institute for Global Labour and Human Rights headquartered in Pittsburgh. It had earned its stripes by exposing alleged Disney-associated labor violations in Bangladesh in 2004.[39]

In January 2006, SACOM successfully nominated The Walt Disney Company for the Public Eye Award 2006 in the category "social rights" (human and labor rights). The Public Eye Awards, according to the group's promotional materials, "mark a critical counterpoint to the annual meeting of the World Economic Forum (WEF) in Davos. Organized since 2000 by Berne Declaration and Friends of the Earth (in 2009 replaced by Greenpeace), Public Eye reminds

Reputation, Stock Price, and You | 177

the corporate world that social and environmental misdeeds have consequences—for the affected people and territory, but also for the reputation of the offender."[40] The 2006 Award, which Disney shared with Citigroup, the banking conglomerate, stated:

> *Serious labor and human rights violations by Walt Disney subcontractors tarnish the carefree image that the entertainment giant tries to present to us through its films and cartoon figures. However the company does not publish the names of its suppliers in China and therefore prevents the verification of working conditions through independent inspectors. SACOM calls on Walt Disney to publish the names of its suppliers and to allow independent NGOs to make regular inspections of their operations.*

SACOM organized a coalition of the committed. The growing list of strategic partners of SACOM included the National Labor Committee, United Students Against Sweatshops, Writers Guild of America—West and East, Sweatshops Watch, Clean Clothes Campaign—Austria, and Réseau-Solidarité—France. In August 2005, the media campaign against Disney broke into the mainstream. One of the videos produced by SACOM landed at the Cable News Network (CNN). Disney said in a statement that its officials "have conducted approximately 20 ILS audits at these factories since 1998."[41]

In fact, by August 2005, The Walt Disney Company's labor standards department was liaising with some 6,000 licensees and vendors and had conducted more than 40,000 audits since 1996. Jim Leung, Walt Disney Company Regional Director of International Labour Standards, met with SACOM and other Hong Kong–based labor coalitions, followed by three more meetings by early January 2006. Nevertheless, the December 2006 SACOM report "revealed gross violations of Chinese labour laws and international codes of conduct relating to work safety and compensation at seven factories that manufactured Disney merchandise in southern China,"[42] and closed with a demand that Disney order its factory representatives to:

- Consult with SACOM and concerned labor groups to provide workers with training programs

- Work out a detailed timetable for participatory training

- Support democratic elections run by workers for the establishment of Workers' Committees

- Collaborate with workers in factory monitoring for the long term

Frustrated with the results of its efforts to effect changes at factories producing its goods, Disney pulled its business. Disney released a statement

Chapter 8 | Boards of Directors

that it had been working with both the licensee and the factory for many months and that "notwithstanding multiple offers by Disney to help the licensee and factory to improve standards, the licensee has chosen to walk away."[42] Because Disney represented 80% of the factory's business, 5 weeks after SACOM's deadline for action, the 800 workers at Huang Xing Light Manufacturing factory in Shenzhen in southern China were dismissed and the factory closed. SACOM criticized Disney's actions as "cut and run." Said Chan: "This is the worst response to workers' rights violations. Disney must take responsibility for the labour rights violations carried out by its suppliers."

Wal-Mart, with well publicized labor issues at around the same time, was losing an estimated 6% top-line sales from potential customers who refused to shop at the retailer out of ethical considerations. It is not clear what economic effects conscience-consumerism and the SACOM campaign had at that time on The Walt Disney Company. But Disney clearly recognized that it was going to be criticized for supporting exploitative factories, and also for abandoning exploitative factories. That criticism targeted the authenticity of the Disney brand, and placed the company's reputation at risk.

Reputation Protection

The strong consumer brand that underpins Disney's value is based on a reputation for child-friendly family value–based entertainment. Disney's board of directors has long appreciated that Disney's reputation confers pricing power, enhances sales volume, helps control employee- and supplier-related expenses, and helps reduce the cost of capital.

Matthew Ryan, Disney Senior Vice President, Brand, Franchise, & Customer Relationship Management, explained in 2001, "a strong consumer brand like Disney is invaluable in attracting the right kind of people to the company: people come to Disney because they love the brand and want to contribute to its legacy…Everyone who works here knows the high standards the Disney brand requires, and that compels our employees whether they are front-line cast members or senior executives, to think through all decisions from the perspective of brand impact. We have a culture that encourages creativity and wise risk-taking, but the cardinal rule we have is to never do anything that will harm the brand."[35]

By late 2005, Disney's kind of leadership in corporate reputation protection was becoming widespread. Enterprise risk managers from multiple companies were increasingly responding to the dark side—reputation risk—as a threat to survival. The Economist Intelligence Unit (EUI) produced a report entitled "Reputation: Risk of Risks" based on surveys of 269 risk managers in companies of varied size.[43] The following were the key findings:

Reputation, Stock Price, and You

- *Corporate reputation is a prized and highly vulnerable corporate asset.*

- *Reputation risk is the single most significant threat to global business operations.*

- *Companies struggle to categorize—let alone quantify—reputational risk.*

In 2007, the Conference Board, the business membership, and research association recommended that boards of directors should:[44]

- *Reach a common understanding of the concept of corporate reputation and tie its discussion to a comprehensive analysis of the firm's stakeholder base.*

- *Become familiar with management's rationale for prioritizing stakeholder relations and be persuaded that the selected relations are instrumental to achieving the firm's long-term objectives.*

- *Discuss and understand the nature of reputation risk as an effect of certain business operational incidents, not a separate and distinct category of uncertainties.*

- *Oversee the design and implementation of a strategic, top-down, and holistic risk management program where all business events with potential consequences on the firm's reputation capital are identified and measured.*

- *Consider adhering to The Conference Board Road Map to Risk Governance to embed reputation risk oversight into a comprehensive risk management program.*

In 2009, the Conference Board returned to the subject of reputation risk,[45] reporting on a survey of 148 executives from companies around the world. Fifty-nine percent indicated that assessing the perceptions and concerns of stakeholders was an extremely or very significant issue, making it the highest-ranked challenge. McKinsey & Company, a management consultancy, asserted that companies had to step up their reputation management efforts: "A company's reputation has begun to matter more now than it has in decades. Companies and industries with reputation problems are more likely to incur the wrath of legislators, regulators, and the public."[46] It's not just talk. "Reputations are built on a foundation not only of communications but also of deeds: stakeholders can see through PR that isn't supported by real and consistent business activity."

A 2009 Blue Ribbon Report on Risk Governance from the National Association of Corporate Directors (NACD) issued a regulatory conversation on requirements for a board-level risk committee with the conclusion that

Chapter 8 | Boards of Directors

delegating to a committee is part of the problem, and recommended that the whole board should take ownership of risk oversight.[47] The Committee of Sponsoring Organizations of the Treadway Commission (COSO), a joint initiative of five accounting societies, produced its own rather audit-centric template.[48] In November 2009, the International Standards Organization (ISO) released ISO 31000:2009–Risk management–Principles and guidelines (US/EU/Other). This standard provides principles, framework, and a process for managing any form of risk in a transparent, systematic, and credible manner within any scope or context.[49] Also in 2009, Standard & Poor's began integrating enterprise risk management issues into credit ratings.[50]

With reputation risk slowly being appreciated as a consequence of operational risk, more corporate boards began to understand its materiality. A brief surge after the Sarbanes-Oxley legislation showed that 99 (20%) of the S&P 500 constituent members disclosed the materiality of reputation risk, but the annual count tapered to a low of 32 (6%) in 2007, and by 2009, the number had risen only slightly to 11%. That year, new rules by the U.S. SEC on required disclosures about corporate risk management shifted responsibility for enterprise risk to the level of the board.[51,52] By the next year, the fraction was up to 32%; and, as of June 2012, 71% of the S&P 500 index constituent members disclosed that reputation risk was material to their business (Figure 8-2).

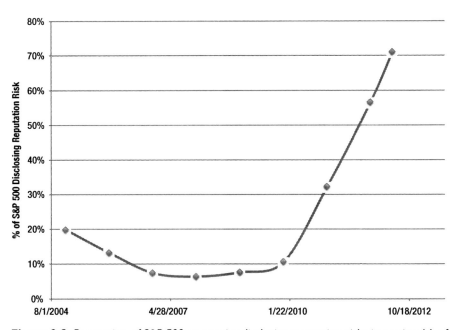

Figure 8-2. Proportion of S&P 500 companies disclosing reputation risks in section 1A of their annual 10K SEC filing.,

Reputation, Stock Price, and You

For members of corporate boards, reputation risk is personal. Under longstanding precepts of corporate law, the business and affairs of a corporation are managed by its board of directors. The board has authority to appoint officers who assume day-to-day management functions under the direction of the board. Directors and officers, in turn, are bound by fiduciary duties to shareholders, generally entailing affirmative, open-ended obligations to act in the best interest of the corporation and its shareholders.

There are two categories of fiduciary duties: the duty of care and the duty of loyalty. As Cathy Reese explains in *Corporate Finance Review*[53]:

> *The duty of care requires that directors and officers exercise disinterested due care in decision making, and act on an informed basis...Further, corporations can indemnify officers and directors against personal liability for losses that the corporation incurs resulting from decisions made in breach of the duty of care.*

> *The duty of loyalty requires that directors and officers serve the interests of the corporation and its shareholders with undivided allegiance. Unlike the duty of care, corporations are not permitted to indemnify officers and directors against personal liability for breaches of the duty of loyalty.*

Provided a director did not breach the duty of loyalty by "standing on both sides" of a transaction in order to benefit personally, Delaware's Business Judgment Rule provided assurance that courts would not second-guess the wisdom or the propriety of their decisions, even if they turn out in retrospect to have been improvident. That safe harbor has been offering directors and officers increasingly less shelter as the implications of two decisions separated by a decade have been appreciated by the market.

The Delaware court's review of *In re Caremark International Inc. Derivative Litigation* in 1996 established the duty of oversight as one expression of the duty of care and ruled that directors should be held liable for directorial indecision as well as the directorial decision.[54] "Specifically, the court said that the board, including officers, could be held liable for 'unconscionable failures of the board to act in circumstances in which due attention would arguably have prevented the loss'—so that's a failure of the board to act—'or in circumstances in which loss eventuates not from a decision but from unconsidered in action.'"[55] This duty of oversight applies to all corporate assets, including reputation. Ten years later, the Delaware Supreme Court upped the ante by formally approving the directors' duty of oversight but upgrading its importance to an expression of the duty of loyalty. "The court is essentially saying in these oversight liability cases that you can't avail yourself of the Business Judgment Rule if you exercise no judgment," added Reese.

Chapter 8 | Boards of Directors

To underscore that point, in December 2010, a shareholder group filed suit against the board as well as managers of Johnson & Johnson, the once-venerated health care conglomerate, for an unspecified amount alleging failure to uphold their duty of oversight, breaching their duty of loyalty, and allowing adverse events to proceed that inevitably "destroyed the company's hard earned reputation."

The suit followed nearly 2 years of adverse publicity arising from the failure of one business process or another: ethical breaches, quality failures, and safety recalls by the bucketful. The depth and breadth of the failures affirms a certain this-is-not-your-father's-Buick sensibility about Johnson & Johnson today.

According to Tony Chapelle, who reports for the *Financial Times' Agenda Week*: "Governance experts say that J&J's board should step in and more closely oversee the company's business processes in three vital areas: quality, safety and ethics." In the spring of 2012, Warren Buffet's Berkshire Hathaway joined in the conversation by cutting its investments in Johnson & Johnson by almost two-thirds to $700 million.[56]

A 2012 review compiled 18 case studies of companies that suffered various crises between 1999 and 2009.[57] The high-profile companies were selected so that there was full maturity in the consequences, explained Professor Alan Punter, one of the authors. The companies included AIG, Arthur Andersen, BP, Cadbury Schweppes, Enron, Firestone, Northern Rock, and Société Générale. Said Punter, "The consequences were fairly severe, and that's just the measurable ones"[58]:

- In 7 cases out of the 18 cases studies, the company collapsed and/or faced a government rescue (AIG, Arthur Andersen, Enron, Independent Insurance, Land of Leather, Northern Rock, and Network rail).

- In 11 cases, the chairman or CEO lost his job.

- In 16 cases, the company and/or senior executives were fined.

- In 4 cases, senior management or board members were jailed.

Corporate directors, when asked, readily disclose their personal concerns about reputation risk. A 2012 survey by the accounting and audit firm Eisner and Amper reported that around 70% of corporate directors identified reputational risk as the most important risk to their boards, noting that reputational risk had overtaken compliance risk as the number one concern. The study observed that "this percentage skyrockets with the addition of their concerns about the elements of reputational risk which include IT risk, product risk, outsourcing risk, privacy and data security, and risk due to

Reputation, Stock Price, and You

fraud."[59] Similarly, a 2011 Lloyd's Risk Index review of 500 C-suite board level executives showed that reputational risk had risen to the 3rd ranking, up from 9th in 2009.[60]

Managing reputation risk is first an operational concern. By direction of the board, several companies have created operational units focused on reputational risk. Goldman Sachs' firm-wide business practice committee (and subordinate regional and divisional committees) monitor and oversee reputational and operational risk events affecting the firm. Scenario analysis is one of the tools they use, employing operational risk expertise within its broader risk management framework. According to its global co-heads of operational risk management, Mark D'Arcy and Spyro Karetsos, now Principal, Enterprise Risk and Control, Vanguard: "While it is not our responsibility to quantify reputational risk, there is an internal process that measures our exposure to those risks that are difficult to quantify, one of which is reputational risk."[61]

Capital One Financial established a department of corporate reputation and governance almost a decade ago. Led by the company's general counsel (who reports directly to CEO Richard Fairbank), the department includes the legal, corporate affairs, regulatory affairs, audit, and government affairs functions of the firm. "We built a discipline for including reputation risk assessments into business decision-making across the enterprise," said Richard Woods, Capital One's senior vice president of corporate affairs.[62]

According to Willis, the insurance brokerage and intermediary, 95% of major corporations in the last 20 years have suffered at least one serious reputation-damaging event based on a survey of 600 publicly held companies. The research used precipitous and sustained loss of market capitalization as a proxy for reputation loss, and showed that these companies had faced 1,853 crisis events, of which 50% were due to a failure of the company's strategy or business model.[63]

For risks to asset value that cannot be otherwise mitigated, there are insurances. Starting in 2011, a number of companies began offering insurance products for reputation risk. Two principal types of coverage are available, all in the $100 million limit range. First are communications solutions, offered by underwriters in cooperation with PR/Communications groups, which provide outsized indemnifications for crisis communications expenses. Underwriters include AIG, Zurich/Aon, and Willis. Second is a reputation value loss policy, offered solely by underwriters in cooperation with Steel City Re, the parent firm of the author. This provides indemnifications for losses due to business process failures that generate adverse publicity. Losses are indexed to an independent measurable parameter—changes in the companies' reputational value metrics.

Chapter 8 | Boards of Directors

Under a parametric system, claim payments are triggered by the occurrence of a specific event that can be objectively verified, such as a hurricane reaching a certain wind speed or an earthquake reaching a certain ground shaking threshold. Underwriting and claims management are greatly simplified.[64]

Losses under Reputational Value Insurance are capped at the lesser of policy limits or fractions of the policy limits depending on the value of the parameter—the magnitude of change of the insured's reputational value metrics.

Insurance is available only to companies that demonstrate they are in control of the business processes whose failures are likely to generate adverse media coverage and reputational events. A useful analogy for the constraint is in fire insurance, a common property insurance product, where measures such as sprinklers and fire extinguishers are required as a condition of underwriting the policy.

Three examples illustrate companies that should consider insurance for reputational value risk:

- When a company has achieved iconic status or is a brand leader, its stakeholders possess elevated expectations. On the downside, its detractors have a more vulnerable target. Iconic firms are preferred targets for activists whose claims, even if libelous, attract significant media attention. Reputational Value Insurance provides a means of independently and credibly refuting false claims, because the insurance fosters reputation-enhancing behaviors and actually protects against losses caused by rogue activities.

- A company may be in a commercial sector that has overarching reputational challenges, where management wishes to differentiate the business from its peers. In a reputationally challenged sector, qualifying for Reputational Value Insurance provides an independent and credible means for signaling exceptional status.

- When a company is recovering from a reputational event, management wishes to signal rehabilitation. The three-step process that is required by the insurance enables stakeholders to recognize that risks going forward are greatly reduced. Qualifying for Reputational Value Insurance informs stakeholders that the business is rehabilitated.

Reputational Value Insurance can be a visible part of the management of reputation risk because it can be readily observed, understood, and valued by all stakeholders.

Since the 2006 letter, SACOM has expanded its range of corporate targets. According to Chan, "Our objective hasn't changed. We still want Disney and other corporations to bear their social responsibility and fulfill their obligations to ensure that workers are properly treated and labour laws are followed."[42] SACOM's Disney Project "promises to persist in monitoring and disclosing any violations of labor laws in Disney's supplier factories in China, [and hopes]... to awaken the conscience of Disney."[65]

John R. Lund, senior vice president of Disney Parks Supply Chain Management for Disney Destinations LLC, epitomizes the company's conscience. Before 2008, when Lund took the top supply chain job at Disney Destinations, the Disney arm that oversees theme parks, resorts, and cruise lines around the globe, the company's supply chain operations focused on cost containment. Now, supply chain operations focus on all six reputational pillars. The company works with suppliers it considers to be of high integrity, and has formed stronger relationships with fewer suppliers. "We have reduced the number of vendors by over 50 percent in the last four years," Lund said. He believes that supply chains can drive shareholder value by improving operating income, asset utilization, and the company's reputation. "The reputation of a company is fundamentally affected by the choices you make in running a supply chain," he said.[66]

Consider This

- Reputation is a valuable corporate asset that takes years to build and could take only moments to destroy.

- An authentic corporate culture of reputation protection engages employees with all the associated financial benefits; it helps build reputational resilience.

- An authentic corporate culture of reputation protection expresses itself in every aspect of the company's operations; reputational metric scorecards help guide the "show of force" (the deployment of marketing and legal muscle).

- Insurances can help stakeholders better appreciate and value the otherwise opaque state of the operational controls for reputation risk protection.

Chapter 8 | Boards of Directors

Business Strategy

The board's duties and responsibilities, for which they are accountable, include reviewing, approving, and guiding corporate strategy.[67] Operational surprises can play havoc with business strategy and they occur with alarming frequency. They can draw management's attention and resources away from core objectives. When they involve reputational risks, they can draw board attention, reduce revenues, and raise expenses as various stakeholders are adversely impacted.

More than two thirds of the 618 companies surveyed by Willis admitted they were caught off guard by an operational surprise "somewhat" to "extensively" in the last 5 years, and an even higher percentage for large organizations and public companies.[68] Yet when asked whether they saw proprietary advantages in integrating risk management with strategy, only 15% felt "mostly" or "extensively" while more than half replied "minimally" or "not at all."

Because the reputation of a business is a critical factor in determining its value, it is at the board level where risk management must be integrated with strategy, and where a culture for reputation risk awareness must reside.[69] Brand-centered firms such as Disney, McDonald's or Apple brought the founders' innate sense for the value of reputation into the boardroom, where it is integrated into business strategy. Rolls-Royce and Goldman Sachs have evolved this sense of reputational risk awareness. The studies below describe in greater detail how three companies—Standard Chartered plc, a financial services firm; Diageo plc, a beverage firm; and Anglo American plc, a mining concern—have integrated reputation risk management into board-level strategic oversight.

Standard Chartered plc

Although the British Empire isn't as global as it used to be, that hasn't stopped Standard Chartered, a company that traces its roots back more than 150 years, to the heyday of the Empire.[70] This U.K.-based banking group, familiarly known as Stanchart, operates primarily in Asia, the Middle East, and Africa, within some of the world's fastest-growing economies, as well as in Europe and the Americas. With more than 1,700 offices in more than 70 countries, the company operates through two business segments: consumer banking (deposit accounts, loans, cards, and investment products) and wholesale banking (capital markets, cash management, international trade, custody, and clearing services).

Differentiating Standard Chartered from the many banks that had experienced reputational crises in the past 5 years, non-executive Chairman Sir John Peace wrote: "We are different because we have a cohesive and distinctive global culture with a strong emphasis on values and leadership. Here for good, our brand promise powerfully sums up who we are and what we stand for."[71]

Standard Chartered has two dedicated board-level committees addressing reputation risk: the Board Risk Committee (BRC) and the Brand and Values Committee (BVC).

The Board Risk Committee, whose membership consists exclusively of non-executive directors of the Group, is responsible for oversight and review of prudential risks including but not limited to credit, market, capital, liquidity, operational, and reputational factors. These are the traditional "hard factors" of finance. The group's Chief Risk Officer reports to this committee.

Added in 2010, the Brand and Value Committee addresses the softer factors. Summarizing the committee's second year of operations, Chairman Paul Skinner wrote: "The Committee continues to make good progress on its key priorities including, but not limited to, the main themes of brand, customer/client focus, reputational risk, sustainability and culture and values."

According to Standard Chartered's 2011 annual report:[71]

> At each Committee meeting, the most significant and forward-looking reputational risks facing the Group are considered and reviewed. A 'heat map' is presented that sets out the forward-looking reputational risk from the lenses of multiple external stakeholders such as Socially Responsible Investors (SRIs) and Non Governmental Organisations (NGOs). The Committee has sought and received assurance from management that the mechanisms in place for monitoring reputational risk remain robust and reporting to the Committee remains fit for purpose.

The board oversees layers of operational controls where reputation risk management is defined at both the strategic and tactical level.

> The GRC provides Group-wide oversight on reputational risk, sets policy and monitors material risks. The Group Head of Corporate Affairs is the overall Risk Control Owner for reputational risk. The BRC and BVC provide additional oversight of reputational risk on behalf of the Board.

> At the business level, the Wholesale Banking Responsibility and Reputational Risk Committee and the Consumer Banking Reputational Risk Committee have responsibility for managing reputational risk in their respective businesses.

> At country level, the Country Head of Corporate Affairs is the Risk Control Owner of reputational risk. It is their responsibility to protect our reputation in that market with the support of the country management team. The Head of Corporate Affairs and Country Chief Executive Officer must actively:

_188_ **Chapter 8 | Boards of Directors**

• _Promote awareness and application of our policies and procedures regarding reputational risk_

• _Encourage business and functions to take account of our reputation in all decision-making, including dealings with customers and suppliers_

Diageo plc

Diageo plc is the leading premium spirits business in the world by volume, net sales, and operating profit. The company produces and sells 8 of the world's top 20 spirits brands and is one of the few international drinks companies that span the entire alcohol beverage market, offering beer, wine, and spirits. Diageo's well-known brands include Smirnoff vodka, Bailey's cream liqueur, Johnnie Walker Scotch whisky, José Cuervo tequila, Tanqueray gin, Captain Morgan rum, Guinness beer, and wines from Sterling Vineyards and Beaulieu Vineyard.[72]

Diageo's products are sold in more than 180 markets around the world. In many countries, there are cultural stigmas associated with its products, and in most countries antisocial behavior is associated with socially irresponsible consumption of its products. Protecting its reputation is central to its ability to enjoy the active support of "customers, consumers and suppliers, together with the confidence of their other stakeholders," wrote its non-executive Chairman Dr. Franz B. Hume. "There can be no compromise on our values and standards of integrity. In the last three years we have devoted much time and energy to ensure that all our employees understand that Diageo must have complete compliance with the high standards of behaviour laid out in our Code of Conduct."[73]

The company's corporate governance report shows reputational risk awareness and the importance of internal controls and risk management in engineering resilience into the system:

> _Diageo's aim is to manage risk and to control its business and financial activities cost-effectively and in a manner that enables it to: exploit profitable business opportunities in a disciplined way; avoid or reduce risks that can cause loss, reputational damage or business failure; support operational effectiveness; and enhance resilience to external events.... Risk management and internal control processes encompass activity to mitigate financial, operational, compliance and reputational risk._

Enterprise-level reputational concerns map into its supply chain management strategies:

> _Responsible sourcing is critical to maintaining Diageo's positive reputation and meeting customers' and consumers' demands. To this end, Diageo manages_

Reputation, Stock Price, and You

social and ethical risk, ranging from labour and human rights to commercial integrity, through a four-stage screening and auditing process. Diageo's expectations of business ethics and sustainability are made clear to suppliers. Minimum compliance and ethics standards as well as aspirational goals are set out in Diageo's Partnering with Suppliers Standards. Additionally, Diageo plays a leading role in AIM-PROGRESS, the collaborative consumer goods sector forum working to improve processes and standards in a more effective way through member organisations' supply chains.

In the year ended 30 June 2011, Diageo launched its Sustainable Agriculture Sourcing Guidelines and subsequently worked to determine how the guidelines could help support broader sustainable development, focusing first on cream. As a part of this initiative, Diageo helped its main cream supplier in Ireland create their sustainability programme, including an advisory committee, on which Diageo sits along with members of the private, independent and public sectors, to help drive sustainability performance in the Irish dairy farming industry.

Anglo American plc

Anglo American's name might be a little misleading—it has never been American.[74] Founded in 1917, the U.K.-based company owns significant stakes in global producers of platinum (75% of Anglo Platinum) and diamonds (45% of De Beers S.A.). Anglo American also has interests in ferrous and base metals and industrial minerals. It ranks among the world's largest iron ore producers and is also a leading copper producer. It is one of the world's largest coal miners and exporters of metallurgical coal, a key raw material in steel production, and also produces thermal coal, used to generate electricity. The founding Oppenheimer family no longer controls Anglo American.

"Good governance," writes non-executive chairman Sir John Parker, "is not merely following a set of rules, but ensuring that the highest standards of behaviour begin at board level and flow throughout the organisation."[75]

"The management of risk is critical to the success of Anglo American," writes David Challen, Chairman of the Audit Committee. "The Group is exposed to a variety of risks which can have a financial, operational, or reputational impact. Effective management of risk supports the delivery of the Group's objectives and achievement of sustainable growth....Understanding our key risks and developing appropriate responses is critical to our future success. We are committed to a robust system of risk identification and an effective response to such risks."[75]

The company in their annual report of 2011 recognizes the direct link between employee behavior and reputation among various stakeholders.

Chapter 8 | Boards of Directors

- *We are committed to our people, who determine how effectively we operate and build our reputation with our investors, partners, and fellow employees every day, and whom we require to uphold our values.*

- *Effective management of occupational health protects our people, enhances productivity, and helps maintain our license to operate and our global reputation.*

Anglo American pays significant attention to the reputational impact of nearly every operational risk.

- *Operational performance and project delivery impact. Failure to meet project delivery timetables and budgets may affect operational performance, delay cash inflows, increase capital costs and reduce profitability, as well as have a negative impact on the Group's reputation.*

- *Infrastructure impact. Failure to obtain supporting facilities may affect the sustainability and growth of the business, leading to loss of competitiveness, market share and reputation.*

- *Failure of rail or port facilities may result in delays and increased costs as well as lost revenue and reputation with customers. Failure to procure shipping costs at competitive market rates may reduce profit margins.*

- *Business Integrity impact: Potential impacts include prosecution, fines, penalties and reputation damage.*

- *Failure to achieve expected standards of health, safety and environment performance in joint ventures impact: higher costs or lower production may result and have a bearing on operational results, asset values or the Group's reputation.*

Culture and Strategy

Family-owned enterprises are the clearest examples of organizations with inbuilt cultural strength. Partnerships are also, historically, fierce guardians of strong cultures.[3] Critics of Goldman Sachs have pinned some of the blame for the perceived decline in its old-fashioned values on its 1999 transformation from a partnership to a publicly listed company.

But while creating a culture—say, at a startup—is relatively easy, sustaining a healthy one as the company grows is more of a challenge. An exemplary company whose culture survived for years after transforming from a family business to a public company is Johnson & Johnson. The Johnson & Johnson

Reputation, Stock Price, and You

Credo protected its culture and its intense focus on the pillars of its reputation, and guided management during its security crisis of 1983.

Penned by then CEO Robert Wood Johnson shortly before the company's initial public offering in 1944, the Credo represents Johnson's philosophy about running a business. The Credo is an active part of the corporate culture and is referenced repeatedly in the Company's major operating and reporting documents. It is a statement of "corporate social responsibility" that was crafted some 40 years before the concept was popularized.

The Credo is written in the first-person plural and recognizes the company's obligations to its stakeholders. The first paragraph sets an unambiguous ethical tone from the top:[76]

"We believe our first responsibility is to the doctors, nurses, and patients, to mothers and fathers and all others who use our products and services. In meeting their needs, everything we do must be of high quality."

The Credo calls for the need to "reduce our costs in order to maintain reasonable prices" and to give suppliers and distributors "an opportunity to make a fair profit." Employees must be respected and treated with dignity, fairly compensated, and "we must provide competent management, and their actions must be just and ethical."

The Credo also acknowledges issues of sustainability and corporate citizenship: "Our final responsibility is to our stockholders. Business must make a sound profit. We must experiment with new ideas. Research must be carried on, innovative programs developed, and mistakes paid for." And, in its last line, the Credo modestly addresses what many have argued is the primary obligation of business, "When we operate according to these principles, the stockholders should realize a fair return."

The Credo and the company's positive reputation obviously served it well at that time. But the company's current saga suggests it may have mislaid the powerful Credo of its founder. The current challenges illustrate a dictum that no corporate leader can afford to neglect. Sustaining an excellent corporate reputation is a never-ending responsibility. It requires unrelenting vigilance and attention to all the processes that create reputation. Resting on laurels is not an option.

Consider This

- A mission statement can reveal much about a company's culture.

Chapter 8 | Boards of Directors

- The structures and processes of governance are the board-level signs of a company's culture.

- A culture that incorporates reputation into its governance increases the likelihood that the operational benefits can be realized.

- Reputational metrics and reputational insurances are indications that a company embraces a culture for reputation risk management and overall business strategy.

Guidance

Corporate governance that demonstrates authentic oversight of the pillars of reputation—ethics, quality, innovation, safety, sustainability, and security—creates value. A recent study by Mercer Investment Consulting found that 46% of institutional asset owners now take environmental, social, and corporate governance analysis into consideration when making investment decisions. And institutional investors demonstrate a willingness to pay a premium of 12%–14% for the shares of well-governed companies in North America and Western Europe, and even higher premiums for the shares of well-governed companies in emerging markets, a McKinsey & Company study reports.[77]

The economic performances of Diageo and Anglo American over the trailing 12 months illustrate the rationale. Diageo returned 46% while the S&P 500 Beverage Index returned 17.25% (Figure 8-3a);[78] and Anglo American lost 12% while the S&P/TSX Global Mining Index lost 20% (Figure 8-3b).[79]

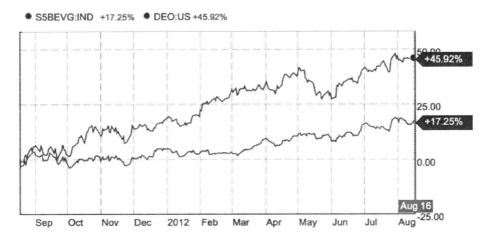

Figure 8-3a. Trailing 12-month returns for Diageo plc and the S&P 500 Beverage Index.

Reputation, Stock Price, and You

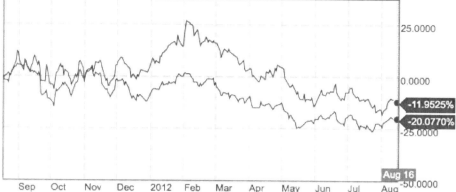

Figure 8-3b. Trailing 12-month returns for Anglo American plc and the iShares S&P/TSX Global Mining Fund.

Three out of four business leaders believe corporate reputation is substantially driven by internal corporate culture, yet only 5% think their organization's culture is strong enough to preclude reputational crisis, according to a recent survey of 100 business leaders and HR professionals conducted by MWW Group.[80] Standard Chartered found itself in a reputational crisis in August 2012. The matter came to a head on 14 August when the British bank agreed to pay New York's top banking regulator $340 million to settle claims that it laundered hundreds of billions of dollars in tainted money for Iran and lied to regulators.[81]

Until the moment of the crisis, Standard Chartered was returning 20% for the trailing 12 months while the S&P Global Financials Sector Index as returning 9.35% (Figure 8-4).[82] Within a few weeks, the major loss of market cap was significantly restored and the trailing 12-month returns were greater than the reference group by the time of the settlement. As discussed more generally in Chapter 10, Standard Chartered's "good fortune" with regulators can be attributed to its board's good faith response and management of the crisis. "Effectively the bank's decision to opt for a fast settlement of the charges allowed it to escape from sinking sand."[83] By the numbers, as this book is fond of noting, the bank's quick actions reduced the magnitude of the potential fine. The bank's payment of $340 million was less than the mid-2012 payment of $619 million by ING, the Dutch bank, for sanctions breaches, while HSBC has set aside $700 million to cover expected fines for money laundering failures.[84] But if an institution's reputation is sullied, those responsible must go. "A big issue is the failure of oversight, which means Standard Chartered needs to act over the make-up of the board," said one top-20 shareholder. "They may need to act quickly over this to prevent a loss of credibility."[85]

Chapter 8 | Boards of Directors

The good news for companies assailed by allegations of bad behavior is that, while it may take as long to create a good culture as it does to establish a good reputation, a strong set of values is usually harder to destroy. Standard Chartered plc, a case in point, is an example of rapid action informed by an appreciation of the value of reputation. All bets are off, however, should the company itself be dismantled or taken over.[3]

Figure 8-4. Trailing 12-month returns for Standard Chartered plc and the iShares S&P Global Financials Sector Fund.

UBS is rebuilding a culture that is part of the company's heritage. It has taken a leadership role in its sector by being the first to publicly and specifically link its CEO's compensation to the firm's reputation.

Disney has a very strong brand-centric culture and a reputation for family values that it is protecting through operational changes in areas many would not consider important to a brand—back office and supply chain operations.

Johnson & Johnson, a reputational bellwether for more than a quarter century, shows the magnitude of reputational resilience a strong culture can create. In the past few years, the culture of Robert Wood Johnson has been diluted by more modern notions that have tolerated, well, greater ethical flexibility. And the chickens have come home to roost as the company faces up to $2 billion in costs to settle hip implant claims[86] and another $2.2 billion for aggressive product marketing that triggered three False Claims Act lawsuits.[87]

In their 1982 book, *In Search of Excellence*—one of the first attempts to identify and explain the correlation between a positive corporate culture and strong performance—Tom Peters and Robert Waterman pointed out that "poorer-performing companies often have strong cultures, too, but dysfunctional ones."[3] The present chapter illustrates practical steps boards can take

Reputation, Stock Price, and You 195

to build strong, positive, and reputationally sensitive cultures through oversight of executive compensation, asset protection, and business strategy.

By the Numbers

Table 8-2. Enterprise-Level Reputation Risks, Board Actions, and Value Created

Risk, Board Action, or Result	Measure
Average change in the number of mentions of the word reputation in UBS' annual report after the 2009 reforms	52% increase
Fraction of CEO bonus at UBS linked to measures of reputation	11%
Most recent annual rate of disclosure of corporate reputational risk	50% per year increase
Fraction of board members who rank reputation as their firm's topmost concern	70%
Fraction of major corporations that have had at least one major reputational event over the past 20 years	95%
Average trailing 12-month economic returns of Anglo American, Diageo and Standard Chartered relative to their benchmark indexes (prior to the 1 August crisis)	18% superior returns

Endnotes

1 Russell D. The BP cast list. *The Daily Beast.* 16 June 2010. Available at: http://www. thedailybeast.com/articles/2010/06/16/bp-oil-disaster-who-is-responsible.html. Accessed 17 July 2012.

2 Libor scandal: Andrew Bailey insists Barclays' problems originated from 'tone at the top.' *Huffington Post.* 16 July 2012. Available at: http://www.huffingtonpost.co.uk/2012/07/16/ libor-diamond-rate-rigging-barclays-bank-diamond_n_1677195.html. Accessed 14 August 2012.

3 Hill A. Corporate culture: Lofty aspirations. *Financial Times.* 15 July 2012. Available at: http://www.ft.com/intl/cms/s/0/d1b4b71a-ccde-11e1-9960-00144feabdc0. html#axzz23GQOLxlr. Accessed 12 August 2012.

4 Klein P. Can say on pay increase social responsibility? *Forbes.* 3 July 2012. Available at: http:// www.forbes.com/sites/csr/2012/07/03/can-say-on-pay-increase-social-responsibility/?goback=. gde_2955795_member_130388605. Accessed 11 August 2012.

5 Pearl Meyer & Partners. Top 10 Compensation Committee agenda items for 2012. Available at: http://www.pearlmeyer.com/top102012. Accessed 4 September 2012.

6 TalkingPoint: Boardroom challenges – executive compensation and say on pay. Financier Worldwide.com. May 2012. Available at: http://www.financierworldwide.com/article. php?id=9379. Accessed 4 September 2012.

Chapter 8 | Boards of Directors

7 Poerlo M. Dodd-Frank's say on pay rules pose triple threat to directors. *American Banker.* 1 June 2012. Available at: http://www.americanbanker.com/bankthink/Dodd-Frank-say-on-pay-golden-parachute-1049805-1.html. Accessed 4 September 2012.

8 U.S. directors jittery about pay committee post. *Reuters.* 12 June 2012. http://www.reuters.com/article/2012/06/12/us-pay-directors-lawsuits-idUSBRE85B1D320120612. Accessed 4 September 2012.

9 UBS Annual Report 2011.

10 Carter A, Protess B. UBS scandal is a reminder about why Dodd-Frank came to be. *The New York Times,* 19 September 2011. Available at: http://dealbook.nytimes.com/2011/09/19/ubs-scandal-is-reminder-of-why-dodd-frank-came-to-be/. Accessed 12 August 2012.

11 Swiss victims of hedge fund collapse. *BBC.* 2 October 1998. Available at: http://news.bbc.co.uk/2/hi/business/184861.stm. Accessed 13 August 2012.

12 Bruner RF. A merger of equals? *Wall Street Journal.* 20 January 2004. Available at: http://online.wsj.com/article/SB107455595079505805.html. Accessed 13 August 2012.

13 Simonian H.UBS's fresh subprime writedown takes its losses for year to $18bn. *Financial Times.* 31 January 2008. Available at: http://www.ft.com/intl/cms/s/0/13f035ba-cf9f-11dc-854a-0000779fd2ac.html#axzz23RZT9lbA. Accessed 13 August 2012.

14 Simonian H, Hughes C. UBS turns to Singapore fund for new capital. *Financial Times.* 11 December 2007. Available at: http://www.ft.com/intl/cms/s/0/3fb9574e-a78b-11dc-a25a-0000779fd2ac.html#axzz23RZT9lbA. Accessed 13 August 2012.

15 Hughes C, Simonian H, Larsen PT. Former UBS chief calls for radical change. *Financial Times.* 4 April 2008. Available at: http://www.ft.com/intl/cms/s/0/040581a4-01e1-11dd-a323-000077b07658.html#axzz23RZT9lbA. Accessed 13 August 2012.

16 Chung J, Guerrera F, Garnham P. UBS settles US tax probes for $780m. *Financial Times.* 19 February 2009. Available at: http://www.ft.com/intl/cms/s/0/ddeae744-fe14-11dd-932e-000077b07658.html#axzz23RZT9lbA. Accessed 13 August 2012.

17 Voreacos D.UBS tax-fraud charge is dropped by U.S. prosecutors. *Bloomberg.* 22 October 2010. Available at: http://www.bloomberg.com/news/2010-10-22/u-s-ends-ubs-deferred-prosecution-accord-in-conspiracy-case.html. Accessed 13 August 2012.

18 UBS replaces chairman Peter Kurer with former Swiss finance minister Kaspar Villiger. *The Telegraph.* 4 March 2009. Available at: http://www.telegraph.co.uk/finance/newsbysector/banksandfinance/4936067/UBS-replaces-chairman-Peter-Kurer-with-former-Swiss-finance-minister-Kaspar-Villiger.html. Accessed 13 August 2012.

19 Quinn J, Dunkley J. Trading scandal claims top scalp at UBS. *The Sydney Morning Herald.* 26 September 2011. Available at: http://www.smh.com.au/business/trading-scandal-claims-top-scalp-at-ubs-20110925-1krst.html. Accessed 13 August 2012.

20 Kaspar Villiger profile. *Forbes.* Available at: http://www.forbes.com/profile/kaspar-villiger/. Accessed 13 August 2012.

21 FSF principles for sound compensation practices. Financial Stability Board, 2009. Available at: http://www.financialstabilityboard.org/publications/r_0904b.pdf. Accessed 14 August 2012.

Reputation, Stock Price, and You | 197

22 Schafer D. No stop to bankers' pay rises, data reveal. *Financial Times*. 24 June 2012. Available at: http://www.ft.com/intl/cms/s/0/abde55a4-bbeb-11e1-9aff-00144feabdc0. html#axzz23RZT9lbA. Accessed 12 August 2012.

23 Sharma K. Financial sector compensation and excess risk-taking: a consideration of the issues and policy lessons. United Nations Department of Economic and Social Affairs. DESA Working Paper No. 115, ST/ESA/2012/DWP/115, April 2012.

24 Fraser M. Kaspar Villiger will leave the bank in May. *Operational Risk and Regulation*,. 3 February 2012. Available at: http://www.risk.net/operational-risk-and-regulation/ news/2143736/ubs-chairman-steps. Accessed 13 August 2012.

25 Godbehere A. *Forbes*. Available at: http://www.forbes.com/profile/ann-godbehere/. Accessed 14 August 2012.

26 RPT-UPDATE 4-UBS names Ermotti CEO to steady bank after scandal. *Reuters*. 15 November 2011. Bart K. Available at: http://www.reuters.com/article/2011/11/15/ubs-idUSL5E7MF02R20111115. Accessed 13 November 2012.

27 Groendahl B, Logutenkova E. UBS chairman says bank's reputation will play role in CEO's pay. *Bloomberg*. 23 April 2012. Available at: http://www.bloomberg.com/news/2012-04-23/ ubs-chairman-says-bank-s-reputation-will-play-role-in-ceo-s-pay.html. Accessed 12 August 2012.

28 New Barclays chairman: I'll review entire business. *Associated Press*, 12 August 2012. Available at: http://abcnews.go.com/International/wireStory/barclays-chairman-review-entire-business-16988751#.UCk9n0SI_-I . Accessed 13 August 2012.

29 Treanor J. David Walker draws up Barclays' to-do list. *The Guardian*. 12 August 2012. Available at: http://hereisthecity.com/2012/08/12/david-walker-draws-up-barclays-to-do-list/. Accessed 13 August 2012.

30 Kim S. Jamie Dimon may meet with janitor about pay. *ABC News*. 19 June 2012. Available at: http://abcnews.go.com/Business/jamie-dimon-defends-wall-street-capitol-hill/ story?id=16598004#.UCpRAkSI_-k. Accessed 14 August 2012.

31 Goldman Sachs' compensation principles. Available at: www.goldmansachs.com/investor.../ compensation-principles.pdf. Accessed 14 August 2012.

32 Marcinek L, Griffin D, Kopecki D. JPMorgan said to consider clawing back bonuses after loss. *Bloomberg*. 15 May 2012. Available at: http://www.bloomberg.com/news/2012-05-15/ jpmorgan-said-to-weigh-bonus-clawbacks-after-loss.html. Accessed 12 August 2012.

33 Kirdahy M. How to rebuild your corporate reputation. *Forbes*. 15 February 2008. Available at: http://www.forbes.com/2008/02/14/corporate-executive-strategy-lead-manage-cx_ mk_0215reputation.html. Accessed 14 August 2012.

34 Gaines-Ross L. Reputation warfare. *Harvard Business Review*. 2010 December, pp. 3–8.

35 Best Global Brands 2011. Interbrand, 2011. Available at: http://www.interbrand.com/en/ best-global-brands/Best-Global-Brands-2011/Disney-MatthewRyan.aspx. Accessed 14 August 2012.

36 Boardroom Liabilities. Special supplement. Corporate Board Member, 2007. Boardroom-Liabilities.pdf. Accessed 4 September 2012.

37 Letter from Jenny Chan, Chief Coordinator, SACOM to Robert Iger, Chief Executive Officer, The Walt Disney Company, dated 8 December 2006. sacom-second-letter-to-disney-ceo-dec-8-2006_.pdf Accessed 15 August 2012.

Chapter 8 | Boards of Directors

38 Paying the price for profit in toyland. *CBC Marketplace*. 5 December 2012. Available at: http://www.cbc.ca/marketplace/pre-2007/files/home/toys/. Accessed 15 August 2012.

39 Walt Disney. Knowmore.org Available at: http://knowmore.org/wiki/index. php?title=Walt_Disney. Accessed 15 August 2012.

40 The Public Eye Awards. About. Available at: http://www.publiceye.ch/en/about/what-are-public-eye-awards/. Accessed 15 August 2012.

41 Disney sweatshops alleged. *CNN Money*. 18 August 2005. http://money.cnn. com/2005/08/18/news/international/disney_china/. Accessed 17 August 2012.

42 Disney sweats over sweatshop charges in China. *Daily News & Analysis*. 16 February 2007. Available at: http://www.dnaindia.com/world/report_disney-sweats-over-sweatshop-charges-in-china_1080420. Accessed 15 August 2012.

43 Reputation: Risk of risk. *Economist Intelligence Unit*. December 2005.

44 Tonello M. *Reputation risk: A corporate governance perspective*. The Conference Board, Report R-1412-07-WG, December 2007.

45 Mitchell C. *Corporate brands. meeting the challenges of changing times*. The Conference Board, Report R-1442-09-RR, August 2009.

46 Bonini S, Court D, Marchi A. Rebuilding corporate reputations. *McKinsey Quarterly*. 2009; June. Available at: http://www.mckinseyquarterly.com/Rebuilding_corporate_reputations_2367. Accessed 15 August 2012.

47 Available at: http://www.mgt.ncsu.edu/erm/index.php/articles/ entry/balancing-risk-reward/. Accessed 15 August 2012.

48 Committee of Sponsoring Organizations of the Treadway Commission. Enterprise risk management — integrated framework (2004). Available at: http://www.coso.org/-ERM.htm. Accessed 16 August 2012.

49 Available at: http://www.iso.org/iso/iso_catalogue/catalogue_tc/ catalogue_detail. htm?csnumber=43170

50 Available at: http://www2.standardandpoors.com/spf/pdf/ media/ERM_for_Corporates_ProgressReport_07_22_ 09.pdf

51 Final rule, proxy disclosure enhancements, SEC. Available at: http://www.sec.gov/rules/final/2009/33-9089.pdf. Accessed 15 August 2012.

52 Kossovsky N. Reputation: the greatest risk. *The Risk Report*. 2010; 33(2):1–8.

53 Reese C, Kossovsky N. Intangibles and the new reality: risk, reputation, and value creation. *Corporate Finance Review*. January/February 2011. Available at: http://www.fr.com/files/Uploads/Documents/Resse.%20Corporate%20Finance%20Review.%20Intangibles%20and%20the%20new%20reality.%20Jan%202011.pdf. Accessed 15 August 2012.

54 In re Caremark International Inc. Derivative Litigation, 698 A.2d 959 (Del. Ch. 1996).

55 Reese CL. Director and officer liability for director and officer liability for mismanagement of intangible assets. Mission Intangible Monthly Briefing, 6 February 2009. Audio recordings available from the Intangible Asset Finance Society, http://iafinance.org/monthly-briefings.

Reputation, Stock Price, and You | 199

56 McCrum D, Jopson B. Berkshire cuts P&G and Kraft holdings. *Financial Times*. 14 August 2012. Available at: http://www.ft.com/intl/cms/s/0/044552d2-e659-11e1-ac5f-00144feab49a.html#axzz23Q66eleu. Accessed 18 August 2012.

57 Roads to ruin. A study of major risk events: their origins, impact and implications. *Airmic*. 21 July 2011. Available at: http://www.airmic.com/jresearch/roads-ruin-executive-briefing. Accessed 16 August 2012.

58 Emerging risks 2012. Allianz. *Commercial Risk Europe*. Emerging Risks Report 2012_low res.pdf Accessed 16 August 2012.

59 Reputational and regulatory risk are top concerns of boards. Press Release. Eisner Amper. 7 May 2012. Available at: http://www.eisneramper.com/IT-Risk-Management-news-0512.aspx. Accessed 15 August 2012.

60 Lloyd's Risk Index 2011. Available at: http://www.lloyds.com/News-and-Insight/Risk-Insight/Lloyds-Risk-Index. Accessed 15 August 2012.

61 Benyon D.Goldman Sachs uses scenarios to study reputation risks. *Operational Risk & Regulation*. 17 March 2010. Available at: http://www.risk.net/operational-risk-and-regulation/news/1596842/goldman-sachs-scenarios-study-reputation-risks. Accessed 14 August 2012.

62 Landy H. The fragile state of bank reputations: results from our 2012 study. *American Banker*. 1 July 2012. Available at: http://www.americanbanker.com/magazine/122_7/annual-consumer-survey-bank-reputations-gained-ground-1050345-1.html. Accessed 14 August 2012.

63 Willis: insurance industry response to reputational risk is inadequate. Press Release. Willis. 21 February 2012. Available at: http://www.willis.com/Media_Room/Press_Releases_%28Browse_All%29/2012/20120221_Phil_Ellis_Risk_Frontiers_Speech_press_release_21-02-2012/. Accessed 15 August 2012.

64 Catastrophes: insurance issues. *Insurance Information Institute*. September 2012. Available at: http://www.iii-insurancematters.org/white_papers/catastrophes-insurance-issues.html. Accessed 6 October 2012.

65 Disney. SACOM. Available at: http://sacom.hk/category/campaigns/disney. Accessed 15 August 2012.

66 Supply chain management the Disney way. *CSCMP's Supply Chain Quarterly*, Quarter 2 2012. Available at: http://www.supplychainquarterly.com/print/20120523-supply-chain-managers-can-promote-customer-experience-says-disney-executive/. Accessed 17 August 2012.

67 Global principles of accountable corporate governance. California Public Employees' Retirement System, 14 November 2011, p. 22.

68 Beasley M, Branson B, Hancock B. *Current State of Enterprise Risk Oversight*. North Carolina State University, July 2012. Available at: AICPA_ERM_Research_Study_2012_Final_Submission_July_16,_2012.pdf. Accessed 16 August 2012.

69 PWC Audit Committee Guide. ac-guide-nov11-intro.pdf

70 Standard Chartered plc. Hoovers. Available at: http://www.hoovers.com/company/Standard_Chartered_PLC/sfcfri-1.html. Accessed 16 August 2012.

71 Standard Chartered plc. Annual Report, 2011.

Chapter 8 | Boards of Directors

72 Diageo plc. Hoovers. Available at: http://www.hoovers.com/company/Diageo_plc/hhrxri-1. html. Accessed 16 August 2012.

73 Diageo plc. Annual Report, 2011.

74 Anglo American plc. Hoovers. Available at: http://www.hoovers.com/company/Anglo_American_plc/crxfsi-1.html#. Accessed 16 August 2012.

75 Anglo American plc. Annual Report, 2011.

76 Our Credo. Johnson & Johnson. Available at: http://www.jnj.com/connect/about-jnj/jnj-credo/. Accessed 6 October 2012.

77 Overview of business and corporate accountability. BSR Issue Briefs. Available at: http://www.bsr.org/BSRResources/IssueBriefDetail.cfm?DocumentID=48907. (http://www.bulentsenver.com/yeditepe/htm/BSR%20%BB%20Business%20for%20Social%20Responsibility%20-%20bOverview%20of%20Business%20and%20Corporate%20Accountability-b.htm#intro). Accessed 4 September 2012.

78 Available at: http://www.bloomberg.com/quote/S5BEVG:IND. Accessed 17 August 2012.

79 Available at: http://www.bloomberg.com/quote/CMW:CN. Accessed 17 August 2012.

80 MWW survey: 3 out of 4 business leaders believe corporate reputation is substantially driven by internal culture. Press Release, 31 May 2012. Available at: http://www.mwwpr.com/pressroom/2012/05/mww-survey-3-out-of-4-business-leaders-believe-corporate-reputation-is-substantially-driven-by-internal-culture/. Accessed 12 August 2012.

81 Silver-Greenberg J. British bank in $340 million settlement for laundering. New York Times. 14 August 2012. http://www.nytimes.com/2012/08/15/business/standard-chartered-settles-with-new-york-for-340-million.html?pagewanted=all. Accessed 6 October 2012.

82 Available at: http://www.bloomberg.com/quote/IXG:US. Accessed 17 August 2012.

83 Hunt P. Let Standard Chartered serve as lessons to others. Mortgage Strategy. 24 September 2012. Available at: http://www.mortgagestrategy.co.uk/analysis/let-standard-chartered-serve-as-lessons-to-others/1058285.article. Accessed 6 October 2012.

84 Scannell K, Goff S. Standard Chartered pushes for settlement. Financial Times. 12 August 2012. http://www.ft.com/intl/cms/s/0/097c53aa-e33d-11e1-bf02-00144feab49a. html#axzz28YgH1eLC. Accessed 6 October 2012.

85 Goff S, Oakley D. Stanch art hastens board shake-up. Financial Times. 17 August 2012. Available at: http://www.ft.com/intl/cms/s/0/fe3b7eca-e879-11e1-8ffc-00144feab49a. html#axzz23tU8qUZz. Accessed 18 August 2012.

86 Voreacos D. J&J said to pay $600,000 to settle first suits over hips. Bloomberg. 21 August 2012. Available at: http://www.bloomberg.com/news/2012-08-21/j-j-said-to-pay-600-000-to-settle-first-suits-over-depuy-hips.html. Accessed 1 September 2012.

87 Voreacos D, Cronin Fisk M. J&J will pay $181 million to settle Dispersal ad claims. Bloomberg. 30 August 2012. Available at: http://www.bloomberg.com/news/2012-08-30/j-j-will-pay-181-million-to-settle-risperdal-ad-claims.html. Accessed 1 September 2012.

CHAPTER

9

Analysts

Budd Beach, an analyst at Raymond James, asked what [Wal-Mart] executives thought the effect [of allegations of corruption in its Mexican operations] on the company's reputation was. 'We will be a better company because of this,' Mr. Duke, the CEO, responded.

—The New York Times, 1 June 2012[1]

Reputation is a consequence of corporate behavior that motivates stakeholders to behave in ways that either reward or punish the corporation. Reputation value is the measure of reward or punishment. This chapter compares and contrasts measures of both the impression and the expression of reputation value that may be useful to financial analysts. Featured are the methods of Transparent Value, *Fortune*, *Barron's*, Harris Interactive, Reputation Institute, and Steel City Re, the author's employer. Consistent with Bernstein's maxim— "the plural of 'anecdote' is not 'data'"—these measures are useful alternatives to scattershot extra-financial reputation information.[2]

Reputation Value

"Congratulations, Mr. Carnegie, you are now the richest man in the world."[3] Thus in 1901, banker J. P. Morgan sealed his purchase of Carnegie's steel company and memorialized for eternity proof that Andrew Carnegie knew how to create value. Not that anyone had doubts. At the time Morgan bought Carnegie's assets to create U.S. Steel, the company produced more of the metal than all of Great Britain.

Carnegie's formula was transparent. "I think Carnegie's genius was first of all, an ability to foresee how things were going to change," says historian John Ingram. "Once he saw that something was of potential benefit to him, he was willing to invest enormously in it."[4]

Chapter 9 | Analysts

Here's the catch. He knew both where to look and how to develop winning strategies. On knowing where to look, he said, "As I grow older, I pay less attention to what men *say*, I just watch what they *do*." As to strategy, Carnegie was a believer in the wisdom of crowds—stakeholders, actually. He called it "a mastermind group."

Carnegie elaborated on this in 1908 to newspaper columnist Napoleon Hill: "Well, if you want to know how I got my money, I will refer you to these men here on my staff; they got it for me. We have here in this business a master mind. It is not my mind, and it is not the mind of any other man on my staff, but the sum total of all these minds that I have gathered around me that constitute a master mind in the steel business."[5]

Steel City Re's approach to measuring reputational value and establishing a reputational value ranking rests on combining these two principles. Steel City Re watches what stakeholders are *expected* to do by watching Carnegie's mastermind watch stakeholders. Before one can determine what stakeholders are expected to do, one has to channel Carnegie and know where the mastermind would watch what they do.

In August 2012, *Bloomberg* reported that there were two thoughts as to whether Boeing would or would not stick to its scheduled development of its 787 airframe.

> *The development of a stretch version of the Dreamliner, called the 787-10X, continues as well, Boeing Commercial Airplanes President Ray Conner wrote in a message to employees. The* Seattle Times *reported, citing unidentified people familiar with the matter, that Boeing had slowed down the development process.*[6]

Boeing's statements and the conflicting comments of insiders present two alternate realities that will impact each of its major stakeholders. For example, customers who may have been expecting the availability of the modified 787 by a certain date may choose to move to a different platform or upgrade existing platforms to extend their life spans a bit longer. Employee pools may shift in number, skill set, and geographic location based on Boeing's production schedules. Supply chains, and the vendors that feed them, will be activated, accelerated, or deactivated depending on the actual changes being implemented by Boeing. Watching the stakeholders and "what they do" can provide indications of Boeing's actual intentions.

As Carnegie proved, there is value in watching what they are doing. A company established in 2003 was based on that premise.

Transparent Value, LLC articulated its dedicated goal: seeking to deliver sustainable investment returns across global equity markets by introducing a

Reputation, Stock Price, and You

new way to measure the equity value of publicly traded companies. Transparent Value, LLC provides a range of financial market services based on an analysis of what stakeholders are doing. Using patent-pending processes, their investment methodology fused the insights of fundamental analysis with the transparency of a disciplined, rules-based stock selection and portfolio construction process.

In May 2009, Guggenheim Partners, LLC, a diversified financial services firm, acquired a controlling interest in Transparent Value and its subsidiaries. Guggenheim, with $125 billion in assets under management, made "substantial" investments in infrastructure and to seed the funds that replicated Transparent Value indexes, according to Julian Koski, their founder.[7] Today, Transparent Value's analysis of what "they are doing" feeds a proprietary algorithm that calculates the probability that what is being done will enable management to deliver the business performance *expected* by shareholders as reflected in current stock price. Transparent Value calls its proprietary measure the Required Business Performance Probability (RBP Probability) metric.[8]

Their analytical process starts with a company's current stock price and most recent financial statements from which they determine expected cash flows, and, from there, the level of sales needed to support the current stock price. Then they statistically determine, using management's past business performance and an analysis of supply chain activity, the probability that there will be sufficient products sold at the expected prices to meet expectations.

Transparent Value observes company behaviors, calculates investor expectations, and then determines the probability that the former will meet the latter. When investor expectations are materially ahead of what a company appears to be capable of delivering, Transparent Value interprets the finding as risky investor behavior. It reports that behavior with a metric called the Behavioral Risk Indicator. Investor behavior in advance of the Facebook IPO, reviewed in Chapter 7, is an example of what Transparent Value would consider material Behavioral Risk.

"RBP tells us the revenue required at the most granular level, such as how many iPods Apple has to sell, or how many stores Starbucks has to open, or how many packages FedEx has to ship to support the price of its stock," Koski explains.[9]

Beyond analyzing probabilities of meeting investor expectations, Transparent Value also invests in companies with the highest RBP Probabilities in select benchmark indexes while avoiding those companies in the benchmark that they believe have the highest likelihood of disappointing and underperforming relative to other companies. The logic is mathematically sound: if you can avoid investing in the worst relative performers, you should outperform the

Chapter 9 | Analysts

benchmark index. "Avoiding losers isn't a glamorous business," Koski admits, and companies that fit Transparent Value's winner profile tend to be a plain Jane. "I noticed that in my family's portfolio, it had always been the unsexy names that made money. Unsexy is better than sexy, but only in stock picking."[7]

Transparent Value provides investment strategies for a range of mutual funds generally investing in large capitalization companies. Two exemplary funds, the Market and Value funds Transparent Val DJ RBP US LC Mkt Idx I (MUTF:TVIMX) and Transparent Val DJ RBP US LC Val Idx I (MUTF:TVVIX) respectively, both underperformed the S&P 500 Composite Equity Index over the trailing 12 months from 4 October 2012 with mean monthly returns of 1.80% and 2.05% compared to the S&P 500's mean monthly return of 2.09% (Table 9-1).

Table 9-1. As of 4 October 2012, Trailing 12-Month Portfolio Characteristics of Exemplary Strategies Informed by Required Business Performance Probability Metrics (Risk-Free Rate [RFR] = 1.17%)

	S&P 500	**TVIMX**	**TVVIX**
Mean monthly return	2.09%	1.80%	2.05%
Standard deviation	5.61%	4.76%	5.99%
Compound monthly return	1.94%	1.70%	1.88%
Annualized return	25.03%	21.63%	24.54%
Annualized standard deviation	19.42%	16.50%	20.75%
Excess return (RFR)	23.86%	20.46%	23.37%
Sharpe ratio	1.23	1.24	1.13
Sortino ratio (0%)	58.41%	57.69%	53.91%
Portfolio beta (relative to S&P 500)	—	0.69	0.93
Portfolio alpha (relative to S&P 500)	—	0.35%	0.11%
Portfolio correlation to S&P 500	—	0.82	0.87
Coefficient of determination	—	0.48	0.86

Transparent Value watches what people do and then uses its proprietary models to estimate the probability that those actions will meet the expectations of investors implied by the stock price. Steel City Re also watches what people do. However, it relies on the other Carnegie tool,

Reputation, Stock Price, and You 205

the mastermind, to watch what people do in the *expectation* of what other people are going to do. For this, Steel City Re looks to decision markets.

Decision markets (also known as predictive markets, information markets, prediction markets, idea futures, event derivatives, virtual markets, or Carnegie's mastermind) are markets created for the purpose of making predictions.[10] They have two key features: each participant makes a prediction independent of influences from any other participant, and the market rewards the participant who made the prediction that most closely approximates the future outcome. Markets may reward participants in two ways: indirectly, through accolades and other external acknowledgments that eventually favorably impact employment and compensation, or through an immediate prize or award. In decision markets that trade future contracts whose value is the reward, current market prices can be interpreted as predictions of the probability of the event or the expected value of the parameter.[10]

Participants cannot have conflicted interests wherein they may be motivated to offer a prediction other than their best guess in order to purposefully distort the market's outcome—an unfortunate condition that existed and distorted the outcome of LIBOR (London InterBank Offered Rate), the product of a decision market currently supervised by its sponsor, the British Bankers' Association (BBA).[11] Nevertheless, the market behind the BBA's LIBOR provides meaningful insight into a key decision market in the world of finance.

The BBA's LIBOR is a benchmark giving an indication, or expectation, of the average rate at which a leading bank can obtain unsecured funding in the London interbank market for a given period in a given currency. Absent manipulation, it therefore represents the lowest real-world cost of unsecured funding in the London market.

Individual LIBOR rates are the end-product of a calculation based upon submissions from a bank panel, made up of the largest, most active banks in each currency LIBOR is quoted for. The panel comprises the decision market. The panel watches what the panelists do in the *expectation* of what global bank lending officers are going to do.

Every decision market participant on the panel is asked to base their LIBOR submissions on the following question:

> At what rate could you borrow funds, were you to do so by asking for and then accepting inter-bank offers in a reasonable market size just prior to 11 am?[12]

Chapter 9 | Analysts

LIBOR is based as much on actual transactions as it is on *expectations* of future transactions. Since not all banks will require funds in marketable size each day in each of the currencies and maturities they quote, it would not be feasible to create a suite of LIBOR rates if this was a requirement.

> However, a bank will know what its credit and liquidity risk profile is from rates at which it has dealt and can construct a curve to predict accurately the correct rate for currencies or maturities in which it has not been active.

In markets that trade future contracts, people who buy low and sell high are rewarded for improving the market prediction, while those who buy high and sell low are punished for degrading the market prediction. Graefe and Armstrong reported recently that the simple averages of forecasts, the method BBA uses to calculate LIBOR, and more structured prediction markets with futures contracts such as the Iowa Election Markets, The simExchange, Hollywood Stock Exchange, NewsFutures, and the Popular Science Predictions Exchange, produce outcomes with similar accuracy.[13]

Steel City Re draws data from prediction markets that capture the expected behaviors of stakeholders that impact the profit and loss (P&L) statement. There are four equally weighted families of data that comprise the pillars of the Steel City Re Reputational Value Metrics: the CRR, a measure of ranking joined arithmetically, and the RVM, a non-financial measure of value joined geometrically. These four families of *expectation* data report on the various P&L elements discussed in prior chapters: stakeholder behaviors responsible for revenue, stakeholder behaviors responsible for expenses, equity investor behaviors, and a measure of the alignment of the various stakeholders' expectations.

The reputational value metrics comprise purely algorithmic arithmetic and logarithmic transformations of those data that are purchased by Steel City Re from a publicly traded commercial vendor. Steel City Re does not create the markets, nor does it influence the decisions reached by the markets. There is one integrated algorithm and it transforms the published data in a repeatable manner. The automated process is monitored to ensure that the outputs are reliable. Steel City Re neither adds nor subtracts information from the calculation.

The calculations generate non-financial measures of value that are recorded as the RVM scaled in a non-financial unit, the Gerken Unit, named after a co-founder of the company. Steel City Re also calculates values that are ordered by rank to generate the CRR scaled four significant digits as a percentile unit (Table 9-2).

Table 9-2. Properties of Steel City Re Reputational Value Metrics

	RVM	CRR
Unit	Gerken	Percentile
Component joining method	Geometric	Arithmetic
Range	Generally $-1.0 \leq x \leq 2.5$	$0.0000 \leq x \leq 1.0000$
Median	0.4301 (23 August 2012)	0.5001
Primary use	Volatility and risk	Relative value

In April 2009, Steel City Re first made available these objective algorithmically generated reputational value metrics to support a range of executive management needs.[14] The metrics helped corporate boards and senior management better communicate with stakeholders, quickly assess stakeholder reactions to major strategic initiatives, enhance oversight including compensation decisions, and better mitigate and manage crises. Steel City Re's reputation metrics have also inspired an investment strategy called RepuStars.[15] The RepuStars Variety Corporate Reputation Index (INDEXDJX: REPUVAR), a stock selection strategy, is calculated and published by S&P/Dow Jones Indexes. The RepuSPX, a similar strategy applied only to the constituent companies of the S&P 500 Composite Index, is privately managed by Technology Option Capital, a financial modeling advisory company.

The Steel City Re reputational value metrics are calculated through a proprietary algorithm that quantifies the expectations held by stakeholders that produce economically relevant behaviors. The behaviors directly impact company revenues and operating costs. Expectations of these behaviors therefore impact expectations of company value. Usually captured by stock price, this value may sometimes deviate.

At times, stakeholders may reasonably disagree and hold different expectations. When equity stakeholders have low expectations, while other stakeholders have high expectations, there are value opportunities.

The selection algorithm underpinning the RepuStars strategy is designed to identify these value opportunities. For REPUVAR, the algorithm selects up to 3 companies from each of 19 commercial sectors companies in which value opportunities are implied by a high reputation value and a low stock price. REPUVAR is denominated in U.S. dollars. The components trade on U.S. exchanges and are screened for price and market cap. The benchmark index is the S&P 500 Composite Equity Index.

Chapter 9 | Analysts

For RepuSPX, the algorithm selects up to 8 companies from members of the S&P 500 composite equity index from each of 19 commercial sectors where value opportunities are implied as previously.

Both REPUVAR and RepuSPX outperformed the S&P 500 Composite Equity Index over the trailing 12 months from 4 October 2012, with mean monthly returns of 2.18% and 3.04% compared to the S&P 500's mean monthly return of 2.09% (Table 9-3).

Table 9-3. As of 4 October 2012, Trailing 12-Month Portfolio Characteristics of Exemplary Strategies Informed by Steel City Re's Corporate Reputation Metrics (Risk-Free Rate [RFR] = 1.17%)

	S&P 500	REPUVAR	RepuSPX
Mean monthly return	2.09%	2.18%	3.04%
Standard deviation	5.61%	6.60%	6.35%
Compound monthly return	1.94%	1.98%	2.85%
Annualized return	25.03%	26.20%	36.48%
Annualized standard deviation	19.42%	22.86%	21.99%
Excess return (RFR)	23.86%	25.03%	35.31%
Sharpe ratio	1.23	1.09	1.61
Sortino ratio (0%)	58.41%	49.88%	80.64%
Portfolio beta (relative to S&P 500)		1.11	1.04
Portfolio alpha (relative to S&P 500)		-0.13%	0.87%
Portfolio correlation to S&P 500		0.94	0.92
Coefficient of determination		1.23	1.11

Other Reputation Metrics

Because reputation has often been conflated with brand, the evolution of reputation measurement and management has been heavily influenced by the analytical framework and measurement tools of market research. As *Forbes* magazine explains, "We live in a world where word of mouth is the No. 1 driver of sales and competitive advantage—and because there's a strong correlation between a company's reputation and consumers' willingness to recommend it, businesses need to focus on building those strong bonds with stakeholders."[16] Most prominent among the tools used to quantify reputation is the market opinion survey and its product, a reputation score.

Fortune

Fortune magazine, working in cooperation with the Hay Group, has been producing since 2001 what they believe is the "definitive report card on corporate reputations."[17] For the 2012 U.S.-based list of Most Admired Companies, Hay Group, a global management consultancy, began with the Fortune 1000, the 1,000 largest companies ranked by revenue. The 10 largest were selected for each of 58 industries. To create the 58 industry lists in 2012, Hay asked executives, directors, and analysts to rate companies in their own industry on nine criteria, from investment value to social responsibility. The nine axes of ranking are:

- Innovation
- People management
- Use of assets
- Social responsibility
- Management quality
- Financial soundness
- Long-term investment
- Product quality
- Global competitiveness

The participant list is compiled in July–September and the surveys sent out annually in October. A second reminder mailing goes out toward the end of November, and all surveys are due back to the Hay Group by mid-December at the latest. Raters are asked to evaluate each eligible company on each attribute by assigning a score from 0 ("Poor") to 10 ("Excellent"). For the purposes of the industry rankings, a company's overall score is determined through a simple average of the individual attribute scores. Companies that rank in the top half of their industry are defined as "most admired" within their industry.[18]

Discussing the 2012 data, Mel Stark, vice president and regional reward practice leader at Hay Group, said, "Over the past 15 years, we have seen the composition of the World's Most Admired Companies (WMAC) list change, but the attributes that enable those companies to excel have remained the same."[19] According to Hay Group's research, the four critical factors for organizational success are the things they do:

- Executing and enabling strategy

Chapter 9 | Analysts

- Building structures and processes to sustain long-term performance
- Achieving success through people
- Placing a high value on leadership and talent

WMAC companies behave differently from their peers. Hay Group reports that 94% of WMAC feel that their efforts to engage employees have reduced turnover vs. 67% of peers, and 81% of WMAC use performance measures to encourage leaders to think short term and into the future vs. 43% of peers.[20]

Fortune notes, tongue in cheek, "The only thing harder than gaining admiration from peers in the corporate world is maintaining it" (Table 9-4). Three of the Most Admired Companies—GE, P&G, and Berkshire Hathaway—have stayed in the top slot of their industry sector every year they were included in the survey.[21] A rather exclusive group we would add.

Table 9-4. 2012 Fortune's Most Admired of the 1000 Largest U.S. Companies: Top 10

2011 Ranking	2012 Ranking	Company
1	1	Apple, Inc
2	2	Google
7	3	Amazon.com
6	4	The Coca Cola Company
12	5	IBM
8	6	FedEx
3	7	Berkshire Hathaway
16	8	Starbucks
5	9	Procter & Gamble
4	10	Southwest Airlines

Barron's

First described in Chapter 6, *Barron's* is a member of *The Wall Street Journal* family of companies owned by Dow Jones, and in turn, by News Corp. Barron's surveys professional money managers annually about the respect they accord the world's 100 largest companies. A more narrowly defined survey population than that used by *Fortune* and Hays Group in their Most Admired list, participants are asked to select one of four statements reflecting their view of

Reputation, Stock Price, and You 211

each company: Highly Respect, Respect, Respect Somewhat, or Don't Respect. A point value is assigned to each response, with the highest accorded to Highly Respect, and a mean score is tabulated for each company. In the case of ties, the higher ranking goes to the company with the most Highly Respect votes (Table 9-5).[22]

When asked to rank the factors they consider most important in determining respect for corporations, 24% of the managers this year offered "strong management" while 20% said "sound business strategy." Both are observable behaviors that underpin management's reputation and about 50% of a company's reputation. Eighteen percent felt ethics were foremost in their minds in terms of respect. Revenue and profit growth was the top concern for only 9% of respondents.

Barron's notes that while "The Most Respected Companies" rankings historically haven't been predictive of stock-trading patterns, the collective opinions of professional investors can serve as one component of evaluating companies.

Table 9-5. 2012 Barron's Most Respected of the 100 Largest Companies: Top 10

2011 Ranking	2012 Ranking	Company
1	1	Apple, Inc
4	2	IBM
5	3	McDonald's
2	4	Amazon.com
NR	5	Caterpillar
7	6	3M
13	7	United Parcel Service
8	8	The Coca Cola Company
19	9	Nestlé
17	10	Intel

Harris Interactive

In contrast to *Barron's* survey of money managers, Harris Interactive, a leading global independent research organization, surveys the general public. Formerly known as the Harris Poll, Harris Interactive has used since 1999 the Harris

Chapter 9 | Analysts

Reputation Quotient (RQ) to measure the reputations of the most visible companies in the United States. The Annual RQ process begins with a Nominations Phase and is followed by a Ratings Phase, where they measure the reputation of the most visible companies in the United States.

For the Nominations Phase, which is used to identify the companies with the most "visible" reputations according to the general public, respondents are asked to name companies that stand out as having the best and worst reputations overall. For the 2012 survey, two open-end questions were asked of about 4,600 people online:

> *Of all the companies that you're familiar with or that you might have heard about, which TWO – in your opinion – stand out as having the BEST reputations overall?*
>
> *Of all the companies that you're familiar with or that you might have heard about, which TWO – in your opinion – stand out as having the WORST reputations overall?*

Nominations from the surveys were tallied with subsidiaries and brand names were collapsed within the parent company. The nominations were then summed to create a total number of nominations for each company, and the final list comprised the 60 most visible companies in the United States as of October 2011.

The RQ Ratings Phase is also driven by survey of the general public. For two weeks in December 2011, approximately 13,000 respondents ranked more than 60 companies on 20 different attributes comprising six major reputational categories and the scores were compressed arithmetically to values where 80 or greater is excellent, and 50 or lower is "critically" poor.[23] The categories are:

- Social Responsibility
- Vision and Leadership
- Financial Performance
- Emotional Appeal
- Products and Services
- Workplace Environment

The 13th annual Harris RQ survey comprising the survey results of December 2011 were reported in February 2012 (Table 9-6). In summary, wrote the market research firm, "It's a complicated world for corporate America as consumer perceptions grow increasingly negative. With the erosion of trust in corporate leadership, consumers have higher expectations and are

Reputation, Stock Price, and You | 213

demanding more information and transparency from companies with which they plan to spend their hard-earned dollars." Companies with which the general public is a stakeholder only indirectly, and therefore likely to be impacted by their "critically" poor reputational standing only through shareholder or regulatory action, included three major financial sector firms.

> Over the lifespan of the RQ study, twelve companies have received scores below 50, and the vast majority of these, like Enron, MCI (formerly WorldCom), Adelphia, and Global Crossing, are now defunct. The 2012 RQ survey shows the reputations of Bank of America, Goldman Sachs and AIG in an equally challenging place. The general public believes that Bank of America has been more concerned with operational and financial recovery than with customers and rates the bank low in levels of trust, ethics, and customer service. In order to rebuild their reputation, Bank of America will need to engage beyond this functional rebound.[24]

Table 9-6. 2012 Harris Interactive Reputation RQ Ranking of the 60 Most Visible Companies: Top 10

2011 Ranking	2012 Ranking	Company
5	1	Apple, Inc
1	2	Google
15	3	The Coca Cola Company
8	4	Amazon.com
7	5	Kraft Foods
10	6	The Walt Disney Company
2	7	Johnson & Johnson
17	8	Whole Foods Market
16	9	Microsoft
13	10	United Parcel Service

Reputation Institute

Similar to the Harris approach, the Reputation Institute, a global management advisory organization, surveys the general public to generate its branded corporate reputation rankings, RepTrak (Table 9-7). Founded in 1997, surveys of the Reputation Institute's RepTrak calculate reputational scores on the basis of seven drivers of reputation that collectively influence the four "brand-like" emotional foundations of reputation: Admiration, Trust, Good Feeling,

Chapter 9 | Analysts

and Overall Esteem. The seven key dimensions that drive corporate reputation in the RepTrak system are: [25]

- Products/Services

- Innovation

- Workplace

- Governance

- Citizenship

- Leadership

- Financial Performance

  The RepTrak System evaluates the degree to which a particular dimension affects the emotional bond between a particular stakeholder group and a company, and it determines which dimensions have the highest impact on support and recommendation. It works across stakeholders providing a single lens to measure and manage reputation. [25]

For the 2012 study of U.S. companies, the largest companies based on revenue data from the *Forbes* Global 2000 list were filtered for firms that were engaged in general public-facing commercial activities and/or had a reasonable amount of familiarity with the general public. Survey results from 10,200 respondents were then tallied and values normalized to allow for multiyear longitudinal studies.

Reported in cooperation with *Forbes* magazine, the 2012 study showed that the influence of perceptions of the enterprise on its overall reputation has continued to increase over the years. In the Reputation Institute survey, governance drove 15.6% of a company's reputation with consumers, followed by corporate citizenship (14.2%). These dimensions were second only to Products & Services (17.7%).

Table 9-7. 2012 Reputation Institute Reptrak150 Ranking of U.S. Companies: Top 10

2011 Ranking	2012 Ranking	Company
15	1	General Mills
2	2	Kraft Foods Inc.
3	3	Johnson & Johnson
5	4	Kellogg's
1	5	Amazon.com

2011 Ranking	2012 Ranking	Company
6	6	United Parcel Service
25	7	The Coca Cola Company
46	8	Apple, Inc.
28	9	Pepsi Co.
20	10	Procter & Gamble

Explaining the data, Kasper Ulf Nielsen, Reputation Institute's executive partner said, "People's willingness to buy, recommend, work for, and invest in a company is driven 60% by their perceptions of the company and only 40% by their perceptions of their products."[16] The data trend, notes the Institute, speaks to our current environment—a "Reputation Economy"—where a company's value is being driven by who they are, not just by what they do.

Although the distinction between who they are and what they do may not be apparent to survey respondents, they, too, ranked four companies in 2012 in the "poor" reputation group with scores below 40 on the RepTrak scales. Those companies were Halliburton, Goldman Sachs, Fannie Mae, and Freddie Mac.

Table 9-8. Characteristics of the Overlapping RepTrak and RQ Public Survey Measures

	2012 RepTrak 150	2012 Harris RQ 60
Mean	67.24	70.79
Standard error	1.57	1.39
Median	71.26	73.19
Standard deviation	10.88	9.66
Sample variance	118.28	93.27
Kurtosis	0.07	0.19
Skewness	−0.89	-0.91
Minimum	36.95	46.18
Maximum	83.30	85.62

Guidance

There is a hunger for reputation metrics. "Evidence is accumulating to show that reputation *is* (emphasis in the original) directly associated with superior

Chapter 9 | Analysts

corporate performance over time, in ways that likely yield benefit both to investors and executives."[26] In a culture that manages what it can measure, and invests according to modern portfolio theory, metrics are essential.

None of the providers of survey data, or Steel City Re with its algorithmic metrics, suggests that reputational metrics alone are good stock picking tools. "Surveys tend to be backward-looking," says Charles Bobrinskoy, research director at Ariel Investments in Chicago. "People look at who has accomplished a lot and rank them highly. As investors, we have to say, 'Is all of it in the stock today?' Conversely, he says, it is important to ask whether a widely hated stock just might be an opportunity.[22] That question is explicit in both the RepuStars and Required Business Performance investment strategies that are informed by the Steel City Re's Reputational Value Metrics and other reputation metrics.

The *Fortune* Most Admired survey data and *Barron's* Most Respected survey data appear to capture the perceptions of investor and business professional stakeholders—peers—while both Harris Interactive and the Reputation Institute reputation scores capture the perception of the general public comprising a mix of customers, vendors, employees, or simply interested parties that vote and may influence regulators. The Steel City Re metrics capture the integrated views of all stakeholders.

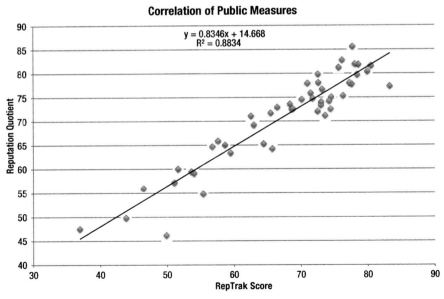

Figure 9-1. Plot of the RQ (y-axis) scores and RepTrak (x-axis) scores for the 2012 metrics. There is a 94% correlation between the RepTrak and RQ public survey measures, while the coefficient of determination (R^2) is 88%.

Reputation, Stock Price, and You

There is a 94% correlation between the scores for the 48 companies found both on the 2012 RepTrak150 list and the 2012 Harris Interactive RQ 60 list (Figure 9-1). This not surprising in light of some common history between the two measures. In 2006, Harris Interactive Inc.; Charles J. Fombrun, founder of the Reputation Institute; and Reputation Institute, Inc. entered into an agreement whereby Harris Interactive acquired all of Fombrun's right, title, and interest in (1) the trademarks "Harris/Fombrun Reputation Quotient," "Reputation Quotient," and "RQ," (2) every corporate measurement tool to which those trademarks refer or have referred, and (3) all data generated from application of such measurement tools. The agreement also contains certain restrictions on the ability of the parties to provide future specified reputation-related services for a period of 24 months, and also contains mutual releases of prior claims. Harris Interactive paid Fombrun $525,000 as consideration for the trademark rights transferred and the exclusive right to use the standardized methodology dating back to 1999 developed by Harris Interactive and Fombrun to measure corporate reputation.[27]

On the other hand, among the 128 companies for which there are overlapping metrics, there is only a 21% correlation between the Reputation Institute's RepTrak metrics reflecting public opinion and the companies most admired by their peers as reported to *Fortune* (Figure 9-2). The most notable outliers: Goldman Sachs and Halliburton, which both scored above 7 among their peers/Most Admired and below 40 among the general public/RepTrak. Among the 43 companies for which there are overlapping metrics, there is a 67% correlation between the *Barron's* Most Respected rankings provided by professional money managers and *Fortune's* Most Admired rankings from a wider cut and larger group of business professionals.

Studies on corporate reputations dating back more than a decade have emphasized the plurality of perceptions and representations around a company, referring to "corporate reputations" as a multifaceted rather than as a monolithic concept.[28] The poor correlation between two distinct communities of stakeholders, the general public as captured by the RepTrak metrics and the business community as captured by the Most Admired metrics, show that this remains true in 2012.

Theoretical work argues that stakeholders tend to pay attention to actions that are perceived as salient to their specific interests and values, and make inferences about corporate dispositions (their trustworthiness, reliability, social responsibility, etc.) based on observed actions that are interpreted as reflections of the former.[29] Empirical research exploring the drivers of reputation among specific categories of stakeholders, however, is relatively scarce, notwithstanding the recent emergence of multi-stakeholder investment strategies.

Chapter 9 | Analysts

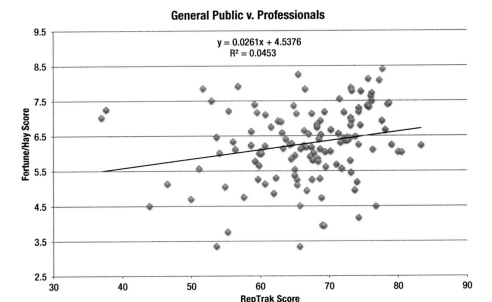

Figure 9-2. Plot of the WMAC scores (y-axis) and RepTrak scores (x-axis) for the 2012 metrics. There is a 21% correlation between the Reputation Institute RepTrak public survey and the *Fortune* Most Admired professional survey measures while the coefficient of determination (R^2) is only 5%.

A relatively recent study looked at the dimensions that affect the judgment of securities analysts, key influencers whose evaluations and behavior affect collective perceptions of critical resource-holders such as institutional as well as retail investors.[30] Results from a survey of 75 analysts operating on the Milan Stock Exchange by Gabioneta et al. indicate that securities analysts tend to judge companies mainly on their financial performance, the configuration of their governance structures, the quality of their financial disclosure, and the quality of their leadership and of their prospects for the future.[31]

The Gabioneta study indicated that four dimensions of corporate reputation—namely Financial Performance, Vision & Leadership, Financial Disclosure, and Corporate Governance following the framework of the Reputation Institute—displayed a high correlation with the overall disposition of securities analysts toward a company. These four dimensions of corporate reputation, however, as suggested empirically by the 2012 survey data, did not seem to have a direct effect on analysts' behavior—that is, on the content of the recommendations they issue. Instead, their influence appears to be mediated by what we termed a company's "emotional appeal"—in other words, the extent to which a company is trusted, liked, admired, and respected by the respondent.

Another study suggested that analysts might view reputation in the context of a corporate financial statement. Under this paradigm, it was suggested, reputation could be parsed on the balance sheet as both an asset and a liability. On the asset side is the increased value of the implicit claims sold by the firm now and in the future, while on the liability side is the present value of honoring these claims in the future. For example, consider a durable-good producer that has built a reputation for superior post-sales service. The present value of the price premiums that the firm receives on sales of its product as a result of the reputation would be an asset. The liability would be the present value of the cost of providing superior after-sales service in the future.[32]

Such a perspective is of academic interest but not necessarily operationally useful to an analyst. This volume has suggested that reputation is best viewed as influencing the magnitude of line items on the profit and loss statement, as reflecting stakeholder impressions of governance, and as will be shown in Chapter 10, influencing regulatory burden. The data in this chapter indicate that what companies do creates different observable quantifiable reputations among different stakeholders. These can be measured through surveys and algorithms, and the various measures of reputation can inform secondary actions among stakeholders ranging from selecting stocks to improving marketing strategies

To be sure, these various approaches to measuring and quantifying corporate reputations vary rather widely. One major point of differentiation among the measures is timeliness. Surveys done well take time; overnight surveys, the staple of election season, yield widely disparate outcomes even on narrowly defined questions.

The two algorithmic measures are more responsive to market timing. Transparent Value's metrics rank discrepancies between equity investor expectations and the likelihood that operations will meet those expectations. High probabilities of failure can serve as early warnings of securities to avoid. Steel City Re's metrics report reputation ranking, value, volatility, and direction of change. Because they reflect the expectations of a broad range of stakeholders, they can help management and boards get timely early warnings of adverse public reactions to policy decisions and perceptions of operational risks—one of the most compelling applications of decision markets.[33]

The greatest consumers of metrics are stakeholders who extract the informational content therein to produce more metrics: market forecasts. More than any other market segment, analysts will find leading indicators in these extra-financial measures of corporate reputational value (Table 9-9).

Chapter 9 | Analysts

Consider This

- Based on what companies do, quantitative measures of reputation report stakeholder perceptions that eventually translate to actions with material economic consequences.

- Depending on how the data are captured, from whom they are captured, and how they are processed, reputation metrics may be leading indicators of customer behavior, investor behavior, or multi-stakeholder behavior. In any case, they represent the "wisdom of crowds."

- Different stakeholders may assign significantly different reputational values to the same company, thereby enabling certain reputation metrics to inform equity selection strategies.

By the Numbers

Table 9-9. Characteristics of Several Measures of Reputation (Returns as of 4 Oct. 2012)

Type	Description	Insight
Expert	Transparent Value's Required Business Performance Probability Metrics primarily for large cap companies. Captures equity investor expectations.	RBP: $0 < x < 100\%$
Algorithmic	Two exemplary large cap funds informed by Transparent Value metrics, Market (TVIMX) and Value (TVVIX).	TTM returns TVIMX: 21.63% TTM returns TVVIX : 24.54% TTM returns SPX: 25.03%
Algorithmic	Steel City Re Corporate Reputation Ranking and Reputation Value Metrics for approximately 7,000 public companies. Captures multi-stakeholder expectations.	Ranking: $0 \leq x \leq 1.0000$ Value: $\sim 1.0 \leq x \leq 2.5$
Algorithmic	Two exemplary equity indexes informed by the Steel City Re metrics, RepuStars Variety (REPUVAR), and RepuStarsSPX.	TTM returns REPUVAR: 26.20% TTM returns RepuSPX: 36.48% TTM returns SPX: 25.03%

Type	Description	Insight
Survey	Fortune/Hay Group Most Admired metrics for the 1,000 largest companies. Captures business and financial professional stakeholder expectations.	Admired: $0 \leq x \leq 10$
Survey	*Barron's* Most Respected metrics for the 100 largest global companies. Captures financial professional stakeholder expectations.	Respected: $1 \leq x \leq 4$
Survey	Harris Interactive Reputation Quotient metrics. Captures general public stakeholder expectations.	RQ: $\sim 40 \leq x \leq 90$
Survey	Reputation Institute RepTrak metrics. Captures general public stakeholder expectations.	RepTrak: $\sim 30 \leq x \leq 90$
Survey	Correlation of reputation rankings from the general public with rankings from the professional business community	21%

Endnotes

1 Clifford S. The annual shareholders' meeting for Wal-Mart, like its stock, is buoyant. *The New York Times*. 1 June 2012. Available at: http://www.nytimes.com/2012/06/02/business/wal-mart-board-challenges-rebuffed.html?_r=2&ref=business. Accessed 12 August 2012.

2 Bernstein IS. Metaphor, cognitive belief, and science. *Behavioral and Brain Sciences*. 1988;11:247–248.

3 Available at: http://scotland.stv.tv/greatest-scot/nominees/118993-andrew-carnegie-1835-1919/. Accessed 4 May 2012.

4 Available at: http://www.pbs.org/wgbh/amex/carnegie/peopleevents/pande01.html. Accessed 4 May 2012.

5 Hill N. *The wisdom of Andrew Carnegie as told to Napoleon Hill*. Napoleon Hill Foundation, 2005.

6 Ray S. Boeing's Conner sticking to 777 jet's upgrade plan. *Bloomberg*. 23 August 2012. Available at: http://www.bloomberg.com/news/2012-08-24/boeing-s-conner-sticking-to-777-jet-s-upgrade-plan.html\. Accessed 24 August 2012.

Chapter 9 | Analysts

7 How Julian Koski's maverick stock picking method led to a merger with Guggenheim. *RIA Biz*. 10 January 2012. Available at: http://www.riabiz.com/a/10528703/how-julian-koskis-maverick-stock-picking-method-led-to-a-merger-guggenheim. Accessed 26 August 2012.

8 Transparent value. Available at: http://www.transparentvaluefunds.com/index.aspx?q=i. Accessed 25 August 2012.

9 Guggenheim Partners launches three transparent value mutual funds. Press Release, 3 May 2010. Available at: http://www.transparentvaluefunds.com/news/Guggenheim%20Press%20Release.pdf. Accessed 25 August 2012.

10 Prediction markets. *Wikipedia*. Available at: http://en.wikipedia.org/wiki/Prediction_market. Accessed 25 August 2012.

11 Jones H. UK sets out terms of urgent Libor review. *Reuters*. 30 July 2012. Available at: http://www.reuters.com/article/2012/07/30/us-britain-libor-idUSBRE86T08320120730. Accessed 25 August 2012.

12 The basics. BBALibor™. Available at: http://www.bbalibor.com/bbalibor-explained/the-basics. Accessed 25 August 2012.

13 Graefe A, Armstrong JS. Comparing face-to-face meetings, nominal groups, Delphi and prediction markets on an estimation task. *International Journal of Forecasting*. 2011; 27:183–195.

14 Steel City Re. Intangible Asset Management: reputation metrics. Available at: http://www.steelcityre.com/finance_management_index.shtml. Accessed 28 August 2012.

15 Technology Option Capital. Guide to RepuStars. Available at: http://www.steelcityre.com/documents/SOP4004GuidetoRepuStarsv720120229.pdf. Accessed 28 August 2012.

16 Smith J. The world's most reputable companies. *Forbes*. 7 June 2012. Available at: http://www.forbes.com/sites/jacquelynsmith/2012/06/07/the-worlds-most-reputable-companies/. Accessed 28 August 2012.

17 How we pick them. World's most admired companies. *Fortune*. 2012. Available at: http://money.cnn.com/magazines/fortune/most-admired/2012/faq/. Accessed 28 August 2012.

18 Hay Group. How we identify and rank the Most Admired. Available at: http://www.haygroup.com/ww/best_companies/index.aspx?id=1582. Accessed 29 August 2012.

19 FORTUNE magazine World's Most Admired companies. Press release, 1 March 2012. Available at: http://www.haygroup.com/ww/press/details.aspx?id=33038. Accessed 28 August 2012.

20 Hay Group. Media fact box. Available at: http://www.haygroup.com/Fortune/media-fact-box/. Accessed 29 August 2012.

21 Most admired industry stars. World's most admired companies. *Fortune*. 2012. Available at: http://money.cnn.com/magazines/fortune/most-admired/2012/longest-streaks/?iid=smlrr. Accessed 28 August 2012.

22 Santoli M. *Barron's* cover: The world's most respected companies. *Barron's*. 25 June 2012. Available at: http://online.barrons.com/article/SB500014240531119038829045774789930577 27490.html#articleTabs_article%3D1. Accessed 28 August 2012.

Reputation, Stock Price, and You

23 The 2012 Harris Poll Annual RQ® Public Summary Report. Available at: http://www. harrisinteractive.com/vault/2012_Harris_Poll_RQ_Summary_Report.pdf. Accessed 28 August 2012.

24 Google slips into second as Apple soars to coveted top spot with highest reputation score in history, according to 13th Annual Harris Poll RQ® Study. Press release, 13 February 2012. Available at: http://www.harrisinteractive.com/NewsRoom/PressReleases/tabid/446/ctl/ ReadCustom%20Default/mid/1506/ArticleId/960/Default.aspx. Accessed 28 August 2012.

25 Reputation Institute. The RepTrak™ system. Available at: http://www.reputationinstitute. com/thought-leadership/the-reptrak-system. Accessed 28 August 2012.

26 Greenberg M. On breaking the logjam: the how and why of corporate reputation leadership. *Corporate Finance Review.* 2012; 17(1):11–17.

27 Purchase/Sale Agreement between the Company, Charles J. Fombrun and Reputation Institute, Inc., dated as of May 15, 2006. Available at: http://apps.shareholder.com/sec/ viewerContent.aspx?companyid=HPOL&docid=4435474. Accessed 28 August 2012.

28 Dowling GR. *Creating corporate reputations: identity, image, and performance.* Oxford: Oxford University Press, 2001.

29 Sjovall AM, Talk AC. From actions to impressions: cognitive attribution theory and the formation of corporate reputation. *Corporate Reputation Review.* 2004; 7(3):269–281.

30 Fombrun CJ. Corporate reputations as economic assets. In Hitt M, et al . (Eds.), *Handbook of strategic management.* Oxford: Blackwell, 2002.

31 Gabbioneta C, Ravasi D, Mazzola P. Exploring the drivers of corporate reputation: a study of Italian securities analysts. *Corporate Reputation Review.* 2007;10(2): 99.

32 Dobson J. Introducing ethics into the finance curriculum: a simple three-level Guide. *Journal of Financial Education.* 2008; Spring: 1–17.

33 Hanson R. The Policy Analysis Market (and FutureMAP) Archive. George Mason University. Available at: http://hanson.gmu.edu/policyanalysismarket.html. Accessed 2 September 2012.

CHAPTER

10

Regulators
By Michael D. Greenberg, JD, PhD[1]

> We do want to have regulators who set the rules. For example, there has to be transparency. One of the things that's clear about JP Morgan Chase and was true about AIG: they didn't know what their losses were. If the rules that we had talked about had been in place, and they will be shortly, then they would not have been surprised by losses that were first 'a tempest in a teapot,' and then $2 billion, and then $5 to 6 billion. That's our job: to put rules in place that govern the way things work.
>
> —Barney Frank[2]

Regulators serve as the long arm of government, acting to set and enforce legal standards that apply broadly to define the landscape of industry and commerce. Federal and state regulators serve to monitor corporate behavior in many different ways. Notable examples range from the regulation of pollution by the Environmental Protection Agency (EPA), to the oversight of domestic aviation activity by the Federal Aviation Administration (FAA), to the supervision of securities markets and the capital formation process by the Securities and Exchange Commission (SEC).

In each instance, U.S. regulators establish and enforce rules that bound and limit the scope of legitimate corporate behavior. Some aspects of regulation (as in the case of the SEC) help to structure basic commercial and financial activities, setting a blueprint for how business itself will be conducted. Other aspects of regulation touch on more operational or peripheral elements of business enterprise, but that nevertheless are closely tied to reputation risk— as illustrated by regulations that target product quality, or workplace safety, or corporate ethical culture.[3]

In all such instances, government standard-setting and enforcement activity imposes a set of obligations with which firms neglect to comply at their own peril. More deeply, regulators also help to generate a set of normative social

Chapter 10 | Regulators

expectations for what responsible and reputable corporate behavior ought to look like. Then too, regulators are themselves consumers of reputational information: the enforcement decisions that regulators make, in particular, can easily be influenced by the reputation of firms that fall under regulatory scrutiny. In sum and for a variety of reasons, regulators are an important reputational stakeholder group for corporations to consider.

At the outset, it's important to recognize that the relationship between regulators and the private sector is complex. Deep questions can be asked about the appropriate scope of regulation, how regulators can and should carry out their functions, and whether or not particular areas of regulation are truly enhancing of social welfare. Meanwhile, many narrow silos of regulatory activity, such as Nuclear Regulatory Commission (NRC) oversight of the nuclear power industry, or Food and Drug Administration (FDA) oversight of the new drug development process, are highly technical and detailed in their own right, and demand close scrutiny simply to understand their intent, much less the specific requirements (and corresponding risks) actually being imposed upon industry.

More broadly and in a somewhat different vein, the relationship between regulators and business enterprises is not a one-way street. Businesses can and do influence regulatory policy and enforcement activity, even as regulators monitor and shape the behavior of the private sector. Here again, another set of normative questions arises, regarding what sort of influence and access corporations ought to have, in connection with the regulatory process. It is notably beyond the scope of this chapter to delve deeply into any of these questions about regulation, other than by acknowledging that the relationship between regulators and corporations is complicated and reciprocal, and particularly so when it comes to the influence and impact of corporate reputation.

For current purposes, the main focus of this chapter is to illustrate three basic ideas about regulators, corporate reputation risk, and material economic costs. First, regulators are indeed a major stakeholder group when it comes to corporate reputation. Regulators are both influenced by reputation in the decisions that they make and influencers of reputation through their own enforcement activities. Second, some elements of regulatory policy are particularly aimed at strengthening the pillars of corporate reputation, and at driving companies to pursue stronger reputational performance. Finally, some of the most catastrophic instances of corporate reputational crisis have involved prominent roles on the part of regulators. Where companies fail to comply with substantive regulatory requirements, or to engage effectively with regulators, major reputational damage can sometimes ensue as a result. We reflect on several examples in the text that follows.

Rewards and Enhanced Reputations

Regulators can reward businesses for behaviors associated with reputation-building or -sustaining processes. In the cases that follow, Morgan Stanley was rewarded for behaviors that fostered an ethical environment, notwithstanding the action of a rogue, and the Centers for Medicare and Medicaid Services was charged to begin rewarding hospitals for delivering quality services.

Morgan Stanley: Prosecution Declined

Chapter 8 of the Federal Sentencing Guidelines for Organizations (FSGO) provides a set of standards to deter and punish organizational crime, while recognizing and encouraging effective compliance programs within firms. The FSGO is a regulatory enforcement document, in several important ways. It notably provides benchmarks for federal judges in criminal sentencing, but has also been influential with regard to Justice Department policy on prosecuting corporate crime, and in deferred prosecution agreements entered into by enforcement authorities.

Perhaps more important, the FSGO has incentivized a range of positive compliance and ethical culture behaviors on the part of corporations, such that firms become entitled to more lenient treatment from judges and prosecutors for having undertaken the behaviors. In this vein, a major amendment to the FSGO in 2004 set out a specific corporate obligation "to promote an organizational culture that encourages ethical behavior and compliance with law." This is an example of a regulatory standard that ties directly to corporate reputational performance, and to efforts by companies to fortify their reputations by improving their values, norms, and internal controls. When instances of corporate crime do indeed occur, fulfillment of FSGO standards can in principle help both to protect a firm's reputation and to secure more lenient treatment on the part of enforcement authorities.

The prosecution of Garth Peterson, a former managing director for Morgan Stanley in China who was sentenced in federal court on 16 August 2012, showcases the point.[4] Peterson, an executive involved in Morgan Stanley's China-based practice, perpetrated a fraudulent real estate deal in Shanghai that circumvented the company's internal controls, and that netted Peterson and his co-conspirators millions of dollars in illicit gains. Peterson's actions were subsequently found to have violated the U.S. Foreign Corrupt Practices Act (FCPA), which forbids U.S. nationals and corporations from bribing foreign officials. Under the provisions of FCPA, Morgan Stanley itself could potentially have been subject to criminal sanction for Peterson's misconduct. Federal prosecutors, however, chose not to follow that course, noting instead that Peterson "used a web of deceit to thwart Morgan Stanley's effort to maintain

Chapter 10 | Regulators

adequate controls designed to prevent corruption." They concluded that because "Morgan Stanley constructed and maintained a system of internal controls, which provided reasonable assurances that its employees were not bribing government officials, the Department of Justice declined to bring any enforcement action against Morgan Stanley related to Peterson's misconduct. The company voluntarily disclosed this matter and has cooperated throughout the Department's investigation."[5]

How does the Morgan Stanley case relate back to corporate reputational risk? The answer is that Morgan Stanley was broadly following both FSGO standards and the requirements of FCPA, through its internal controls designed to prevent bribery. The Justice Department investigation of Peterson ultimately exonerated Morgan Stanley of any wrong-doing, and held up Morgan Stanley's internal controls and cooperation as an example of good conduct on the part of the company. Thus, Morgan Stanley avoided the potential for significant fines and penalties under the FCPA, while enhancing its own reputation for honesty with the Department of Justice, and perhaps with other reputational stakeholder groups as well. The outcome of the Peterson case represents a potential reputational crisis that was avoided by the company. It also reflects a series of management controls and internal investments that were made by Morgan Stanley, at least in part, in response to regulatory standards for corporate compliance programs, the latter being embedded in the FSGO, and subsequently adopted by the Department of Justice in its criminal enforcement efforts.

The costs avoided by Morgan Stanley were material. Drawing on DOJ published statistics for all FCPA settlements reached and fines imposed during 1998–2010, the average associated costs in criminal and other penalties in that period was $69.4 million. Higher costs were associated with guilty pleas, and lower with deferred prosecution agreements (Table 10-1).[6]

Table 10-1. Top Ten Foreign Corrupt Practices Act Settlements, 1998–2010. DPA=Deferred Prosecution Agreements.

Company Name	Year	Amount of Settlement (in Millions)	Disposition
Siemens	2008	$800	Guilty Plea
KBR/Halliburton	2009	$579	Guilty Plea
BAE	2010	$400	Guilty Plea
Snamprogetti Netherlands	2010	$365	DPA

Reputation, Stock Price, and You — 229

Company Name	Year	Amount of Settlement (in Millions)	Disposition
Technip S.A.	2010	$338	DPA
Daimler AG	2010	$185	Guilty Plea; DPA
Panalpina	2010	$82	Guilty Plea; DPA
ABB Ltd	2010	$58	Guilty Plea; DPA
Pride	2010	$56	Guilty Plea; DPA
Shell	2010	$48	DPA

The willingness of the Department of Justice to decline prosecution because of existing controls illustrates how challenging it can be to police rogues. In part, the argument goes, this is because every individual under the right circumstances has his price. "The commercialism of the last two decades has displayed a distinctive kind of boundlessness, emblematic of a world in which everything is for sale," writes political philosopher Michael J. Sandel.[7]

When he was an Illinois attorney, the story goes, Abraham Lincoln represented a poor widow who was suing the president of the local bank and asking for $5 in damages. Struggling then to earn a living, Lincoln would become the 16th president of the United States on the basis of, among other things, his reputation for propriety and ethics.

The bank president, a pillar of his community, is alleged to have visited Lincoln's office and, in the presence of Lincoln's partner, offered Abe a bribe to throw the case. Lincoln is reported to have said, "No, the lady deserves her day in court." The banker responded that it would be humiliating if he lost to this widow, so he raised his bribe to $25. Lincoln refused. "$50," said the banker. Abe refused again.

The banker stood up, started reaching for his wallet and said, "Mr. Lincoln, you drive a hard bargain. I'll give you $100 cash right now." Abe jumped up, grabbed the banker and threw him out the door, pitching him into the mud outside. Lincoln's partner was astonished. "Abe, he tried to bribe you three times and you didn't mind. Then the fourth time you just seem to blow up," he said. Abe responded, "He was getting too close to my price."[8]

Hospital Reputation: Quality Encouraged

Responding to the mandates of the Affordable Care Act (ACA), the Centers for Medicare and Medicaid Services (CMS) enacted regulations in 2011 to establish a "Value-Based Purchasing Plan" for hospital services, which ties hospital reimbursement under Medicare to a series of performance metrics, the latter notably including patient survey feedback describing the quality of patients' own experiences in hospital.[9] In a related vein, CMS issued a 2012 final rule under the ACA designed to reduce 30-day readmission rates at hospitals, under which Medicare would penalize hospitals through reductions in their reimbursements of up to 1% during the 2013 program year, based on hospitals' failure to meet specified targets in their own readmission rates.[10] It was anticipated that approximately 2,200 hospitals will be immediately affected by the new rule on readmission rates, collectively facing financial penalties of $300 million. In out years under the new CMS regulation, the potential reimbursement penalties for faulty hospital readmission rates will grow substantially from the initial $300 million base figure.

CMS rules under the ACA provide another example of the reciprocal relationship between regulatory action and corporate reputation. On one hand, the use by CMS of patient feedback in determining hospital reimbursement rates is fundamentally a reputation-driven process, and one that involves a regulator drawing on patient survey metrics in order to make basic decisions about whether to reward or punish specific institutions. Financial penalties based on high hospital readmission rates, meanwhile, correspond to a different high-profile regulatory intervention, and one that will likely generate a reputational impact of its own on targeted institutions (in parallel with the adverse revenue effect). In sum, new CMS rules for the reimbursement of hospitals are at once influenced by hospital reputations, and at the same time are likely to become significant influencers of those reputations. All controversy concerning the reasonableness of the new CSM rules set aside, there is one thing that can be said with confidence about the rules: They seem almost certain to drive a new reputational focus among hospitals, as the latter seek to protect their reimbursements by responding effectively to the CMS reimbursement regime.

Punishments and Diminished Reputations

Regulators can punish businesses for failures in reputation-building or sustaining processes. Punishments may come in the form of penalties, fines, or prohibitions from doing business. Punishments may also come in the form of

Reputation, Stock Price, and You

denials of requests for relief. In the cases below, BP was penalized for a host of failures; and, for its business process failures, Knight Capital was denied relief.

BP: Failures Punished

As we've already discussed at length in Chapters 1 and 2, the BP Deep Water Horizon drill rig disaster is an example of a highly material reputational crisis event. The Deep Water catastrophe involved multiple levels of operational problems and challenges in the lead-up to the spill, but one notable dimension involved regulatory standards and monitoring, and their relationship to the spill. Prior to 2011, off-shore oil drilling in the United States was generally subject to the oversight of the Minerals Management Service (MMS), an agency within the U.S. Department of the Interior.[11] In the decades prior to the Deep Water Horizon event, regulatory policy concerning offshore oil drilling and transportation had notably seesawed between intervals of intense scrutiny and stronger regulation (as in the aftermath of the Exxon Valdez event) vs. intervals of deregulation and a more permissive government stance.[12]

Although the MMS had regulatory responsibility for offshore oil drilling activities on the U.S. continental shelf at the time of the disaster, subsequent reviewers have noted that there was no "comprehensive set of regulations specifically addressing deep water technology, drilling, or well design" at the time of the Macando blow out.[13] Perhaps for this reason, the MMS notably did not detect the problems at the Macando well-site through ordinary inspection processes prior to the event. The post-event investigation nevertheless revealed a series of regulatory violations associated with the Deep Water Horizon disaster, including failure to perform operations in a safe and workmanlike manner, failure to take necessary precautions to keep the well under control at all times, and failure to use appropriate pressure integrity tests as specified by regulations.[14] Although BP was not directly fined by the regulator for these and other regulatory violations, the violations themselves arguably set the stage for the oil spill and for the $20-billion settlement fund that eventually followed it.

The Deep Water Horizon case illustrates an important dimension of regulatory impact on reputation risk and costs from compliance failures. Particularly where the focus of a regulator is on safety, security, or product quality issues, then the risk associated with violating the rules may have less to do with the threat of investigation and prosecution by the regulator than with injury and harm that follows from a major industrial accident. In the Deep Water instance, stronger regulatory monitoring and enforcement in the

Chapter 10 | Regulators

lead-up to the crisis plausibly might have helped to prevent the calamity (and the associated reputational crisis), even though it might also have been perceived by the company as burdensome and punitive.

So what's the right way to understand the role of the regulator, and of corporate reputation, in the Deep Water Horizon case? The regulator set broad safety and operating standards that applied to offshore drilling activity. The regulator did not discover the violations at the Macando site until after the crisis. Meanwhile, the regulatory violations of BP and its affiliates were associated with a catastrophic accident and billions of dollars in damages. Ex post investigation of the accident spotlighted the regulatory violations and deficiencies.

Among the negative consequences to BP was a serious blow to its reputation, across all of its major reputational stakeholder groups—including, but not limited to, the federal regulator. Note that major safety and environmental disasters can always be understood as involving reputational crisis for the firms involved in them. In this instance, the failure to follow regulatory guidelines (and to institute effective controls and compliance) was arguably a proximate cause for an environmental catastrophe, and for the corporate reputational hurricane that accompanied it.

Knight Capital Group: "Mulligan" Denied

Knight Capital is a U.S.-based financial services firm that engages in a variety of institutional trading and market-making activities. The firm was well known and reasonably well regarded until August of 2012, when, as recounted in Chapter 7, a glitch in a newly activated automated trading program led to wildly erratic and unintended securities trading activities. The firm found itself unable to shut down the rogue software quickly, and trading losses of approximately $440 million resulted within a matter of minutes. The losses threw the firm into turmoil, led to a collapse in the price of its own common stock, and largely wiped out the equity position of Knight Capital's existing shareholders, forcing a crisis intervention and recapitalization of the firm by a new group of investors.[15] In the wake of the episode, confidence in the broader stock market (not to speak of Knight Capital itself) reportedly deteriorated to its lowest point in several years.[16]

The automated trading disaster at Knight Capital would have caused a reputational crisis for the company in any event, but regulatory oversight and intervention (or lack thereof) played an important role in both the lead-up to and aftermath of, the crisis.

Reputation, Stock Price, and You 233

Only hours following the "frolic and detour" perpetrated by Knight's rogue trading software, the CEO of the company reportedly called Mary Schapiro, chairman of the SEC who was vacationing in Maine, to request that the firm be allowed to unwind its unintentional acquisition of more than $4 billion of securities positions, in a manner analogous to the cancellation of bogus trades that was permitted following the "flash crash" of 2010. Knight's request for a professional Mulligan[17] was rejected by the SEC, which then forced the company to seek rapid intervention from new investors in order to recapitalize. *The Wall Street Journal* reported: "Ms. Schapiro's willingness to stand firm on a decision that would imperil a large firm was partly a reflection of the changes in place since the market collapse on May 6, 2010, known as the flash crash. Exchanges canceled hundreds of trades afterward, angering market participants who said the decision was arbitrary and hurt market integrity. Under SEC pressure, exchanges instituted more specific rules governing when trades could be canceled. Ms. Schapiro stood by those guidelines, say people briefed on the discussion."[18]

In a related vein and in the days following the episode, the SEC began to investigate whether Knight had violated the SEC's "Market Access Rule," which promulgated standards to require broker-dealers and market makers to install new control systems to prevent automated trades that either violate capital and credit thresholds, or else that appear to be erroneous.[19] The Market Access Rule was itself enacted in the wake of the flash crash of 2010, and was specifically intended to prevent episodes like the recent Knight Capital trading debacle.

As of later summer 2012, the SEC investigation of Knight Capital remained ongoing—but it once again reflects a situation in which the behavior of a firm arguably violated a regulatory standard pressing for more rigorous compliance and controls, with disastrous financial and reputational consequences for the firm. Further regulatory fallout both for Knight Capital, and for the securities markets more broadly, could easily spin out of this episode downstream.

Guidance

The preceding cases illustrate that regulators are sometimes either strongly influenced by, or else exert strong influence upon, corporate reputation. The cases also show that regulators often set standards that can be associated with tremendous reputational risk to firms, and that that risk often goes beyond the simple threat of enforcement.

Notably absent from our list of cases in this chapter are the many episodes in which regulatory enforcement and intervention have themselves been directly associated with fines and penalties of tens or hundreds of millions of dollars

Chapter 10 | Regulators

to corporations (Siemens, Alcatel-Lucent, Daimler-Chrysler, Eli Lilly, Johnson & Johnson, etc.). Those episodes are surely important too, but they obscure the fact that regulation, and the behavior of regulators, can often have a more subtle, but equally important, effect on firms.

Whenever regulatory standards are violated by a corporation and significant harm to external stakeholder groups results, then the potential for a reputational disaster is close at hand. The regulator often sets the stage for corporate reputational risk in these instances, and may shine the investigative spotlight after the fact of a crisis episode, even though regulatory enforcement in itself is not the precipitating factor of the crisis. A similar reputational pattern can be observed in a wide array of regulatory examples and fact patterns, drawing on substantive regulators as disparate as the SEC and the Minerals Management Service.

In a somewhat different vein, it's important to recognize that some key elements of regulatory policy are particularly aimed at strengthening the antecedents of corporate reputation, and driving companies to pursue stronger reputational performance. The FSGO (with respect to Morgan Stanley) and CMS examples described in this chapter are both cases in point.

The FSGO is in one sense a back-handed regulatory document seeking to drive a corporate compliance agenda, at the same time that it also serves as a blueprint for federal sentencing decisions in corporate criminal cases. The FSGO provides a set of detailed instructions to companies for how to mitigate an important precursor to reputational risk, while also establishing incentives to press companies actually to do so.

The CMS example, by contrast, spotlights a regulatory effort to drive stronger reputational performance for hospitals with another major stakeholder group: patients. In this case, the regulator is a direct consumer of reputational information about the institutions, and is using that information to incentivize new hospital-based quality improvement efforts. Here again, regulators play an important role on both sides of the corporate reputational spectrum. Regulators set standards that directly influence reputational risk and prophylactic activity on the part of firms. But regulators are also consumers of reputational information, and can themselves be strongly influenced by it in their enforcement and standard-setting activities. To put it another way, regulators and firms are like the partners in an elaborate minuet, constantly moving back and forth in intricate patterns, with a choreography that is partly scripted by institutional reputations.

Given all of the foregoing, we would be remiss not to remember that there is a deep and fundamental relationship between what regulators do and what firms do through their compliance programs. In some sense, compliance

Reputation, Stock Price, and You 235

efforts undertaken within companies are a mirror reflection of the standards and enforcement undertaken by regulators. Compliance in a vacuum would have little meaning or purpose without regulation to give structure and substance to related corporate efforts. Again, regulators are one of the basic landscape features of the business environment, in helping to determine how commerce and industry will be conducted. Many facets of the relationship between regulators and the private sector move beyond considerations of corporate reputation. Nevertheless, corporate reputation and reputational risk are underlying ghosts in the machine, whenever and wherever the government becomes involved in the regulation of business enterprise.

What are some practical action items for firms and executives to consider, based on all of this? First, know your regulator. A firm needs to understand the substantive regulatory standards that apply to it, and the enforcement posture of the corresponding regulators, in order to assess and manage its related risks. Second, engage your regulator. The fact that regulators are themselves a reputational stakeholder group, and a consumer of reputational information about business, means that firms have some power to influence them through the scope of their own behavior. Formulating a plan for how best to do this is partly a compliance activity, but also an activity with deeper strategic and cultural significance for firm management.

Finally, firms should appreciate the Socratic maxim: "The way to gain a good reputation is to endeavor to be what you desire to appear."[20] Meeting the demands of regulators is only partly about the technical exercise of fulfilling outside legal requirements. On a more important level, it is about internalizing and embodying a set of substantive standards that define product quality, workplace safety, environmental sustainability, good labor practice, and many of the other hallmarks of corporate reputational excellence. To really do this well is to maximize corporate reputational assets, while reducing reputational risks, and the financial costs arising, to a minimum (Table 10-2). And that is the fundamental challenge for corporations in seeking to deal most effectively with their regulators.

Consider This

- Regulators are both influenced by reputation in the decisions that they make and are also influencers of reputation through their own enforcement activities.

- Some elements of regulatory policy are particularly aimed at strengthening the antecedents of corporate reputation and at driving companies to pursue stronger reputational performance.

Chapter 10 | Regulators

- Some of the most catastrophic corporate reputational crises were precipitated by corporate failures to comply with substantive regulatory requirements, or to engage effectively with regulators.

By the Numbers

Prosecution with imprisonment, fines, and penalties are among the punishments regulators use to foster conformance with business practices that are acceptable under the law. Conformance as evidenced by intent—an authentic reputation—even in the setting of a process failure can mitigate punishment and avoid costs.

Table 10-2. Exemplary Benefits and Costs of Regulatory Compliance or Failure

P&L Impact	Regulator	Action	Example	Value
Cost avoided	Department of Justice	Criminal prosecution averted	Morgan Stanley	$69.4 million (est.)
Cost avoided	CMS	Penalties averted	Meeting Medicare quality standard for hospital readmission	$300 million (aggregate anticipated hospital penalties for 2013)
Cost incurred	Multiple	Fines and penalties	BP	$20 billion
Cost incurred	SEC	Relief denied	Knight Capital	$440 million

Endnotes

1 Michael Greenberg is a Senior Behavioral Scientist with the RAND Corporation and Director of the RAND Center for Corporate Ethics and Governance. He is a lawyer and a psychologist by training. He received his PhD in clinical psychology from Duke University and his law degree from Harvard, and spent several years in corporate law practice at Ropes & Gray in Boston prior to joining RAND.

2 Representative Barney Frank (D-Mass.) speaking on Bloomberg TV, 2 August 2012. Available at: http://hereisthecity.com/2012/08/03/rep-barney-frank-congress-cant-write-laws-to-stop-errors-like-kn/. Accessed 12 August 2012.

3 It is not a coincidence that these examples of regulatory focus correspond directly to several of the basic pillars of business reputation that we outlined in Chapter 1.

Reputation, Stock Price, and You   237

4 See discussion in Department of Justice press release dated April 25, 2012, Former Morgan Stanley managing director pleads guilty for role in evading internal controls Required by FCPA." Available at: http://www.justice.gov/opa/pr/2012/April/12-crm-534.html. Accessed 2 September 2012.

5 Ibid.

6 See Department of Justice, *Appendix B – Chart 5, Sanctions imposed upon legal persons for FCPA violations since 1998*. Available at: http://www.justice.gov/criminal/fraud/fcpa/docs/response3-appx-b.pdf. Accessed 2 September 2012.

7 Olster S. One nation, ruled by money. *Fortune*. 20 April 2012. Available at: http://features.blogs.fortune.cnn.com/tag/ethics/. Accessed 3 September 2012.

8 Tsukerman Y. He was getting close to my price. Available at: http://ytspar.tumblr.com/post/45832759l/he-was-getting-too-close-to-my-price. Accessed 3 July 2012.

9 See 76 *Federal Register* 26490 (May 6, 2011). CMS, hospital inpatient value-based purchasing program: final rule.

10 See generally Fiegl C. AMEDNEWS.com, August 27, 2012. 2,200 Hospitals face Medicare pay penalty for readmissions. Available at: http://www.ama-assn.org/amednews/2012/08/27/gvsb0827.htm; and Rao J. NPR blog, August 13, 2012, Thousands of Hospitals face penalties for high readmission rates. Available at: http://www.npr.org/blogs/health/2012/08/13/158711121/thousands-of-hospitals-face-penalties-for-high-readmission-rates?sc=ipad&f=1001. Accessed 2 September 2012.

11 Subsequent reorganization within the Department of Interior has replaced the old MMS with two new administrative entities, the Bureau of Ocean Energy Management and the Bureau of Safety and Environmental Enforcement. See discussion at http://www.boemre.gov/. Accessed 2 September 2012.

12 See discussion in King & Johnson. An oil thirsty America divided into 'dead sea.' *The Wall Street Journal*. 8 October 2010.

13 See Bureau of Ocean Energy Management, Regulation and Enforcement. Report regarding the causes of the April 20, 2010 Macando well blowout, 14 September 2011, at 172.

14 Ibid.

15 See Wall Street to bail out Jersey City's Knight Capital with $400 million package. *Bloomberg News*. August 6, 2012. Available at: http://www.nj.com/business/index.ssf/2012/08/wall_street_to_bail_out_jersey.html. Accessed 2 September 2012.

16 See Cheng J. *The Wall Street Journal*. 21 August 2012 Knight Capital's woes chip away at Wall Street confidence. Available at: http://blogs.wsj.com/marketbeat/2012/08/21/knight-capitals-woes-chip-away-at-wall-street-confidence/. Accessed 2 September 2012.

17 Milligan. *Wikipedia*. Available at: http://en.wikipedia.org/wiki/Mulligan_%28games%29. Accessed 3 September 2012.

18 Patterson S, Strasburg J, Bunge J. SEC nixed Knight's plea for a do-over. *Wall Street Journal*. 6 August 2012. Available at: http://online.wsj.com/article/SB10000872396390444246904577571113923528168.html. Accessed 3 September 2012.

19 Rule 15c3-5 under the Securities Exchange Act of 1934, enacted November 15, 2010 (see Exchange Act Release No. 63241, Nov. 3, 2010, 75 FR 69792). See also discussion in Lynch

Chapter 10 | Regulators

SN. *Reuters.* August 3, 2012, U.S. SEC examining risk controls at Knight Capital. Available at: http://news.yahoo.com/u-sec-examining-risk-controls-knight-capital-213115172--sector.html. Accessed 2 September 2012.

20 Socrates (470 BC–399 BC) quotes. ThinkExist.com. Available at: http://thinkexist.com/quotations/reputation/2.html. Accessed 2 September 2012.

PART IV

Perspectives

CHAPTER

11

Cultural Context

By Robert C. Brandegee[1]

The ability of a company to execute its strategy and bring new products and services to market, are directly linked to a company's understanding of the social and environmental context in which this happens.

—Aron Cramer[2]

We have shown how reputation is a consequence of corporate behavior that motivates stakeholders to behave in ways that either reward or punish the corporation. We've argued that reputation crises—instances in which markets punish companies—are often consequences of operational failures in one or more of the six business processes that are the pillars of reputation (Table 1-1). The factor precipitating market punishment is the magnitude of the market's disappointment when expectations are not met.

While the behaviors of companies help set those expectations, cultural norms—local expectations of citizenship behavior—also play a role.[3] To appreciate the complex interplay among cultural norms, corporate values, and stakeholder expectations, it is helpful to look at cases in which reputational crises have arisen in the absence of any overt business process failure.

This chapter presents only a superficial mention of controversies over some of the most passionate modern-day social struggles. It is enough for our purpose of illustrating the cultural context, but it makes no judgment about the issues these companies encountered in these cases. Although the cases may touch on readers' personal sensitivities, as Chapter 1 indicated, this book observes and explains in the spirit of American pragmatism and avoids moralizing.

Chapter 11 | Cultural Context

Society, Expectations, and Reputation

Corporate behaviors are shaped by a company's values and reflect its culture. This is especially the case in companies still led by their founders or closely held by related family members.

At the time companies are formed, their cultures reflect the values of the time as well as the strategic and operating processes for meeting market needs. These are the foundation of corporate cultures. For every company, corporate boards are stewards of those cultures. As society's expectations evolve, the standards by which corporate behaviors are judged by a company's stakeholders also evolve. Corporate cultures, however, are usually slower to evolve, and therein lies a significant endemic reputational risk: Corporate culture, company values, and company operations can lose touch with the evolving expectations of both stakeholders and society at large.

Four cases—News Corp, Chick-fil-A, Susan G. Komen, and Target—illustrate the diversity of perspectives in society that can transform operational decisions into reputational crises. Individually, they demonstrate pitfalls to steer clear of in operating a business so as to minimize market friction. Collectively, they underscore the many ways that daily debate centers on the question: What should society expect from businesses that are formed and operate under its laws?

News Corp: The Great Debate

Elisabeth Murdoch, daughter of News Corp Chief Executive Rupert Murdoch and chairman of News Corp's U.K. television production firm Shine, declared on 23 August 2012 that "profit without purpose is a recipe for disaster."[4] Delivering the annual James MacTaggart Memorial Lecture (the keynote address at the MediaGuardian Edinburgh International Television Festival), which both her father and brother had delivered in prior years, Elisabeth said, "It is increasingly apparent that the absence of purpose—or of a moral language—within government, media, or business could become one of the most dangerous 'own goals' for capitalism and for freedom."

Three years and a $4.4-billion reputational crisis earlier (see Chapter 4), Elisabeth's brother James—then heir presumptive to their father Rupert's Global News Corporation empire—expressed a decidedly different view: "The right path is all about trusting and empowering consumers. It is about embracing private enterprise and profit as a driver of investment, innovation, and independence. And the dramatic reduction of the activities of the state in our sector... The only reliable, durable, and perpetual guarantor of independence is profit."[5]

Reputation, Stock Price, and You | 243

James was certainly right about the importance of profit. Without it, a company cannot survive, no matter how worthy its purpose. Yet that pursuit ended in a precipitous fall. So Elisabeth was right too. Businesses whose aims extend no further than making a profit can end up destroying themselves.[6] Yet, were it not for its profits then, as well as now, News Corp would not have survived the fall, and Elisabeth would not have been invited to deliver the keynote.

The debate between the Murdoch siblings is one regal contest in the great debate on the role of business in society waged by armies of adversaries on countless fields and issues. It is a debate on which companies speak daily through their actions as much as their words, as they struggle to address profitably the common expectations of their markets without antagonizing any of the various sets of adversaries who compose those markets.

Chick-fil-A: Unnecessary Controversy

In the early 1960s, Truett Cathy founded Chick-fil-A, now the second largest quick-service chicken restaurant chain in the United States. With more than 1,615 locations in 39 states and Washington, DC, sales topped $4.1 billion in 2011. Large as it is, it remains a family business. Truett is the chairman and CEO, his son Dan is president and COO, and his son Don (Bubba) is senior vice president.

Family businesses are built around family values, and nonagenarian Truett Cathy, author of five motivational books, is a devout Southern Baptist with strong religion-focused family values. Since 1946, all of his restaurants have been closed on Sunday.[7] One of the missions of the WinShape Foundation, a charity funded by the family, is supporting marriage enrichment retreats—between a man and a woman. A Foundation spokesperson stated, "We do not accept homosexual couples because of the statement in our contract."[8]

Marriage, gay rights, and religion are flashpoint issues on which different groups with strong social convictions passionately disagree. In a June 2012 radio interview, President Dan Cathy elaborated on his company's values and its "support of the traditional family" and declared that "legalizing same-sex marriage would invite God's judgment on our nation."[9,10] In an election year already seething with politically stoked culture wars, a media firestorm erupted. *US News and World Report* described the reactions of several unlikely stakeholders[11]:

> First the Jim Henson Co., which provided Muppets toys for Chick-fil-A kids meals, pulled its toys and its partnership with the restaurant. Then the (Democratic) mayors of Boston and Chicago expressed opposition to new

Chapter 11 | Cultural Context

Chick-fil-A outlets opening in their cities…On the other side, Republican politicians such as presidential candidate Rick Santorum and former Arkansas Gov. Mike Huckabee defended the restaurant chain and its policies….

Same-sex marriage activists called a boycott and Governor Huckabee countered by calling a national Chick-fil-A Appreciation Day that increased the chain's business that day by 30%—countered in turn 2 days later by a nationwide Same Sex Kiss Day at the restaurants.[12]

Truett Cathy is proud of his inherently uncontroversial chicken sandwich, a food product that his market—customers, employees, suppliers, and creditors—understands. It is not clear how Dan Cathy's radio pronouncements improved that product's reputation beyond a limited portion of these stakeholders. The son's ill-considered remarks ignited a potentially damaging controversy that had nothing to do with the core business his father had built.[13]

Susan G. Komen: Lurking Controversy

Chick-fil-A was not the only battle in the culture wars of 2012. In January, the Susan G. Komen for the Cure Foundation announced the elimination of its funding of breast cancer education and screening by Planned Parenthood pursuant to a new internal rule that organizations under Congressional investigation, as Planned Parenthood was at the time, were ineligible for Komen funding. This decision outraged women's health advocacy groups and triggered an immediate surge in donations and grants to Planned Parenthood. Three days later, Komen restored the funding and the senior anti-abortion Komen executives behind the decision to defund Planned Parenthood resigned, but the damage had been done. Attendance and revenues at Komen events across the nation fell by a third. In August, Komen founder Nancy G. Brinker, having presided over an organization that had raised more than $740 million for breast cancer research since 1982, stepped down as CEO in the hope that it would "help Komen get past the bad publicity."[14,15]

Women's health is not uncontroversial.[16] Few will find fault with improving the health of women in general, and curing breast cancer is a noble cause. But the potentially explosive issue of abortion has always lurked beneath the surface.[17] It is to Nancy Brinker's credit that for three decades she succeeded in sidelining the abortion issue from the benefits of the foundation to women's health.[18] Through a few decisions, a handful of Komen executives unleashed a latent debate that grew in intensity and severely damaged the foundation's core business.[19]

Target Corp: Stumbling into Controversy

In 2010, Target Corp. angered gay-marriage supporters with a $150,000 political donation that benefited a gay-marriage opponent running for Minnesota governor, setting off protests and calls for a boycott from a constituency that had previously seen Target as an ally. Two years later, the retailer drew the ire of opponents of same-sex marriage by supporting a promotion organized by a group of gay Target employees.[20]

In the spring of 2012, Target introduced several "Pride"-themed shirts, with proceeds to benefit the Family Equality Council, a group fighting a proposed amendment to the Minnesota constitution to ban gay marriage.[21] In response, the American Family Association mobilized its supporters to urge Target to pull the shirts. Andy Parrish of Minnesota for Marriage, a pro-family group leading the fight for traditional marriage in Minnesota, said, "Target has alienated the strong majority of Minnesotans who support traditional marriage. They also risk alienating the overwhelming majority of their customers in the 32 states in this country that have voted to support traditional marriage."[22]

As a retailer of general merchandise, Target sells products and services that are hardly controversial. For fifty years, social justice and community service have been planks of its business platform.[23] The company's consistent "socially responsible" behavior created market expectations for which it has been widely acknowledged. It is a company Elisabeth Murdoch could appreciate. In 2010, the business side—thinking like James Murdoch—supported a candidate who called for lower business taxes, but who also had strong social views inconsistent with the expectations of Target's market. Through one ill-considered decision, the company stumbled into a social controversy that could leave observers with the impression that its 48-year track record of social responsibility never existed.

Guidance

The Chick-fil-A, Komen, and Target social controversies illustrate how contending social-issue groups and individuals express their values and direct their capital—whether by purchase decisions, by direct donation to social-issue advocacy groups, or by investment decisions in the equity markets. The lesson in these three cases is that no corporate action goes unobserved, and that it is foolish to neglect society's expectations. The lesson in the News Corp. case of the debate between siblings underscores the diversity of emotional issues related to these expectations.

Chapter 11 | Cultural Context

"Doing the right thing is the right thing to do," advises Paul Liebman, formerly Chief Compliance Counsel for Dell, Inc.[24] Knowing there is a diversity of opinions as to what constitutes the right thing is the first step toward understanding the social context for business operations. Finding the least controversial path through a shifting minefield of socially volatile issues is the second. Making a misstep along that path is an operational failure that does not necessarily have to mature into a reputational crisis if the market accepts the company's authenticity. Building the business case for doing that, with a few how-tos, is what the first 10 chapters of this book are all about.

Consider This

- The culture of the times and the company's founders shape its initial culture. The steward of corporate culture, the board, tends to want to protect and preserve that culture—a posture that can actually prevent it from evolving to respond to changes in society's expectations.

- Many social value perspectives expressed by key corporate figures may cut two ways, strengthening positive reputation among those stakeholders who agree, and vice versa.

- Making key business decisions that are mindful of society's expectations can reduce the likelihood of inadvertently triggering a reputational crisis.

Endnotes

1 Robert C. Brandegee is a management consultant, retired, with Brandegee Incorporated.

2 Aron Cramer President and CEO, BSR (a CSR consultancy)_as quoted in Klein P. Can say on pay increase social responsibility? *Forbes.* 3 July 2012. http://www.forbes.com/sites/csr/2012/07/03/can-say-on-pay-increase-social-responsibility/?goback=.gde_2955795_member_130388605 Accessed 11 August 2012.

3 Gardberg NA, Fombrun CJ. Corporate citizenship: creating intangible assets across institutional environments. *Academy of Management Review.* 2006; 31:329–346.

4 Jannarone J. Elisabeth Murdoch slams 'profit without purpose.' *The Wall Street Journal.* 23 August 2012. Available at: http://online.wsj.com/article/SB10000872396390444812704577607642320827980.html. Accessed 31 August 2012.

5 Murdoch J. 2009 Edinburgh International Television Festival MacTaggart Lecture. 28 August 2009.

6 Skapinker M. Murdochs' schism has lessons for companies. *Financial Times.* 29 August 2012. Available at: http://www.ft.com/intl/cms/s/0/be886812-ee2b-11e1-b0e4-00144feab49a.html#axzz259xfuRiL. Accessed 31 August 2012.

Reputation, Stock Price, and You 247

7 Chick-fil-A. Why we're closed on Sunday. Available at: http://www.chick-fil-a.com/ Company/Highlights-Sunday. Accessed 9 August 2012.

8 Yes, Chick-fil-A says, we Explicitly do not like same-sex couples. Available at: Change.org, 26 January 2011. Jones M. http://news.change.org/stories/yes-chick-fil-a-says-we-explicitly-do-not-like-same-sex-couples. Accessed 9 August 2012.

9 Dan Cathy, Chick-Fil-A president, on anti-gay stance: 'guilty as charged.' *Huffington Post.* 17 July 2012.

10 Zimmerman N. Ed Helms takes high-profile stand against Chick-fil-A for anti-same-sex-marriage stance [UPDATE: Chick-fil-A Relents?]. *Gawker.* 19 July 2012. Available at: http://gawker.com/5927438/ed-helms-takes-high+profile-stand-against-chick+fil+a-for-anti+same+sex+marriage-stance. Accessed 9 October 2012.

11 Cline S. Chick-fil-A's controversial gay marriage beef. *US News and World Report.* 27 July 2012. Available at: http://www.usnews.com/news/articles/2012/07/27/chick-fil-as-controversial-gay-marriage-beef. Accessed 9 August 2012.

12 Gay rights activists hold 'kiss day' at Chick-fil-A restaurants. CNN. 4 August 2012. Available at: http://www.cnn.com/2012/08/03/us/chick-fil-a-kiss-day/index.html. Accessed 10 October 2012.

13 White MC. Chick-fil-A waffles on gay marriage rights, fries brand image. *NBC News,.* 21 September 2012. Available at: http://bottomline.nbcnews.com/_news/2012/09/21/14009108-chick-fil-a-waffles-on-gay-marriage-rights-fries-brand-image?lite. Accessed 10 October 2012.

14 Schwirtz M. Breast cancer group changes leaders. *The New York Times.* 8 August 2012. Available at: http://www.nytimes.com/2012/08/09/us/susan-g-komen-for-the-cure-changes-leadership.html. Accessed 9 August 2012.

15 Will Nancy Brinker's resignation help Komen Race for the Cure? *Palm Beach Post.* 10 August 2012. Available at: http://blogs.palmbeachpost.com/opinionzone/2012/08/10/will-nancy-brinker%E2%80%99s-resignation-help-komen-race-for-the-cure/. Accessed 1 September 2012.

16 Papuga C. Why have women's health issues become a leading issue in this election? *Huffington Post.* 11 September 2012. Available at: http://www.huffingtonpost.com/casey-papuga/womens-health-leading-issue_b_1875463.html?utm_hp_ref=elections-2012. Accessed 10 October 2012.

17 Melnick M. Why a Christian group pulled pink bibles for breast cancer awareness. *Time.* 16 December 2011. Available at: http://healthland.time.com/2011/12/16/why-a-christian-group-pulled-pink-bibles-for-breast-cancer-awareness/. Accessed 10 October 2012.

18 Moyers R. Komen needs a strong board that can Stand up to its founder. *Philanthropy.* 11 September 2012. Available at: http://philanthropy.com/blogs/against-the-grain/komen-needs-a-strong-board-that-can-stand-up-to-its-founder/28254. Accessed 10 October 2012.

19 Feder JL. Can Susan G. Komen recover from Planned Parenthood funding fiasco? *Politico.* 3 February 2012. Available at: http://www.politico.com/news/stories/0212/72435.html. Accessed 10 October 2012.

20 Corporate decision renews Target gay rights controversy. *Fox8 News.* 15 June 2012. Available at: http://www.fox8live.com/story/18680499/target. Accessed 1 September 2012.

Chapter 11 | Cultural Context

21 Waldron M. Target's "Pride' T-shirts stir controversy. *KTNV Action News*. 1 June 2012. Available at: http://www.ktnv.com/news/national/156531285.html. Accessed 1 September 2012.

22 Bohon D. Target Corp. announces t-shirt campaign for homosexual marriage. *The New American*. 28 May 2012. Available at: http://thenewamerican.com/culture/family/item/11525-target-corp-announces-t-shirt-campaign-for-homosexual-marriage. Accessed 1 September 2012.

23 Target Corporation. Culture. Available at: http://corporate.target.com/careers/culture. Accessed 10 October 2012.

24 Liebman P. Is ethics a valuable intangible asset? Mission Intangible Monthly Briefing. 9 April 2010. Audio recordings available from the Intangible Asset Finance Society: http://iafinance. org/monthly-briefings. Accessed 8 October 2012.

CHAPTER

12

Metrics

There are two possible outcomes: If the result confirms the hypothesis, then you've made a measurement. If the result is contrary to the hypothesis, then you've made a discovery.

—Enrico Fermi[1]

If your stock price is sensitive to your company's reputation, then managing the business processes that are the pillars of reputation is a managerial imperative and board oversight duty. Reputation scores and reputational value metrics can help. Clearly, senior management needs more detailed measurements than the board does. But, as Chapter 8 shows, there are three board-level duties—CEO compensation, asset protection, and business strategy—whose fulfillment could be enhanced with measures of reputation.

Reputation scores and reputational value metrics are covered in Chapter 9 at a level of granularity interesting to quantitatively inclined readers, and this chapter begins where Chapter 9 ended. A qualitative discussion frames the picture for all readers and proceeds to a quantitative presentation via charts and graphs.

Metrics: Qualitative Edition

There are two kinds of measures of reputation, and they differ from one another in the same way that a company's book value differs from its market capitalization. The first is based on surveys and resembles a company's book value as determined by a standard transparent accounting procedure. Surveys have been done for decades, reflect the marketing mindset from which they arose, and provide a measurement of reputation at the time the survey is conducted. They are historic snapshots of mindshare and appear to be good predictors of brand awareness and related consumer behaviors. This book cites reputation scores from four different surveys. The World's Most

Chapter 12 | Metrics

Admired Companies (WMAC) survey from *Fortune* magazine and World's Most Respected Large Companies (MRC) from *Barron's* magazine capture the mindshare of a business-oriented survey population. The Reputation Quotient (RQ) survey from Harris Interactive and the RepTrak survey from the Reputation Institute capture the mindshare of a broader general population.

The second kind of measure, resembling market values, involves dynamic processes algorithmically driven by measurements of business performance. Algorithmic processes have been developed over the past decade, reflect the analyst mindset from which they arose, and provide a near real-time measurement of reputation. They are current calculations of expected business performance, harness the "wisdom of crowds," and can be good predictors of stock price behavior. Hence, these can be useful as early warning signals that might guide managers in responding to problems and opportunities.

This book introduces measures from two algorithmic sources. Relative Business Performance probability scores from Transparent Value capture the probabilities that companies will achieve the business performance expected by investors as implied by current stock price. Reputational Value Metrics from Steel City Re (the author's employer) capture the expected economically relevant behavior of the diverse stakeholders who have been covered in the earlier chapters of this book.

The distinction boils down to this:

Survey-based reputation scores quantify what a company has done to create stakeholder opinions; **algorithmic-based reputational value metrics** quantify what the aggregate of company stakeholders can be expected to do.

Survey-based reputation scores, not unlike book value, benefit from transparent methodologies. Based on relatively large samples, they draw statistically valid inferences from questions as simple as, "Rank your respect for this company on a scale of 1–5." They may also delve deeper into psychological aspects of reputation to elicit opinions on matters such as vision and leadership, social responsibility, financial performance, emotional appeal, products and services, and workplace environment. The survey-based measures are disadvantaged, like book values, by their lack of timeliness, inherent backwards view, and inability to capture the economic value of the opinions. Empirically, they have not correlated well with going-forward equity performance.

Algorithmic-based reputational value metrics benefit from high-frequency volumes of timely data that enable the measures to report both spot and dynamic time-series data on reputational value ranking, volatility (risk), and

Reputation, Stock Price, and You

projected rate and direction of change. They capture forward-looking expectations related to economic value that are useful measures for financial instruments. Today, Transparent Value's metrics appear publicly only in investable mutual funds such as the two described in Chapter 9 (tickers: TVIMX, TVVIX). Insurers and hedge funds use Steel City Re's reputational value metrics to underwrite reputation risk and to direct reputation-focused investment strategies. Reputational Value Insurance, underwritten by syndicates at Lloyd's and various insurance companies led by Kiln Group, and the RepuStars Variety composite equity index calculated by S&P/Dow Jones indices (ticker: REPUVAR), are examples. Because of their use in financial instruments, the algorithmic-based metrics—not unlike market values—are disadvantaged by their lack of transparent methodology.

Algorithmic data avoid potential systematic biases in survey data that can unduly shape the reputation scores.[2] Whereas the data underpinning the algorithmic measures of reputation are captured passively, survey data are captured from volunteers who are aware of their contributions. These biases can exacerbate biases already evident in the different populations being surveyed and help explain why the reputation metrics do not necessarily correlate well between and among the different instruments.

Following nearly identical methodologies, the two general public-oriented surveys, RQ and RepTrak, showed a 94% correlation among the 48 companies that were ranked by both reputation scoring systems. But, whereas the correlation between the general public and business-focused survey populations in the 128 companies common to both the RepTrak and WMAC measurement systems was a meager 21%, the correlation between the algorithmic measures and the business-focused survey populations in the 126 companies common to both the Steel City Re and the WMAC measurements was 58% (Table 12-1).

Table 12-1. Stepwise Paired Correlations among Five Reputation Measures

WMAC (118)	100%	68%	36%	21%	58%
MRC (100)	68%	100%	72%	67%	65%
RQ (60)	36%	72%	100%	94%	46%
RepTrak (150)	21%	67%	94%	100%	32%
Ranking (142)	58%	65%	46%	32%	100%
	WMAC	MRC	RQ	RepTrak	Ranking
	Fortune Magazine	Barron's Magazine	Harris Interactive	Reputation Institute	Steel City Re

Chapter 12 | Metrics

These different properties suggest that the algorithmic measures of reputational value may be more useful for day-to-day managerial and oversight functions, while the survey-based reputation scores may be more useful for reviews of historical performance and the types of managerial reviews for which historical financials are most useful. Whichever objective is to be served, for executives who must manage reputation, measurement is a must.

Case discussions of Steel City Re's algorithmic measures of reputation covering nearly four years of observations can be found on the blog of the Intangible Asset Finance Society, *Mission: Intangible*, at http://www.iafinance.org/BlogRetrieve.aspx?BlogID=419.

Survey-based reputation scores from all four of the aforementioned providers and algorithmic reputational value metrics from Steel City Re are available publicly and are compared and contrasted in the text that follows. Some of the graphics draw upon actuarially and mathematically advanced techniques and may require significant time for inspection and dissection. Such attention will ensure a level of comfort for operational and oversight decision-making. However, if you're already saturated or prefer to look at case studies published in color online,[3] this would be a good time to jump to the "Consider This" section at the end of this chapter.

Metrics: Quantitative Edition

Of the approximately 35 public companies discussed in this volume, there are 7 for which there exist 2012 public reputation scores from all 4 providers of survey-based measures and Steel City Re's algorithmic reputational value metrics. Transparent Value's metrics today are shown publicly only through the mutual funds they drive.

Each of the measurement systems uses a different scale. To simplify the comparison of values, the measurements from all five systems were converted to rank-order percentile values whose denominator is reported in the row labeled "Percentile rank denominator." Although they are refreshed weekly, Steel City Re's algorithmic reputational value metrics for the one date of 5 January 2012 are presented to enable tabular comparison with the survey groups (Table 12-2).

Reputation, Stock Price, and You | 253

Table 12-2. Reputation Scores for Seven Companies Converted to Rank-Order Percentile Values and Ordered by Their WMAC Ranking

Source		Fortune Magazine	Barron's Magazine	Harris Interactive	Reputation Institute	Steel City Re
Name	TCKR	World's Most Admired Companies	Most Respected Company	Reputation Quotient	RepTrak	Reputation Ranking 5 January 2012
Percentile rank denominator		118	100	60	150	142
American International Group	AIG	6%	4%	0%	4%	18%
Johnson & Johnson	JNJ	40%	68%	89%	98%	90%
The Coca- Cola Company	KO	65%	92%	96%	95%	96%
PepsiCo	PEP	71%	69%	72%	94%	92%
JP Morgan Chase	JPM	81%	51%	6%	10%	19%
The Walt Disney Company	DIS	98%	89%	91%	89%	59%
Apple Inc.	AAPL	100%	100%	100%	95%	98%

While current reputation rankings are familiar concepts, the Steel City Re reputational value metrics introduce additional measures that are explained here and illustrated in the labeled schematic, which, like a map, will help navigation through the detailed charts that follow (Figure 12-1). First, labeled A–E, is a five-bar chart called "Vital Signs" comprising the reputational metrics for a company as benchmarked against peers in the same standard industry group. The chart provides a snapshot of the company relative to its peers. Historic Volatility, A, reports on the 1-year average standard deviation of the reputational value metric. The Current Volatility, B, reports the exponentially weighted average of the same parameter over only the trailing 12 weeks. It is meaningful when the Current Volatility is significantly different than the Historic Volatility. Current Ranking and return on equity (ROE), C and D,

Chapter 12 | Metrics

report in the charts below the Reputation Ranking as of 23 August 2012 (the tabular values are from 5 January 2012 corresponding to the date of the survey measures) and the trailing 12-month return on equity as of that same date. Last, the Forecast Stability, E, reports on the volatility trend. Higher values suggest less change going forward.

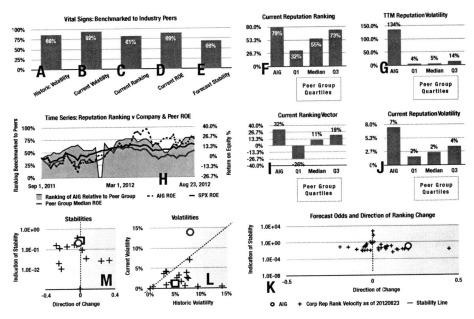

Figure 12-1. Guide to the understanding of representative algorithmically derived reputational value metrics from Steel City Re and are provided here for educational purposes only. TTM = trailing twelve months.

The Time Series chart, H, also reports benchmarked data. It gives the company's reputational value ranking over time relative to peers. The terminal value corresponds to the value shown in Vital Signs–C. Also shown on the time series graph are the ROE of the company, the median of its peer group, and the S&P 500 Composite Index serving as a proxy for the broad market. The terminal value for ROE corresponds to the value shown in Vital Signs–D.

The four additional bar charts, F–J, report the same values shown in the vital signs, but with greater detail. Also, rather than benchmarking to peers, the percentile values reflect the company's standing relative to approximately 7,300 companies in the Steel City Re database. The values for the peer group quartiles are also reported. The metrics include Current Reputation Ranking, F; Trailing Twelve Month (Historic) Reputation Volatility, G; Current Reputation Volatility, J; and an indicator of reputational stability, the Ranking

Reputation, Stock Price, and You | 255

Vector, I. Last, a flag chart, K, displays the indication of reputational ranking stability and the expected direction of change.

Flag graphs L and M are two of four graphs introduced in the Guidance section of this chapter. They illustrate how rapid changes in reputational value standing and value can be discovered, and potentially spur management to take action.

American International Group (AIG)

World's Most Admired Companies	Most Respected Company	Reputation Quotient	RepTrak	Reputation Ranking 5 January 2012
6%	4%	0%	4%	18%

Parameter	Metric	Description
Sector & Count	1312	Finance
Industry & Count	43	Multi-Line Insurance
SubIndustry & Count	179	Insurance Companies

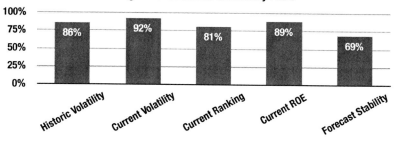

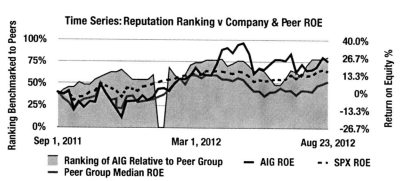

Chapter 12 | Metrics

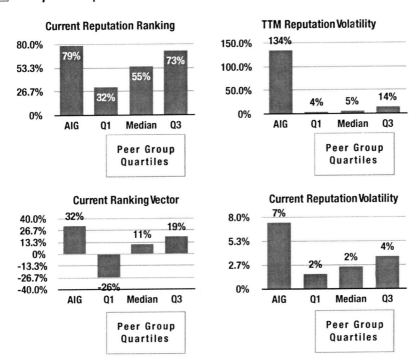
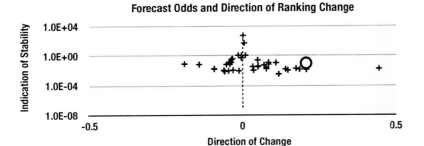

Johnson & Johnson (JNJ)

World's Most Admired Companies	Most Respected Company	Reputation Quotient	RepTrak	Reputation Ranking 5 January 2012
40%	68%	89%	98%	90%

Parameter	Metric	Description
Sector & Count	557	Health Technology
Industry & Count	32	Pharmaceuticals: Major
SubIndustry & Count	33	Diversified Health Care

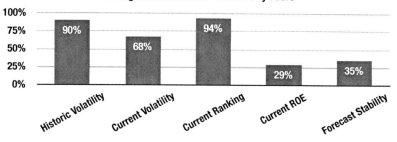

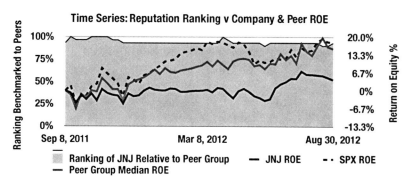

Chapter 12 | Metrics

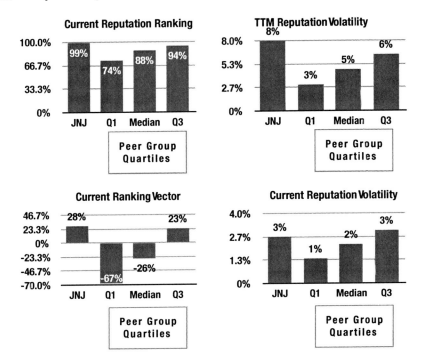
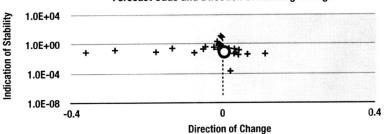

The Coca-Cola Company (KO)

World's Most Admired Companies	Most Respected Company	Reputation Quotient	RepTrak	Reputation Ranking 5 January 2012
65%	92%	96%	95%	96%

Parameter	Metric	Description
Sector & Count	345	Consumer Non-Durables
Industry & Count	20	Beverages: Non-Alcoholic
SubIndustry & Count	20	Soft Drink Producers & Bottlers

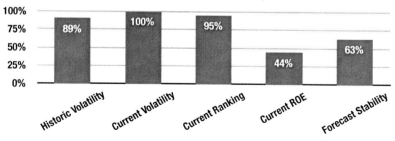

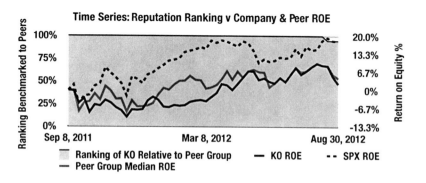

Chapter 12 | Metrics

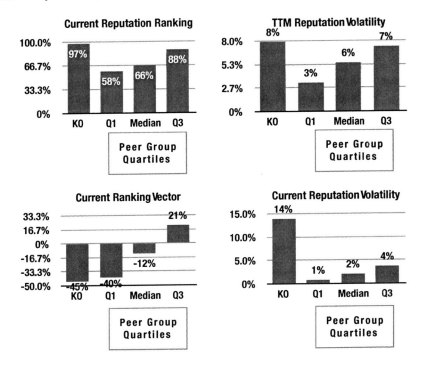

PepsiCo (PEP)

World's Most Admired Companies	Most Respected Company	Reputation Quotient	RepTrak	Reputation Ranking 5 January 2012
71%	69%	72%	94%	92%

Parameter	Metric	Description
Sector & Count	345	Consumer Non-Durables
Industry & Count	20	Beverages: Non-Alcoholic
SubIndustry & Count	20	Soft Drink Producers & Bottlers

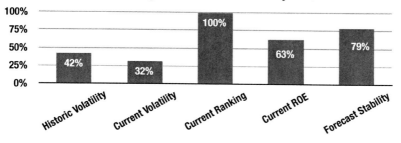

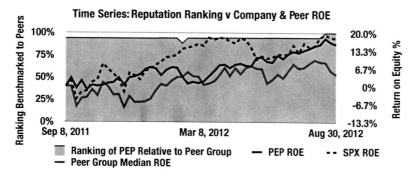

Chapter 12 | Metrics

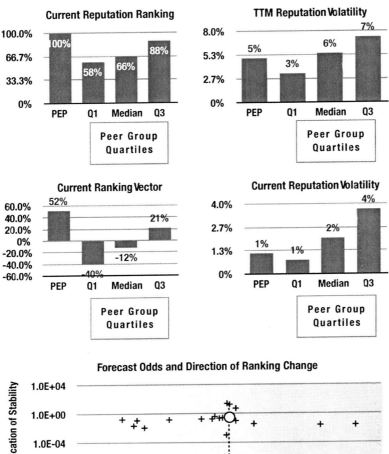

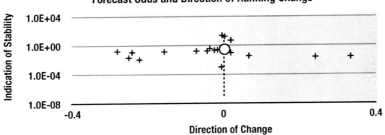

JP Morgan Chase (JPM)

World's Most Admired Companies	Most Respected Company	Reputation Quotient	RepTrak	Reputation Ranking 5 January 2012
81%	51%	6%	10%	19%

Parameter	Metric	Description
Sector & Count	1307	Finance
Industry & Count	50	Financial Conglomerates
SubIndustry & Count	249	Commercial Banks /-Bank Hldg Co's

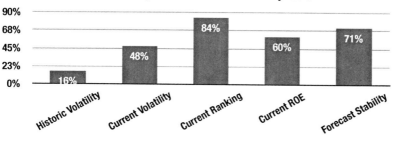

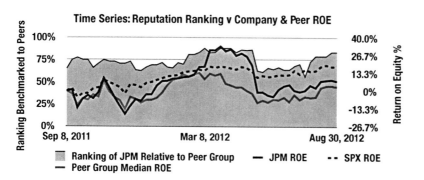

Chapter 12 | Metrics

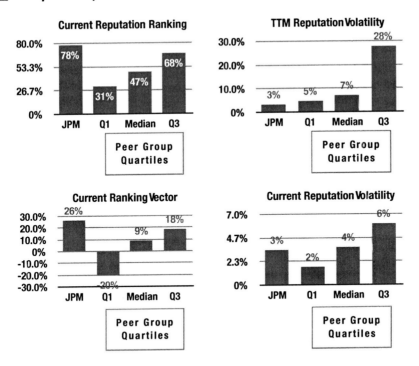

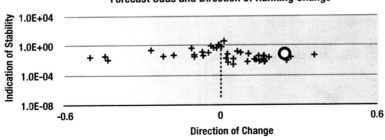

The Walt Disney Company (DIS)

World's Most Admired Companies	Most Respected Company	Reputation Quotient	RepTrak	Reputation Ranking 5 January 2012
98%	89%	91%	89%	59%

Parameter	Metric	Description
Sector & Count	420	Consumer Services
Industry & Count	11	Media Conglomerates
SubIndustry & Count	64	Miscellaneous Recreation

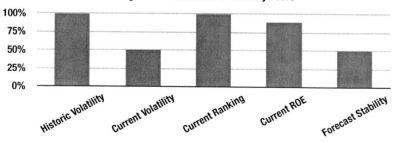

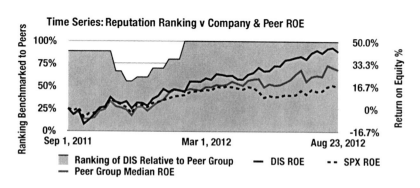

Chapter 12 | Metrics

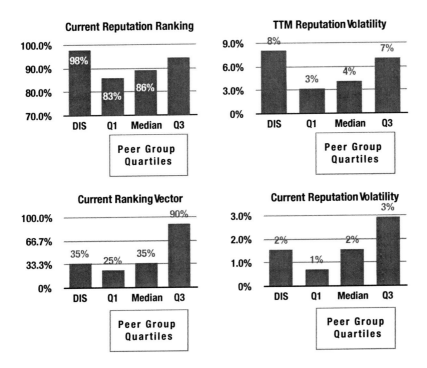

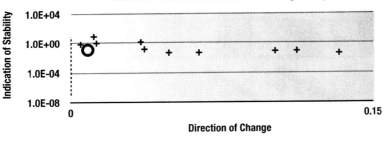

Apple Inc. (AAPL)

World's Most Admired Companies	Most Respected Company	Reputation Quotient	RepTrak	Reputation Ranking 5 January 2012
100%	100%	100%	95%	98%

Parameter	Metric	Description
Sector & Count	623	Electronic Technology
Industry & Count	25	Computer Processing Hardware
SubIndustry & Count	47	Electronic Data Processing Equipment

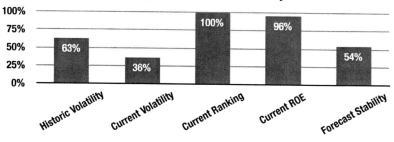

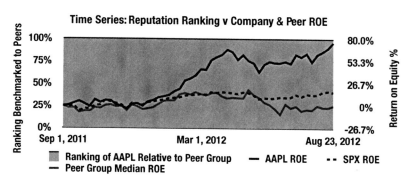

Chapter 12 | Metrics

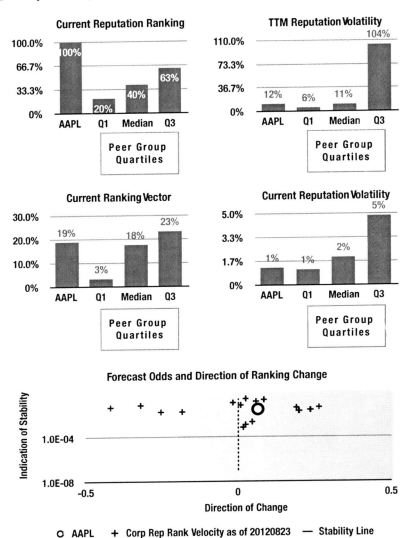

Guidance

One of the other benefits of the data frequency and density of the algorithmic metrics from Steel City Re is the ability to analyze reputational value trends and identify deviations that may be the harbingers of a looming crisis.

For example, the metrics for Pepsi and Coke, both members of the 20-member Non-Alcoholic Beverages sector, show that as of 23 August 2012 the reputational value volatility for Coke increased significantly among the entire peer group and began to trend negative (Figure 12-2). These data suggest a

Reputation, Stock Price, and You 269

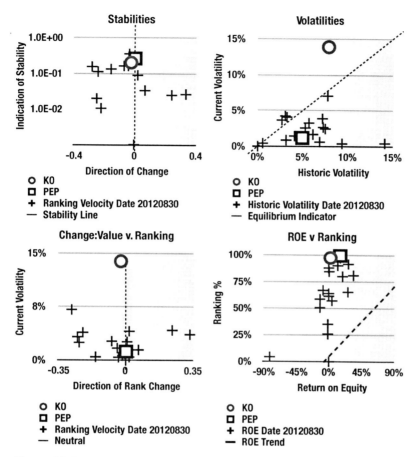

Figure 12-2. Flag graphs of reputational value spot data for both Pepsi and Coca-Cola dated 30 August 2012 shows a sudden spike in Coca-Cola's reputational ranking volatility and a negative change of rank associated with a stock split and a surprised market. Concurrently, Pepsi's trailing 12-month return on equity, if only briefly edged past Coke. In short order, the fundamental differences discussed in Chapter 5 returned Coke to its usual dominance.

recent major operational change reduced Coke's reputation among a significant fraction of its stakeholders, and is a signal to management that something recently destabilized the situation. Further examples of alerts evidenced by changes in the Steel City Re reputational metrics can be found on the *Mission: Intangible* blog of the Intangible Asset Finance Society.

Another benefit of the data frequency and density of the algorithmic metrics from Steel City Re is the ability to characterize the severity of a reputational crisis in real time. In early May 2012, JP Morgan Chase reported a $2 billion loss from a failed hedging strategy. The media declared it a reputational crisis. "The dollar loss, though, could be less significant than the hit to Dimon and

Chapter 12 | Metrics

the bank's reputation," reported Reuters.[4] The insight provided by the Steel City Re Reputational Metrics and reported 19 May in the *Mission: Intangible* blog contradicted the pronouncements of the media: "On the basis of JP Morgan Chase's historical reputational value metrics, and in the context of the three-year long view, this current event could be viewed as just one more bump in a long and volatile history of bumps."[5]

Four months later, the expectations reported by the reputational metrics were realized. By mid-September 2012, the market capitalization decline had been erased and the reputational measures had almost all returned to prior values. "The events made for great media fodder, but it never really was a reputational crisis, as the metrics showed then, and affirm now. And notwithstanding the personal abuse of...[Congressional]...hearings, etc., by mid September CEO Jamie Dimon had reaped a 22.6% gain from his $17.1 million bet on JP Morgan Chase's reputational resilience for a cool $3.86 million in less than two months."[6]

Consider This

- Because managing and overseeing reputation is a managerial activity, reputation metrics can be helpful.

- High-frequency algorithmically-produced reputational value metrics provide insights more useful for day-to-day administration, risk management, and crisis management while annually generated survey-based scores may be more useful for historical reviews assessing past performance.

- Colorful charts, graphs. and reputation case studies of companies recently in the news can be found on the *Mission: Intangible* blog of the Intangible Asset Finance Society: http://www.iafinance.org/BlogRetrieve.aspx?BlogID=419.

By the Numbers

The top reasons for measurement are improving business performance and enhancing communications. Whether you are an operating executive, communications executive or market analyst, reputation scores and reputational value metrics have been, are, or soon will be part of your daily fare. The table below displays a sample of the cross-correlations of data in this chapter.

Reputation, Stock Price, and You | 271

Table 12-3. Representative Pairwise Correlations between Various Measures of Reputation

Metric 1	Source	Metric 2	Source	Number of Common Companies	Correlation (%)
RepTrak	General survey	RQ	General Survey	48	94
MRC	Investor survey	SCRE Ranking	Algorithmic	42	65
WMAC	Business survey	SCRE Ranking	Algorithmic	126	58
RepTrak	General survey	SCRE Ranking	Algorithmic	136	32
WMAC	Business survey	RepTrak	General survey	128	21

Endnotes

1 Fermi E. (Nobel laureate in physics, 1938) Available at: http://www.brainyquote.com/ quotes/keywords/measurement.html#dGcXkLYDr7wmheGD.99. Accessed 12 August 2012.

2 Wright KB. Researching Internet-based populations: Advantages and disadvantages of online survey research, online questionnaire authoring software packages, and web survey services. *Journal of Computer-Mediated Communication*, 2005;10(3): article 11. Available at: http://jcmc.indiana.edu/vol10/issue3/wright.html. Accessed 7 October 2012.

3 Visit the Mission:Intangible blog of the Intangible Asset Finance Society at http://iafinance. org/.

4 Henry D, Rothacker R. JPMorgan has $2 billion trading loss, reputation hit. *Reuters*, 10 May 2012. http://www.reuters.com/article/2012/05/10/us-jpmorgan-trading-idUSBRE8491H020120510. Accessed 18 September 2012.

5 JP Morgan Chase: Is there a metric in the house? *Mission: Intangible.* 19 May 2012. Available at: http://www.iafinance.org/_blog/MISSION_INTANGIBLE/post/JP_Morgan_Chase_Is_there_a_metric_in_the_house/. Accessed 18 September 2012.

6 JP Morgan Chase: Got better. *Mission: Intangible.* 18 September 2012. Available at: http://www.iafinance.org/_blog/MISSION_INTANGIBLE/post/JP_Morgan_Chase_%5BI%5D_got_better/. Accessed 18 September 2012.

CHAPTER

13

Consider These

A business can simultaneously enhance its reputation and demonstrate its responsibility by meeting stakeholder expectations.

—Carola Hillebrand and Kevin Money[1]

An uninitiated came before Hillel, the famed Judean sage and scholar who lived more than 2,000 years ago, and said to him, "Make me wise in your ways, on the condition that you teach me the whole Torah while I stand on one foot." Hillel answered him: "What is hateful to you, do not to your neighbor. That is the whole Torah; the rest is the commentary thereof; now go and learn it."[2]

Watch What They Do

Corporate reputation is a multi-stakeholder concept that is reflected in the perceptions that stakeholders have of an organization based on what they experience personally or discover from all other sources.[3] These interactions trigger economic behaviors that impact the profit and loss (P&L) statement in many ways and ultimately affect enterprise value. There are effects too on governance, regulators, and analysts.

Much evidence in the literature and reaffirmed here shows that reputations with different stakeholder groups create complex reciprocal behaviors in other groups that are then again reflected in reputation. In particular, reputation with employees is seen to have an impact on reputation with customers and communities.[4]

This complexity of interplay suggests, further to the words of Hillel, that the prudent way to manage stakeholder interactions is to foster ethical conformance, ensure quality, drive innovation, promote sustainability, and

Chapter 13 | Consider These

optimize both safety and security—the six drivers of reputation. Authentic behaviors will be observed by all, and reputation will follow.

We have shown that corporate culture enables board-level decisions and operating-level actions that help create value through these six drivers, and that the standards by which stakeholders measure success are sensitive to societal norms. These norms are dynamic, and a culture appropriate for certain times may not remain so, even if the corporate culture is strong and unchanging—indeed sometimes *because* it is strong and unchanging.

Stakeholders are always watching; the tint of their glasses, however, may shift without advance notice. Because of the complex perceptual interplay, organizations managing their corporate reputation should take into account not only their direct interactions and relationships with stakeholders, but also the influences stakeholders have on each other.[5]

In short, do the right thing for your stakeholders and meet their expectations. The rest is commentary thereof; now go and learn it.

Final Guidance

This book is organized to present the origins of reputation, a dynamic consequence of a complex web of reciprocal relationships among many different stakeholders (Figure 13-1). But rather than risk irrelevance as an academic discourse, this book offers readers a financial journey of actions they may emulate. The key is to couple corporate behavior to its reputation, appreciate that stakeholder behavior translates to measurable reputational value, and recognize that the diverse effects of market behaviors yield profit and loss, which then links to a company's stock price.

This book doesn't grant reputation the status of an "air ball" by leaving it without an owner. It purposefully shifts responsibility for the management of reputational value from risk and PR managers to the board of directors, COO, and CFO by providing frameworks for governance, measurement, and financial risk transfer.

Last, this book takes pains to clarify what is *not* reputational value. It distinguishes between reputation and measurable reputational value; between brand (a promise), and reputation (an expectation of behavior) and between generalized market cap loss on one hand and granular details of gains or losses in revenue and expenses on the other.

Briefly, Parts 1 and 2 are organized to help the reader appreciate how various business processes shape a company's reputation and trigger behaviors in stakeholders that impact specific line items on the P&L statement. The most important of these processes are the six drivers of reputational value.

Part 3 shows how the business environment for those business processes is influenced by corporate culture, judged by equity investors, governed by the company's directors, observed by analysts, and overseen by regulators. A case is made for supporting the board's oversight duties with reputational metrics and signaling value to stakeholders through insurances.

The first two chapters of Part 4 show how appreciation of corporate actions with respect to the six drivers of reputational value is sensitive to evolving societal expectations in a qualitative sense, and how the market can observe, interpret, and value those behaviors through quantitative measures of reputation and reputational value.

This concluding chapter returns the financial journey to the executive suite and boardroom. It is here that reputational value figures in three distinct conversations on business strategies: increasing, protecting, and restoring reputational value. Here we conclude the journey as we began—with metrics and cases, to reinforce the principle that we manage best that which we measure.

Corporate Reputation

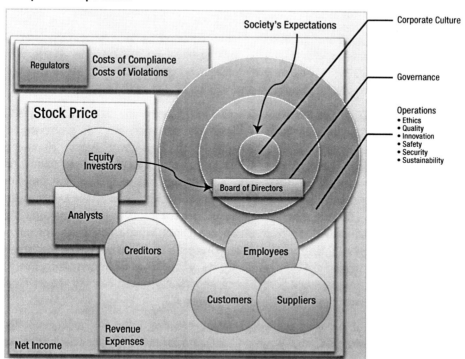

Figure 13-1. Complex multi-stakeholder interactions, observable actions, and expectations collectively establish corporate reputation value and stock price.

Chapter 13 | Consider These

Increasing Reputational Value

The average company has an average reputation. "[To increase its reputational value,] start with what seems to be almost intuitive," suggests Paul Liebman, formerly Chief Compliance Counsel for Dell Inc., an electronic technology company. "Doing the right thing is the right thing to do."[6] Then communicate what you are doing in a way that stakeholders can recognize, appreciate, and value. The company that successfully transforms itself from an average company to one with a superior reputation can expect to realize on average an additional 6.5% in market capitalization, all other things being equal.

The "right thing" is for management to put in place systems that advance the performance of the six business drivers of reputation enumerated in detail in Table 1-1 and listed again in the preceding section. Systems include policies, conformance monitoring solutions, and enforcement mechanisms. "I learned a long time ago," shares Robert Rittereiser, formerly CFO of Merrill Lynch and CEO of EF Hutton, both financial service companies, "whatever policies you have, ultimately, you must have in place processes that enforce those policies." Having been tasked by the courts to unwind complex failed structures from financiers ranging from Michael Milken to Bernie Madoff, Rittereiser adds, "If you have a policy you can't enforce, you really don't have a policy."[7]

The key success metric for these performance systems is that they provide management with an integrated, holistic view of corporate operations. The measure of value is the degree with which the transparency created through these systems can be appreciated and valued by the market.

George Long, Chief Governance Counsel and Corporate Secretary for PNC, speaking on an unofficial basis, whimsically referred to the gathering of enterprise-wide data as "sideloading."[8] With Dr. Urmi Ashar (formerly president of the Three Rivers Chapter of the National Association of Corporate Directors), he describes "sideloading" as a system for building dynamic networks both intra - and extra-organizationally to share information and developing efficient, knowledge-based processes that can transcend the capabilities of an individual. "For those out there who enjoy both anagrams and business jargon," Long quips, "I'll say that sideload also has a nice feature— it turns into 'silo dead.'" More seriously, he adds, "Silos of information [are] a bad thing in general because [they] keep information hermetically sealed from other parts of the organization that may need it."

Just as executives protect potentially value-creating information in silos, the C-suite sequesters potentially value-creating information from the market to everyone's loss. "It's really to a company's advantage to explain its behavior— to explain why it's doing things—because in the void…analysts are going to make their own decisions and come to their own conclusions," observes

Reputation, Stock Price, and You | 277

Jonathan Low, a founder and partner of Predictiv, LLC, a management consultancy.[9] Transparency can be a source of value. "Our belief has always been that the returns to transparency exceed the returns to secrecy," says Low. "The social graph requires that companies communicate frequently, openly, honestly," affirms Linda Locke, founder and principal with Reputare Consulting, a corporate reputation consulting firm.[10]

Changes begin at the top and involve building a corporate culture that acknowledges the expectations of all stakeholders, including society at large. A culture that incorporates reputation into its governance increases the likelihood that the operational benefits can be realized. "I think you have to get to the conversation early enough at the board level," says Herbert Winokur, Jr., CEO of Capricorn Holdings Inc., a private equity group.[11] This way the board can "make sure that management is thinking about the reputation—the most valuable asset of almost every company—when they make decisions," adds Winokur, who's more-than-300 board meetings included time with financial service, energy, and nonprofit groups such as the Harvard Corporation.

Executive compensation today is a variable in reputation and one of the processes that boards of directors can change in many companies to increase reputational value. Linking reputation and compensation at the highest levels of corporation reflects best practices for driving a reputation-focused risk culture throughout the organization. Linking compensation and clawbacks to a company's reputation is made easier by systems that quantitatively monitor, measure, and report reputation to the board's compensation committee.

Systems to help management gain transparency in a company whose board is setting a reputation-centered tone at the top are tools. The goal, Locke offers, is to create reputational value by pleasantly surprising the market "Reputation is built on meeting and exceeding stakeholder expectations."[10]

Employees are among the many key stakeholders whose improved alignment can help create reputational value. They chart their course in an institution and adjust their ethical standards on the basis of an institution's culture and how that culture evolves in the course of their employment.

While it may be intuitive that an average company can exceed stakeholder expectations, it appears that even a company at or near the top can do so as well. Apple Inc. is an exemplary firm with a reputation that has so far proven resilient beyond the mortality of its founder, Steve Jobs.

In transitioning leadership successfully from Steve Jobs to Tim Cook, Apple communicated to stakeholders that its processes for innovation and operational excellence were institutional and not located solely in one individual. To do so was critical and explains how Apple was able to create

Chapter 13 | Consider These

unexpected reputational value. When the market's expectations are exceeded, reputational value increases. The operational benefits associated with Apple's multi-stakeholder focus have helped even this extremely valuable and successful company further exceed investor's expectations.

By the numbers, in 2012 Apple Inc. ranked no. 1 in three of four reputation surveys and one algorithmic reputation metric described in Chapter 9. Although in 2011 it also ranked no. 1 among the World's Most Admired Companies, Most Respected Companies, and Corporate Reputation Rankings, it ranked no, 8 in the Reputation Quotient (RQ) rankings and no. 48 in the RepTrak rankings—suggesting that, at least among members of the general public, there was room for increasing reputation value. Its Steel City Re reputation metrics are presented in Chapter 12.

For the trailing 12 months from 23 August 2012, Apple Inc. outperformed the average of the top 10% of its 25-member industry computer processing hardware peer group[12] (excluding Apple) by 8.3%. The only peer company to outperform $621 billion Apple's 75% return on equity was $0.48 billion Cray Inc. On 30 August 2012, Cray's P/E ratio was 15.61.

Protecting Reputational Value

A reputation whose value is worth protecting must be authentic and not conflated with a brand. To underscore a key concept in this book, brand *promise* and reputation *expectation* are not the same. Brand is an emotional construct. Reputation is a cognitive expectation of behavior held by stakeholders. Investing in the former at the expense of the latter, as shown in the case studies throughout this book, will not create long-term value and can degrade reputational value. It risks an inauthentic reputation among customers, which can lead to great disappointment.

Authentic means understanding what the key drivers of reputational value are, above and beyond ethics. For example, in the technology sector case study in Chapter 4, innovation was the dominant reputation pillar. In the aircraft power plant business case study in Chapter 3, safety was the critical reputation asset. In the jewelry case study in Chapter 3, a reputation for quality meant a consistent customer experience with a trustworthy salesperson.

Protecting an authentic reputation means having systems to align the global workforce with the best interests of the company, provide operational transparency, and provide visibility. It also means having media-monitoring systems that can provide indications of pending reputational crises. It is important to remember that operational failures will invariably happen. With proper preparation and quick action, reputational crises do not necessarily have to follow them.

Reputation, Stock Price, and You

In a globally integrated manufacturing operation, a reputation is the product of superior engineering design and risk management, which includes top notch supply chain oversight and operational control—systems comprising policies, conformance-monitoring solutions, and enforcement mechanisms. In a global service operation, a reputation similarly rests on supplier engagement and earning the designation of a "preferred customer." Disney explicitly believes that its supply chain is a source of reputational value. The company has an ongoing initiative to "operationalize a holistic strategy on the supply-chain resilience side that we believe is [already] helping to protect our reputation," says Scott Childers, Director, Integrated Trade Management at The Walt Disney Company.[13] Total global operational visibility, the next frontier in risk management, will help the company build on processes that Disney has had in place for many years and further "increase the value of that risk mitigation and [help] communicate the value upwards and outwards related to Disney's value overall," adds Childers. "The resilient organization manages its entire supply chain from the perspective of its customers," explains Locke, "because a failure at any point is blamed on the company."[10]

One strong motivation for developing systems that capture information from all supply chain partners is that the volume of information is beyond the management capacity of humans. Long notes that McKinsey, the consulting firm, "estimates that enterprises stored more than 7 exabytes of new data in 2010." One exabyte is equal to 4,000 times the information in the U.S. Library of Congress. "You need to identify where all the points of information come in," adds Long.[8]

When a reputation is compromised, the value proposition for a stakeholder may vanish. When multiple stakeholders perceive failure, a firm's once stellar reputation may be permanently damaged, with diminished enterprise value—if not overall company viability.

Organizational culture, the driver of reputation, is a force that can reduce the variances of otherwise unconstrained behaviors—but only to the extent that management and the board take the care (technically, a duty of loyalty) to both oversee and enforce it. Ignorance, under U.S. Delaware corporate law, is tantamount to culpability. A strong culture that establishes organizational norms, and a board of directors that will support management even in the face of placing revenue at risk, are essential for driving consistently ethical behavior and mitigating the risk from "rogues."

Nevertheless, operational failures will occur. They are not crises, according to Winokur, who served for 15 years on the board of Enron, the failed energy services company. "Crises arrive, by definition, when you're not expecting them. They are something outside the status quo."[11] Knowing when an

Chapter 13 | Consider These

operational failure is becoming a reputational crisis is a key reputational value protection strategy.

"There are several signs of a pending reputational crisis," says Richard S. Levick, president and CEO of Levick Strategic Communications:[14]

- Search engine results on terms specific to a company's business, products, or people, and linked to websites belonging to the plaintiff's bar, regulators, and activist nongovernmental organizations (NGOs) appear at higher levels of relevance.

- High-impact bloggers use terms specific to a company's business, products, or people in an adverse context.

- Terms specific to a company's business, products, or people appear with Twitter hashmarks.

- Reputational value metrics that sense the economic consequences of media effects on stakeholders show increased volatility. (item added by author).

These cardinal signs tell "you that things are starting to heat up." It's pack journalism just like Timothy Crouse described in *The Boys on the Bus.*[14] Christopher Teas, managing director of Southport Lane, a private equity firm, explains it this way. "As the vast volume of information from the Internet overwhelms people's ability to process, they end up parroting the views of those they trust."[15]

Monitoring the evolution of an operational crisis and being ready to address the fallout are managerial imperatives. "Having a rapid cross-functional response team ... is crucial," noted Long.[8] Levick agreed that a key success factor is preparing well in advance of a crisis.[14] The mantle of leadership in a crisis, however, needs to shift to the board, says Winokur. "When something unusual happens, the executive floor becomes essentially a third- or fourth-grade soccer team where everybody goes for the ball." Boards need to take early ownership of the crisis response so that management can continue running the company.[11]

The board's assumption of crisis management is essential when the reputation of the C-suite is at risk. In many cases, the CEO is held to a higher standard than other employees, notes William Hernandez, a director of Kodak, Black Box, and several other firms.[16] It may be "unfair," but as Low declares, "Personal behavior of every kind is increasingly a public matter. Get used to it."[17]

The Walt Disney Company has had its surprises from the supply chain, and its CEO has been the object of scorn from Institutional Shareholder Services. The company has successfully protected its reputation, as shown by the numbers. Disney, an $88-billion media and entertainment conglomerate, ranks highly among the various reputation surveys and algorithmic measures. In 2012, it ranked 13th among the World's Most Admired, 11th among the World's Most Respected, in the 97.7th percentile in the Corporate Reputation Rankings, 6th in the RQ rankings, and 17th on the RepTrak rankings.

According to the Steel City Re reputational value metrics reported in Chapter 12, Disney raised its Reputation Value measure over the trailing 12 months by 0.17 Gerken Units (GU), an increase of 25%. Its reputational value volatility of 1.5% was at the median of its 11-member media conglomerate peer group,[12] and its return on equity of 42.4% was at the 88th percentile and 18.4% greater than the median return of its peer group. On 30 August 2012, its P/E ratio was 16.34.

Restoring Reputational Value

Because a reputational crisis will shave an average 7% from a company's market capitalization, reputational value restoration can yield a net additional average of 13.5% in market capitalization. The incentives are transparent; the pathway is formulaic—provided that its execution is authentic by the following measures.

- Identify the root cause of the process failure that precipitated the adverse media events that are central to reputational damage.

- Identify key stakeholders and assure them that, having identified the root cause, the company is taking immediate action to rectify the problem while mitigating risks to all stakeholders. Implementing authentic operational controls linked to reputation risk and value is an exemplary demonstration of ongoing restoration of reputation. Davia Temin, president and CEO of Temin and Company Incorporated, a communications consultancy, says "Any time you have a reputational crisis of any kind the best companies, the best organizations, and the best industries take that seriously and start putting in fixes themselves."[18]

- Develop, implement, and promote industry-wide adoption of process controls that can ensure that neither your firm, nor

Chapter 13 | Consider These

others in the industry, will have to suffer the consequences of a similar failure in the future.

As with all reputation-related activities, they must be authentic and they must be executed so as to be recognized and valued by stakeholders. The challenge with financial service firms after the 2008 crisis, adds Temin, is that the industry waited "to have the government put in the 'fixings' for them and vilify them some more."

When trust is violated, as it was with the financial industry, authenticity may require a third party's validation. Properly designed reputational insurances can help signal authenticity to stakeholders.

By the numbers, AIG, a $58 billion insurance company, ranks poorly in reputational surveys. In 2012, it ranked only in the 6th percentile among 138 of the World's Most Admired, 60th—a "critically poor" ranking—in the RQ rankings and 144th on the RepTrak rankings.

On the other hand, it ranked in the 78th percentile of the Steel City Re Corporate Reputation Rankings and appears by those algorithmic metrics to be on track to restoring its reputation. Similarly to Disney, it raised its Reputation Value measure over the trailing 12 months by 0.10 GU or 23%. Its reputational value volatility of 7.4% was at the 92nd percentile of its 43-member multi-line insurance company peer group. Its reputational value velocity was a strong 20.6%, and its return on equity of 24% was at the 88.5th percentile and 24.7% greater than the median return of its peer group. Additional reputational metrics indicating reputation restoration are reported in Chapter 12.

The reputation metrics suggested that AIG was making changes. With its P/E ratio of 2.99 in mid-August 2012, there was ample reward available if that multiple were to be raised through the full spectrum of reputational value restoration efforts.

By the Numbers—Highlights

Mindful of Bernstein's maxim—"the plural of 'anecdote' is not 'data'"—this book provides quantitative data evidencing the reputational value to be gained, placed at risk, or lost, in the context of a diversity of stakeholder behaviors.[19] Table 13-1 highlights some of these data.

Reputation, Stock Price, and You 283

Table 13-1. Selected Measures Discussed in Prior Chapters

Chapter	Source	Description	Measure			
2	BP's 2010 crisis	Regulatory burden	50 hearings; 80 bills; and $15–$25 billion in fines and penalties			
2	BP's 2010 crisis	Creditor response	Liquidity crisis; net cost of credit 16% increase over 2009; credit default swap spreads August 2012 about 35 basis points higher (70% higher) than March 2010			
2	BP's 2010 crisis	Investor response	Two board members not reelected; three derivative lawsuits; and friction over future CEO compensation; net $54 billion in lost market capitalization			
3	Rolls-Royce reputational value dividend	*Sustained* sales volume and pricing power	Stock price effect—Interval Gains (Losses)			
				Rolls-Royce	S&P500	
			01-Nov-10	0	0	01-Nov-10
			15-Nov-10	(–8.7%)	1.1%	15-Nov-10
4	Apple Inc. reputational value dividend	Employee productivity and costs	Store sales are 280% more efficient than the average of a reference group. Selling, General, and Administrative Expenses (SG&A) costs are 65% lower than at Microsoft			
4	Goldman Sachs reputational value dividend	Employee productivity and costs	Average deal size 15% larger than the average of its peers; total deal value 42% greater than the average of its peers. Operating costs per $/revenue no less than 4% lower than average of rivals			
5	Supply chain reputational value dividend	Customer of choice status	2%–4% lower cost of goods sold			

Chapter 13 | Consider These

Chapter	Source	Description	Measure
5	Toyota Motors crisis	P&L effects	Credit default swap prices up 0.6%–0.7% 16% fall in monthly sales 14% fall in annual market share 3% fall in secondary market pricing power (inventory value) Total P&L impact $2 billion
6	Creditor reputational value dividend	Credit costs	All other things being equal: Credit spreads for the largest companies with the best reputations (*Fortune*) are ~0.75% lower than the prices for those with the worst reputations. CDS prices for the largest companies with the best reputations (*Barron's*) are ~0.60% lower than the prices for those with the worst reputations.
7	Equity investor reputational value dividend	Market cap effects of an unexpected boost in reputation	Average annual market cap boost of 6.5% over 10-year study period
7	Equity investor reputational value dividend	Effects on CEO pay	Correlation of investor respect metric with CEO salary: $800,000 per full notch up.
8	Board-level reputation risk awareness	Most recent annual rate of disclosure of corporate reputational risk	50% per year increase 71% of the S&P 500 as of June 2012
8	Compensation committee adoption of reputation-linked incentives	Fraction of CEO bonus at UBS linked to measures of reputation	11%

Chapter	Source	Description	Measure
9	Survey-based reputation rankings	Correlation of rankings from the general public with rankings from the professional business community	21%
10	Regulatory costs	Estimated average fine for Foreign Corrupt Practices Act violations	$69.4 million
12	Metrics	Correlation among a diversity of reputation ranking and reputational value metrics	21%–94%

Endnotes

1 Hillenbrand C, Money K. Corporate responsibility and corporate reputation: two separate concepts or two sides of the same coin? *Corporate Reputation Review.* 2007; 10:261–277.

2 Modern lessons from Hillel. *NPR.* 7 September 2010. http://www.npr.org/templates/story/story.php?storyId=129706379. Accessed 29 August 2012.

3 Smidts A, Pruyn TH, Van Riel CBM. The impact of employee communication and perceived external prestige on organizational identification, *Academy of Management Journal.* 2001; 44(5):1051–1062.

4 Carmeli A. Perceived external prestige, affective commitment, and citizenship behaviors. *Organization Studies.* 2005; 26(3):443–464.

5 Dutton JE, Dukerich JM, Harquail CV. Organizational images and member identification. *Administrative Science Quarterly.* 1994; 39:239–263.

6 Liebman P. Is ethics a valuable intangible asset? Mission Intangible Monthly Briefing. 9 April 2010. Audio recordings available from the Intangible Asset Finance Society: http://iafinance.org/monthly-briefings. Accessed 5 October 2012.

7 Rittereiser RP. Process-driven reputation risk in supply chains. Mission Intangible Monthly Briefing. 7 May 2010. Audio recordings available from the Intangible Asset Finance Society: http://iafinance.org/monthly-briefings. Accessed 18 October 2012.

Chapter 13 | Consider These

8 Long G. Who knows what institutional memory and the role of the sideload. Mission Intangible Monthly Briefing. 4 November 2011. Audio recordings available from the Intangible Asset Finance Society: http://iafinance.org/monthly-briefings. Accessed 5 October 2012.

9 Low J. Is ethics a valuable intangible asset? Mission Intangible Monthly Briefing. 9 April 2010. Audio recordings available from the Intangible Asset Finance Society: http://iafinance.org/monthly-briefings. Accessed 5 October 2012.

10 Locke L. Creating reputation value. Mission Intangible Monthly Briefing. 2 March 2012. Audio recordings available from the Intangible Asset Finance Society: http://iafinance.org/monthly-briefings. Accessed 8 October 2012.

11 Winokur HS. Protecting reputation value. Mission Intangible Monthly Briefing. 13 April 2012. Audio recordings available from the Intangible Asset Finance Society: http://iafinance.org/monthly-briefings. Accessed 5 October 2012.

12 Industry standard groupings provided by FACTSET.

13 Childers S. Process-driven reputation risk in supply chains. Mission Intangible Monthly Briefing. 7 May 2010. Audio recordings available from the Intangible Asset Finance Society: http://iafinance.org/monthly-briefings. Accessed 5 October 2012.

14 Levick RS. Protecting reputation value. Mission Intangible Monthly Briefing. 13 April 2012. Audio recordings available from the Intangible Asset Finance Society: http://iafinance.org/monthly-briefings. Accessed 10 October 2012.

15 Teas C. Wall Street, volatility, and reputation. Mission Intangible Monthly Briefing. 4 May 2012. Audio recordings available from the Intangible Asset Finance Society: http://iafinance.org/monthly-briefings. Accessed 5 October 2012.

16 Hernandez W. Sex and the CEO. Mission Intangible Monthly Briefing. 8 June 2012. Audio recordings available from the Intangible Asset Finance Society: http://iafinance.org/monthly-briefings. Accessed 5 October 2012.

17 Low J. Sex and the CEO. Mission Intangible Monthly Briefing. 8 June 2012. Audio recordings available from the Intangible Asset Finance Society: http://iafinance.org/monthly-briefings. Accessed 5 October 2012.

18 Temin D. Wall Street, volatility, and reputation. Mission Intangible Monthly Briefing. 4 May 2012. Audio recordings available from the Intangible Asset Finance Society: http://iafinance.org/monthly-briefings. Accessed 5 October 2012.

19 Bernstein IS. Metaphor, cognitive belief, and science. Behavioral and Brain Sciences. 1988;11:247–248.

Index

I

A

Aberdeen Asset Management, 153
Affordable Care Act (ACA), 230
American Cancer Society, 106
American International Group (AIG), 255–256
Aon, 151
Apple Inc. (AAPL), 267, 278
  BASIC, 69
  CEO, 65
  Eichenwald writes, 71
  garage-built hardware product, 65
  IBM marketing muscle, 69
  innovation powerhouse, 70
  iPad mini, 64
  iPhone and iPad, 69
  Microsoft, 69
  MVP, 71
  proven model, 66
  recruiting engaged employees, 67–68
  reputational value, 283
  retail employees, 66, 67
  retaining engaged employees, 68–69
  sales, corporate and administrative costs, 71
  Super Bowl, 66
  tablet computer, 64, 65
Asset protection
  corporate reputation value, 174
  reputation protection
    Blue Ribbon Report, 179
    Capital, 183
    COSO, 180

Customer Relationship Management, 178
Delaware court, 181
Enterprise risk managers, 178
failure, 182
fiduciary duties, 181
insurance brokerage, 183
losses, 184
operational risk, 180
reputational value insurance, 185
reputation risk, 182, 183
research association recommendation, 179
stockpiling credentials, 175
third parties, 175
Walt Disney Company
  audits report, 177
  labor conditions, 175
  Public Eye Award, 176
  SACOM, 176
  UNICEF, 176
  workers' rights violations, 178
Automobile Industry Supply Chain, 114

B

Barclays, 62
Barron's Respect scores, 154
Beginner's All-purpose Symbolic Instruction Code (BASIC), 69
Board-level reputation risk awareness, 284
Boards of Directors
  asset protection (see Asset protection)

Index

Boards of Directors (*cont.*)
  business strategy
    Anglo American plc, 189–190
    culture and strategy, 190–191
    Diageo plc, 188–189
    Standard Chartered plc, 186–188
  by the numbers, 195
  compensation committee
    Personal reputation risk, 167
    sensitivity to reputation, 166
    UBS (see Union Bank of Switzerland (UBS))
  compensation to reputation
    CEO's compensation, 172
    Equity awards, 173
    fund managers and financial advisers, 173
    JP Morgan Chase, 173
    reputational value metrics, 174
  guidance
    Diageo and Anglo American, 192
    Johnson & Johnson, 194
    Mercer Investment Consulting, 192
    Standard Chartered, 193–194
    UBS, 194
BP's 2010 crisis, 283

C

Center for Corporate Ethics and Governance (CCEG), 59
Centers for Medicare and Medicaid Services (CMS), 230
Chick-fil-A, 243–244
Coase's theorem, 95–96
Coca-Cola Company (KO), 259
  beverage company, 107
  caramel coloring, 105
  carbon dioxide gas, 106
  contaminated product, 106
  designs business models, 108
  filtered water and sweeteners, 107
  global ethics issues, 108
  market capitalizations, 105
  production and distribution, 111, 112
  product safety, 108
  profit and loss statement, 111
  reputation management implications, 110
  reputation risk disclosures, 108
  symptoms, 106
Committee of Sponsoring Organizations of the Treadway Commission (COSO), 180
Corporate reputation, 146
Corporate Responsibility Magazines, 102–103
Credit default swaps (CDSs), 117, 128, 130
Credit Market Analysis (CMA), 128
Creditor reputational value, 284
Creditors
  commercial credit, 127
  credit risk, 127
  guidance, 134–136
  Johnson & Johnson
    business media, 133
    corporate ethics, 132
    ethical culture, 131
    lower credit costs, 133
    news coverage, 132
    phone query, 132
    stakeholders, 132
  Morgan's statement, 127
  reputation matters
    Barron's survey data, 130
    business processes, 129, 136
    CDSs, 130
    Debt/EBITDA ratio, 130
    economic competencies, 129
    environmental benefits, 129
    Fortune survey, 130
    gauging reputation, 130
    OCEG, 129
    reputational damage, 131
    sin industries, 129
    survey-based ranking, 130
    traditional balance sheets, 129
  Volkswagen Group's, 128
Cultural context
  Chick-fil-A, 243–244
  corporate culture, 242
  guidance, 245–246
  News Corp, 242

Index 289

strategic and operating processes, 242
Susan G. Komen, 244
Target Corp, 245
Customer and company relationship, 31
Customer-Driven Revenue, 48
guidance, 46–47
innovation
impact on enterprise, 45
research in motion (RIM), 43–44
retrospective, 44–45
safety, 32
reputation management (see
Reputation management)
Rolls-Royce, 32
Zale corporation
CEO, 39
customer sentiments, 40, 41
fine jewelers, 38
retrospective, 40–41
Customer-Driven Revenue, 48

D

Deepwater Horizon disaster, 4
Deferred Prosecution Agreements (DPA),
228–229
Domino pizza redux
McIntyre, vice president, 82
secret sauce process, 82–83
Seeking Alpha, 82
Dow Jones indexes, 150

E

Employees
definition, 53
domino pizza redux (see Domino pizza
redux)
ethics
aggressive editor, 57
alpha female, 57
barclays, 62
benefits, 63
ethical failure, 54
expenses, 60–61
international playboy, 57

journalistic, 56
Malcolm Gladwell theorizes, 54
Milly Dowler affair, 61
muddled gray area, 56
Murdoch empire, 59–61
Murdoch's personal challenges, 61
News Corp., 54
organizational culture, 64
Rebekah schmoozes, 57
guidance, 83–85
innovation
Apple Inc. (see Apple Inc. (AAPL))
engagement and alignment, 64
Goldman Sachs Group (see Goldman
Sachs Group)
reputation effect, 85
Environmental Protection Agency (EPA), 225
Equity investor reputational value, 284
Equity investors
buying/selling shares, 143
ExxonMobil Corporation and Koch
Industries, 158
Facebook Inc. (see Facebook)
Lipman, Frederick D., 158
message, 159
proxies, 143
reputation effects, 143, 159
WPP plc. (see WPP)
European Aeronautic Defence and Space
Company (EADS), 34

F

Facebook
equity investors perspective, 150–151
innovation, 158
IPO, 144
professional investors, 158
reputation and information processing
advertising-linked revenue model, 146
advertising revenues, 146
brands, 146
corporate events, 146
ego premium, 146
individual investors, 146
Johnson & Johnson, 147, 158

Index

Facebook, reputation and information processing (*cont.*)
  Knight Capital Group, 147
  macroeconomic events, 146
  retail investors, 146
  risk management, 149
  S&P 500 index, 147, 150
  stakeholders, 146
  Vanity Fair, tongue-in-cheek indictment, 145
  warrant, 145
Federal Aviation Administration (FAA), 225
Federal Sentencing Guidelines for Organizations (FSGO), 227–228, 234
Financial Stability Board's (FSB), 168–169
Foreign Corrupt Practices Act (FCPA), 227–228

G

Gartner annual Supply Chain, 102
George Long, 276
Goldman Sachs Group
  Company, 72–73
  financial institutions, 74
  financial services, 72
  financial success metrics, 74–76
  global powerhouse, 74
  IPO market, 74
  non-stakeholders, 77
  passion and engagement
    bonuses and profits, 78
    financial service employees, 77
    MBA students, 78
    operating costs, 80
    reputation, 79
    retrospective, 81
    turnover rate, 79
Goldman Sachs reputational value, 283

H

Hara-Kiri avoidance
  cacophony, 6
  company-generated communications, 7

Deepwater Horizon disaster, 4
reputation
  BP reputation story, 7
  corporate behaviors, 5–6
  risk management, 7
  stakeholders, 5
Harvard Corporation, 277
Herbert Winokur, 277

I

Initial public offering (IPO), 74, 144
Insurers and hedge funds, 251
International Financing Review (IFR), 75

J

Johnson & Johnson (JNJ), 147, 257–258
Jonathan Low, 277
JP Morgan Chase (JPM), 263–264
Justice Department policy, 227

K

Knight Capital Group, 147, 232–233

L

Linda Locke, 277
London Interbank Offered Rate (LIBOR), 154, 205

M

McDonalds Corporation
  consumers and suppliers, 100
  Corporate Responsibility Committee, 100
  fast-food franchises, 98
  food and paper goods cost, 103
  frozen French fry, 99
  Gartner survey, 102
  Harvard Business School, 99
  milk-shake mixers, 98
  multi-stakeholder, 103
  reputation factors, 100–101

Index 291

restaurants, 98
retrospective, 104
RHM, 99
trust and commitment, 100
well-oiled machine, 102
Metrics, 285
Minerals Management Service (MMS), 231
Morgan Stanley
corporate reputational risk, 228
DPA, 228–229
FCPA, 227
federal court, 227
federal prosecutors, 227
FSGO, 227
illinois attorney, 229
Lincoln's partner, 229
Peterson's misconduct, 228
Most Admired Company, 130
Most Respected Large Companies (MRC), 250
Most Valuable Property (MVP), 71
Multi-stakeholder concept, 273–275

N

News Corp, 242
Nuclear Regulatory Commission (NRC), 226

O

Occupational Safety and Health
Administration (OSHA), 14
Open Compliance and Ethics Group
(OCEG), 129
Organizational culture, 279

P

Paul Liebman, 276
Peet's Coffee & Tea Inc., 119–122
PepsiCo (PEP) Inc., 261
caramel coloring, 105
global food and snack, 109
market capitalizations, 105
production and distribution, 112
profit and loss statement, 111

reputation management implications, 110–111
reputation risk, 110
Walton family stores, 109
Percentile rank denominator, 252
Pittsburgh-based Littlearth Productions, 135

Q

QF32 engine explosion, 33

R

Regulators
benefits and costs, 235, 236
business, 226
CMS, 234
corporate reputation, 226
enforcement activity, 225
enforcement and intervention, 233
firms and executives, 235
FSGO, 234
government standard-setting, 225
hospital reputation, 230
landscape features, 235
Morgan Stanley (see Morgan Stanley)
NRC, 226
policy, 235
punishments, 236
punishments and diminished reputations
BP Deep Water Horizon, 231
Knight Capital, 232–233
reputation-building/sustaining processes, 227
Socratic maxim, 235
stakeholder groups, 234
Regulatory costs, 285
Relative Business Performance probability
scores, 250
RepTrak survey, 250
RepuStars Variety algorithm (RepuSPX), 150
RepuStars Variety Corporate Reputation
Index, 150
Reputation
authenticity, 24
loss, 21

Index

Reputation (*cont.*)
  measurability and magnitude, 24
  process failure
    BP executives and Board of Directors, 20
    capital market analysts, 21
    creditors, 18–19
    customers, 16
    employees, 17
    equity investors, 19–20
    regulators, 21
    suppliers, 17–18
  retrospective, 22–23
  risk
    company's 2009 Annual Report, 13
    explosion at BP's Texas refinery, 12
    morale decline at BP, 15
    omissions, 14–15
    OSHA, 14
    stakeholders' expectations, 12, 13
Reputational value
  business drivers, 276
  market capitalization, 276
  operational benefits, 278
  protection
    authentic reputation, 278
    brand, 278
    C-suite, 280
    reputational crisis, 280
  reputation-centered tone, 277
  restoration, 281
  risk culture, 277
  sideloading, 276
  social graph, 277
  unexpected reputational value, 278
  value-creating information, 276
Reputational value insurance, 251
Reputational value metrics, 250
Reputation-linked incentives, 284
Reputation management
  mission-critical, 32
  process controls, 33–34
  retrospective, 36–37
  Rolls-Royce, 36
  Trent 900 explosion-and-aftermath timeline, 34–35

Reputation measurement
  AAPL, 267–268
  AIG, 255–256
  algorithmic reputational value metrics, 250, 252
  bar charts, 254
  business performance, 270
  communication enhancement, 270
  DIS, 265–266
  dynamic processes, 250
  flag graphs, 255, 269
  JNJ, 257–258
  JPM, 263–264
  KO, 259–260
  MRC, 250
  PEP, 261–262
  percentile rank denominator, 252
  rank-order percentile values, 252, 253
  Relative Business Performance probability scores, 250
  representative pairwise correlations, 271
  RepTrak survey, 250
  reputational value metrics, 250
  RQ survey, 250, 251
  spot and dynamic time-series data, 250
  Steel City Re's algorithmic reputational value metrics, 252–254, 269
  stepwise paired correlations, 251
  survey-based reputation scores, 250, 252
  time series chart, 254
  vital signs chart, 253
  WMAC, 250, 251
Reputation Quotient (RQ) survey, 250
Reputation value
  Barron's, 210–211
  Carnegie's steel company
    formula, 201
    stakeholders, 202
    Steel City Re's approach, 202
    winning strategies, 202
  decision markets, 205
  exemplary funds, 204
  financial statements, 203
  fortune
    Admired Companies, 210
    company rating, 209

Index 293

factors for organizational success, 209–210

WMAC, 209

guidance

agreement, 217

asset and liability, 219

business professional stakeholders, 216

Financial Disclosure and Corporate Governance, 218

Milan Stock Exchange, 218

stakeholders, 217

stock picking tools, 216

Harris Interactive

Nominations Phase, 212

RQ Ratings Phase, 212, 213

Harris Reputation Quotient (RQ), 211–212

investor expectations, 203

LIBOR, 205–206

probabilities, 203

RepTrak

data trend, 215

key dimensions, 214

survey, governance, 214

RepuStars strategy, 207

REPUVAR, 207–208

Steel City Re

commercial vendor, 206

executive management needs, 207

properties of, 207

stakeholders, 206, 207

Robert Rittereiser, 276

Rolls-Royce aircraft engines, 31, 32

Rolls-Royce reputational value, 283

Royal Bank of Scotland Group plc, 152

S

Scott Childers, 279

Securities and Exchange Commission (SEC), 225

S&P 500 index, 147

Steel City Re's algorithmic reputational value metrics, 252–254, 269, 281

Students & Scholars Against Corporate Misbehavior (SACOM), 176

Supplier and vendor-associated costs, 122

Supplier Tracking and Recognition (STAR), 102

Supply chain

business model, 94

buyer's aggregate revenue, 94

Coase's theorem, 94–95

Coca-Cola Company (see Coca-Cola Company (KO))

external/internal linkage, 96

iconic firms, 95

interconnectedness, 95

IT system security, 96

Mactavish report, 95

McDonalds Corporation (see McDonalds Corporation)

operational and reputation benefits, 96–97

operational inflexibility, 96

operational risks, 96

Peet's Coffee & Tea Inc., 119–122

penultimate buyer, 94

PepsiCo Inc. (see PepsiCo (PEP) Inc.)

scarcity, 94

siloed structures, 96

supplier and vendor-associated costs, 122

Toyota Motor Corporation (see Toyota Motor Corporation)

Yum! Brands (see Yum! Brands)

Supply chain reputational value, 283

Survey-based reputation rankings, 285

Survey-based reputation scores, 250, 252

Susan G. Komen, 244

T

Target Corp, 245

Time series chart, 148

Toyota Motor Corporation

automotive industry, 113

business philosophy, 115–116

CDSs, 117

cost reduction strategy, 116

ethics, safety and quality, 117

financial performance indicators, 113

food and beverage industries, 112

Index

Toyota Motor Corporation (cont.)
  Income Statement Impact, 118
  manufacturing process, 114
  operating costs, 118
  parts and components, 114
  reputation loss, 117
  risk and reputation management, 117
  trusted automaker, 112
  vehicle production, 115
Toyota Motors crisis, 284
Tricon Global Restaurants, 101

U, V

Union Bank of Switzerland (UBS)
  CHF21.6 billion ($18 billion), 168
  disgorgement of profits, 168
  eurozone sovereign debt, 167
  fictitious trade, 167
  FSB standards, 169
  G20 leaders, 168
  Human Resources and Compensation Committee, 171
  Kaspar Villiger, 168
  LIBOR, 172
  Long-Term Capital Management, 167
  Oscar Grubel, CEO, 168
  reputation risk, 170
  Securities and Exchange Commission (SEC), 168
  SFr19.4 billion ($17.2 billion), 168
  strategic risk factor, annual reports, 170, 171
  UniCredit Deputy Chief Executive Officer, 171–172
  word reputation, 169
U.S. Delaware corporate law, 279

W

Walt Disney Company (DIS), 265–266
World's Most Admired Companies (WMAC) survey, 249–250
World's Most Respected Large Companies, 250

WPP
  Aon, 151
  Aspesi, Claudio, 152
  business process failure, 151
  economic responsibilities, 151
  Gaines-Ross, Leslie, 152
  global retrenchment, 151
  Goodwin, Fred, 152
  pay packages, 152
  pension plan, 152
  remuneration packages of directors, 152
  respect and pay correlation
    Barron's Respect scores, 154
    Brossy, Semler (compensation advisor), 157
    Cincinnati Bell Inc., 157
    compensation consultancy, 156
    cost of director, 158
    Dodd-Frank Act, 157
    executive compensation systems, 156, 157
    explicit communication channel, 157
    ISS, 157
    KeyCorp and Occidental Petroleum, 158
    negative say-on-pay assessment, 157
    officers' liability insurance, 158
    shareholder spring, 157
    Walt Disney Company, 156
    Watson, Towers, 156
  Rosen, Jeffrey, 152
  say-on-pay and other vocalizations, 153–154
  Sir Martin Sorrell, 151
  Zurich Financial Services, 151

X

Xerox's Palo Alto Research Center, 65

Y

Yum! Brands
  food and paper goods cost, 103

Kids Meal branded products practice, 102
reputationally related processes, 101
restaurant company, 101
STAR, 102

Z

Zale Corporation, 38–42
Zurich Financial Services, 151

CPSIA information can be obtained at www.ICGtesting.com
Printed in the USA
LVOW102218181112

307904LV00003B/1/P